Simulating Humans

Simulating Humans

Computer Graphics Animation and Control

NORMAN I. BADLER, CARY B. PHILLIPS,
BONNIE LYNN WEBBER

Department of Computer and Information Science
University of Pennsylvania

New York   Oxford
OXFORD UNIVERSITY PRESS
1993

Oxford University Press

Oxford New York Toronto
Delhi Bombay Calcutta Madras Karachi
Kuala Lumpur Singapore Hong Kong Tokyo
Nairobi Dar es Salaam Cape Town
Melbourne Auckland Madrid

and associated companies in
Berlin Ibadan

Published by Oxford University Press, Inc.,
200 Madison Avenue, New York, New York 10016

Oxford is a registered trademark of Oxford University Press

Library of Congress Cataloging-in-Publication Data
Badler, Norman I.
Simulating humans : computer graphics animation and control /
Norman I. Badler, Cary B. Phillips, Bonnie L. Webber.
p. cm.   Includes bibliographical references and index.
ISBN 0-19-507359-2
1. Human engineering.   2. Virtual reality.
3. Body, Human—Computer simulation.
4. Human mechanics—Computer simulation.
I. Phillips, Cary B.   II. Webber, Bonnie Lynn.   III. Title.
TA166.B32   1993
620.8′2—dc20   93-12061

9 8 7 6 5 4 3 2 1

Printed in the United States of America
on acid-free paper

To Ginny, Denise, and Mark

Preface

The decade of the 80's saw the dramatic expansion of high performance computer graphics into domains previously able only to flirt with the technology. Among the most dramatic has been the incorporation of real-time interactive manipulation and display for human figures. Though actively pursued by several research groups, the problem of providing a virtual or synthetic human for an engineer or designer already accustomed to Computer-Aided Design techniques was most comprehensively attacked by the Computer Graphics Research Laboratory at the University of Pennsylvania. The breadth of that effort as well as the details of its methodology and software environment are presented in this volume.

This book is intended for human factors engineers requiring current knowledge of how a computer graphics surrogate human can augment their analyses of designed environments. It will also help inform design engineers of the state-of-the-art in human figure modeling, and hence of the human-centered design central to the emergent notion of Concurrent Engineering. Finally, it documents for the computer graphics community a major research effort in the interactive control and motion specification of articulated human figures.

Many people have contributed to the work described in this book, but the textual material derives more or less directly from the efforts of our current and former students and staff: Tarek Alameldin, Francisco Azuola, Breck Baldwin, Welton Becket, Wallace Ching, Paul Diefenbach, Barbara Di Eungenio, Jeffrey Esakov, Christopher Geib, John Granieri, Marc Grosso, Pei-Hwa Ho, Mike Hollick, Moon Jung, Jugal Kalita, Hyeongseok Ko, Eunyoung Koh, Jason Koppel, Michael Kwon, Philip Lee, Libby Levison, Gary Monheit, Michael Moore, Ernest Otani, Susanna Wei, Graham Walters, Michael White, Jianmin Zhao, and Xinmin Zhao. Additional animation help has come from Leanne Hwang, David Haynes, and Brian Stokes. John Granieri and Mike Hollick helped considerably with the photographs and figures.

This work would not have been possible without the generous and often long term support of many organizations and individuals. In particular we would like to acknowledge our many colleagues and friends: Barbara Woolford, Geri Brown, Jim Maida, Abhilash Pandya and the late Linda Orr in the Crew Station Design Section and Mike Greenisen at NASA Johnson Space Center; Ben Cummings, Brenda Thein, Bernie Corona, and Rick Kozycki of the U.S. Army Human Engineering Laboratory at Aberdeen Proving Grounds; James Hartzell, James Larimer, Barry Smith, Mike Prevost, and Chris Neukom of the A^3I Project in the Aeroflight Dynamics Directorate of NASA Ames Research Center; Steve Paquette of the U. S. Army Natick Laboratory; Jagdish Chandra and David Hislop of the U. S. Army Research Office; the Army Artificial Intelligence Center of Excellence at the University of Pennsylvania and its Director, Aravind Joshi; Art Iverson and Jack Jones of the U.S. Army TACOM; Jill Easterly, Ed Boyle, John Ianni, and Wendy Campbell of the U. S. Air Force Human Resources Directorate at Wright-Patterson Air Force Base; Medhat Korna and Ron Dierker of Systems Exploration, Inc.; Pete Glor and Joseph Spann of Hughes Missile Systems (formerly General Dynamics, Convair Division); Ruth Maulucci of MOCO Inc.; John McConville, Bruce Bradtmiller, and Bob Beecher of Anthropology Research Project, Inc.; Edmund Khouri of Lockheed Engineering and Management Services; Barb Fecht of Battelle Pacific Northwest Laboratories; Jerry Duncan of Deere and Company; Ed Bellandi of FMC Corp.; Steve Gulasy of Martin-Marietta Denver Aerospace; Joachim Grollman of Siemens Research; Kathleen Robinette of the Armstrong Medical Research Lab at Wright-Patterson Air Force Base; Harry Frisch of NASA Goddard Space Flight Center; Jerry Allen and the folks at Silicon Graphics, Inc.; Jack Scully of Ascension Technology Corp.; the National Science Foundation CISE Grant CDA88-22719 and ILI Grant USE-9152503; and the State of Pennsylvania Benjamin Franklin Partnership. Martin Zaidel contributed valuable LaTeX help. Finally, the encouragement and patience of Don Jackson at Oxford University Press has been most appreciated.

Norman I. Badler
University of Pennsylvania

Cary B. Phillips
PDI, Sunnyvale

Bonnie L. Webber
University of Pennsylvania

Contents

Simulating Humans

Chapter 1

Introduction and Historical Background

People are all around us. They inhabit our home, workplace, entertainment, and environment. Their presence and actions are noted or ignored, enjoyed or disdained, analyzed or prescribed. The very ubiquitousness of other people in our lives poses a tantalizing challenge to the computational modeler: people are at once the most common object of interest and yet the most structurally complex. Their everyday movements are amazingly fluid yet demanding to reproduce, with actions driven not just mechanically by muscles and bones but also cognitively by beliefs and intentions. Our motor systems manage to learn how to make us move without leaving us the burden or pleasure of knowing how we did it. Likewise we learn how to describe the actions and behaviors of others without consciously struggling with the processes of perception, recognition, and language.

A famous Computer Scientist, Alan Turing, once proposed a test to determine if a computational agent is intelligent [Tur63]. In the Turing Test, a subject communicates with two agents, one human and one computer, through a keyboard which effectively restricts interaction to language. The subject attempts to determine which agent is which by posing questions to both of them and guessing their identities based on the "intelligence" of their answers. No physical manifestation or image of either agent is allowed as the process seeks to establish abstract "intellectual behavior," thinking, and reasoning. Although the Turing Test has stood as the basis for computational intelligence since 1963, it clearly omits any potential to evaluate physical actions, behavior, or appearance.

Later, Edward Feigenbaum proposed a generalized definition that included action: "Intelligent action is an act or decision that is goal-oriented, arrived at by an understandable chain of symbolic analysis and reasoning steps, and is one in which knowledge of the world informs and guides the reasoning." [Bod77]. We can imagine an analogous "Turing Test" that would have the

1

subject watching the behaviors of two agents, one human and one synthetic, while trying to determine at a better than chance level which is which. Human movement enjoys a universality and complexity that would definitely challenge an animated figure in this test: if a computer-synthesized figure looks, moves, and acts like a real person, are we going to believe that it is real? On the surface the question almost seems silly, since we would rather not allow ourselves to be fooled. In fact, however, the question is moot though the premises are slightly different: cartoon characters are hardly "real," yet we watch them and properly interpret their actions and motions in the evolving context of a story. Moreover, they are not "realistic" in the physical sense – no one expects to see a manifest Mickey Mouse walking down the street. Nor do cartoons even move like people – they squash and stretch and perform all sorts of actions that we would never want to do. But somehow our perceptions often make these characters *believable*: they appear to act in a goal-directed way because their human animators have imbued them with physical "intelligence" and behaviors that apparently cause them to chase enemies, bounce off walls, and talk to one another. Of course, these ends are achieved by the skillful weaving of a story into the crafted images of a character. Perhaps surprisingly, the mechanisms by which motion, behavior, and emotion are encoded into cartoons is *not* by building synthetic models of little creatures with muscles and nerves. The requisite animator skills do not come easily; even in the cartoon world refinements to the art and technique took much work, time, and study [TJ81]. Creating such movements automatically in response to real-time interactive queries posed by the subject in our hypothetical experiment does not make the problem any easier. Even Turing, however, admitted that the intelligence sought in his original test did not require the computational *process* of thinking to be identical to that of the human: the external manifestation in a plausible and reasonable answer was all that mattered.

So why are we willing to assimilate the truly artificial reality of cartoons – characters created and moved entirely unlike "real" people – yet be skeptical of more human-like forms? This question holds the key to our physical Turing Test: as the appearance of a character becomes more human, our perceptual apparatus demands motion qualities and behaviors which sympathize with our expectations. As a cartoon character takes on a human form, the only currently viable method for accurate motion is the recording of a real actor and the tracing or transfer ("rotoscoping") of that motion into the animation. Needless to say, this is not particularly satisfying to the modeler: the motion and actor must exist prior to the synthesized result. Even if we recorded thousands of individual motions and retrieved them through some kind of indexed video, we would still lack the freshness, variability, and adaptability of humans to live, work, and play in an infinite variety of settings.

If synthetic human motion is to be produced without the benefit of prior "real" execution and still have a shot at passing the physical Turing Test, then models must carefully balance structure, shape, and motion in a compatible package. If the models are highly simplified or stylized, cartoons or caricatures will be the dominant perception; if they look like humans, then they will be expected to behave like them. How to accomplish this without a real actor showing the way is the challenge addressed here.

Present technology can approach human appearance and motion through computer graphics modeling and three-dimensional animation, but there is considerable distance to go before purely synthesized figures trick our senses. A number of promising research routes can be explored and many are taking us a considerable way toward that ultimate goal. By properly delimiting the scope and application of human models, we can move forward, not to replace humans, but to substitute adequate computational surrogates in various situations otherwise unsafe, impossible, or too expensive for the real thing.

The goals we set in this study are realistic but no less ambitious than the physical Turing Test: we seek to build computational models of human-like figures which, though they may not trick our senses into believing they are alive, nonetheless manifest animacy and convincing behavior. Towards this end, we

- Create an interactive computer graphics human model.

- Endow it with reasonable biomechanical properties.

- Provide it with "human-like" behaviors.

- Use this simulated figure as an agent to effect changes in its world.

- Describe and guide its tasks through natural language instructions.

There are presently no perfect solutions to any of these problems, but significant advances have enabled the consideration of the suite of goals under uniform and consistent assumptions. Ultimately, we should be able to give our surrogate human directions that, in conjunction with suitable symbolic reasoning processes, make it appear to behave in a natural, appropriate, and intelligent fashion. Compromises will be essential, due to limits in computation, throughput of display hardware, and demands of real-time interaction, but our algorithms aim to balance the physical device constraints with carefully crafted models, general solutions, and thoughtful organization.

This study will tend to focus on one particularly well-motivated application for human models: human factors analysis. While not as exciting as motion picture characters, as personable as cartoons, or as skilled as Olympic athletes, there are justifiable uses to virtual human figures in this domain. Visualizing the appearance, capabilities and performance of humans is an important and demanding application (Plate 1). The lessons learned may be transferred to less critical and more entertaining uses of human-like models. From modeling realistic or at least reasonable body size and shape, through the control of the highly redundant body skeleton, to the simulation of plausible motions, human figures offer numerous computational problems and constraints. Building software for human factors applications serves a widespread, non-animator user population. In fact, it appears that such software has broader application since the features needed for analytic applications – such as multiple simultaneous constraints – provide extremely useful features for the conventional animator. Our software design has tried to take into account a wide variety of physical problem-oriented tasks, rather than just offer a computer graphics and animation tool for the already skilled or computer-sophisticated animator.

The remainder of this chapter motivates the human factors environment and then traces some of the relevant history behind the simulation of human figures in this and other domains. It concludes with a discussion of the specific features a human modeling and animation system should have and why we have concentrated on some and not others. In particular, we are not considering cognitive problems such as perception or sensory interpretation, target tracking, object identification, or control feedback that might be important parts of some human factors analyses. Instead we concentrate on modeling a virtual human with reasonable biomechanical structure and form, as described in Chapter 2. In Chapter 4 we address the psychomotor behaviors manifested by such a figure and show how these behaviors may be interactively accessed and controlled. Chapter 5 presents several methods of motion control that bridge the gap between biomechanical capabilities and higher level tasks. Finally, in Chapter 6 we investigate the cognition requirements and strategies needed to have one of these computational agents follow natural language task instructions.

1.1   Why Make Human Figure Models?

Our research has focused on software to make the manipulation of a simulated human figure easy for a particular user population: human factors design engineers or ergonomics analysts. These people typically study, analyze, assess, and visualize human motor performance, fit, reach, view, and other physical tasks in a workplace environment. Traditionally, human factors engineers analyze the design of a prototype workplace by building a mock-up, using real subjects to perform sample tasks, and reporting observations about design satisfaction. This is limiting for several reasons. Jerry Duncan, a human factors engineer at Deere & Company, says that once a design has progressed to the stage at which there is sufficient information for a model builder to construct the mock-up, there is usually so much inertia to the design that radical changes are difficult to incorporate due to cost and time considerations. After a design goes into production, deficiencies are alleviated through specialized training, limits on physical characteristics of personnel, or various operator aids such as mirrors, markers, warning labels, etc. The goal of computer-simulated human factors analysis is not to replace the mock-up process altogether, but to incorporate the analysis into early design stages so that designers can eliminate a high proportion of fit and function problems before building the mock-ups. Considering human factors and other engineering and functional analyses together during rather than after the major design process is a hallmark of Concurrent Engineering [Hau89].

It is difficult to precisely characterize the types of problems a human factors engineer might address. Diverse situations demand empirical data on human capabilities and performance in generic as well as highly specific tasks. Here are some examples.

- Population studies can determine body sizes representative of some group, say NASA astronaut trainees, and this information can be used to determine if space vehicle work cells are adequately designed to fit the individuals expected to work there. Will all astronauts be able to fit through doors or hatches? How will changes in the workplace design affect the fit? Will there be unexpected obstructions to zero gravity locomotion? Where should foot- and hand-holds be located?

- An individual operating a vehicle such as a tractor will need to see the surrounding space to execute the task, avoid any obstructions, and insure safety of nearby people. What can the operator see from a particular vantage point? Can he control the vehicle while looking out the rear window? Can he see the blade in order to follow an excavation line?

- Specific lifting studies might be performed to determine back strain limits for a typical worker population. Is there room to perform a lift properly? What joints are receiving the most strain? Is there a better posture to minimize torques? How does placement of the weight and target affect performance? Is the worker going to suffer fatigue after a few iterations?

- Even more specialized experiments may be undertaken to evaluate the comfort and feel of a particular tool's hand grip. Is there sufficient room for a large hand? Is the grip too large for a small hand? Are all the controls reachable during the grip?

The answers to these and other questions will either verify that the design is adequate or point to possible changes and improvements early in the design process. But once again, the diversity of human body sizes coupled with the multiplier of human action and interaction with a myriad things in the environment leads to an explosion in possible situations, data, and tests.

Any desire to build a "complete" model of human behavior, even for the human factors domain, is surely a futile effort. The field is too broad, the literature immense, and the theory largely empirical. There appear to be two directions out of this dilemma. The first would be the construction of a computational database of all the known, or at least useful, data. Various efforts have been undertaken to assemble such material, for example, the NASA sourcebooks [NAS78, NAS87] and the *Engineering Data Compendium* [BKT86, BL88]. The other way is to build a sophisticated computational human model and use it as a subject in simulated virtual environment tests. The model will utilize an ever-expanding human factors data set to dictate its performance. Upon some reflection, it appears that database direction may start out as the smoother road, but it quickly divides into numerous sinuous paths pot-holed with data gaps, empirical data collection limitations, and population-specific dependencies. The alternative direction (using a computational model underlying any data) may be harder to construct at first, and may have many detours for awhile, but gradually it leads to more destinations with better roads.

This metaphor carries a philosophy for animating human movement that derives from a computer science rather than an empirical point of view. We cannot do without the efforts of the human factors community, but we cannot use their work *per se* as the starting point for human figure modeling. Computer scientists seek computationally general yet efficient solutions to problems. Human factors engineers often analyze a succession of specific tasks or situations. The role we play is transforming the specific needs of the engineer or analyst into a generalized setting where some large percentage of situations may be successfully analyzed. There is sufficient research required to solve general yet difficult problems to justify building suitable software in a computer science environment. The expectation is that in the long run a more specific case-by-case implementation approach will be economically impractical or technologically infeasible.

As we continue to interact with human factors specialists, we have come to appreciate the broad range of problems they must address: fit, reach, visibility, comfort, access, strength, endurance, and fatigue, to mention only some of the *non-cognitive* ones. Our approach is not a denial of their perception and *analysis*, rather it is an alternative view of the problem as *modeling*. Broadly speaking, modeling is the embodiment within computer databases or programs of worldly phenomena. Models can be of many types:

- Mathematical formulations: physical equations of motion, limb strength in tables of empirical data, evaluation formulas measuring workload or fatigue.

- Geometric and topological models: structures representing workplace objects, human body segments, paths to follow, joints and joint limits, spaces that can be reached, attachments, and constraints.

- Conceptual models: names for things, attributes such as color, flexibility, and material, relationships between objects, functional properties.

Of course, modeling (especially of the first sort) is a significant and fundamental part of many studies in the human factors domain, but it has been difficult to balance the needs of the engineer against the complexity of the modeling software. Often, the model is elaborated in only a few dimensions to study some problem while no global integration of models is attempted. Clearly the broadest interpretation of modeling draws not only from many areas of computer science such as artificial intelligence, computer graphics, simulation, and robotics, but also from the inherently relevant fields of biomechanics, anthropometry, physiology, and ergonomics.

The challenge to embed a reasonable set of capabilities in an integrated system has provided dramatic incentives to study issues and solutions in three-dimensional interaction methodologies, multiple goal positioning, visual field assessment, reach space generation, and strength guided motion, to name a few. The empirical data behind these processes is either determined from reliable published reports or supplied by the system user. By leaving the actual data open to the user, the results are as valid as the user wishes to believe. While this is not a very pleasant situation, the inherent variability in human capability data makes some error unavoidable. Better, we think, to let the user know or control the source data than to hide it. This attitude toward validation is not the only plausible one, but it does permit flexibility and generality for the computer and allows final judgment to be vested in the user.

Lest there be concern that we have pared the problem down so far that little of interest remains, we change tactics for awhile and present an historical view of efforts to model humans and their movements. By doing so, we should demonstrate that the human factors domain mirrors problems which arise in other contexts such as dance, sports, or gestural communication. The criteria for success in these fields may be more stringent, so understanding the role and scope of human movement in them can only serve to strengthen our understanding of more mundane actions.

1.2 Historical Roots

Interactive computer graphics systems to support human figure modeling, manipulation, and animation have existed since the early seventies. We trace relevant developments with a sense more of history and evolution rather than of exhaustive survey. There are numerous side branches that lead to interesting topics, but we will sketch only a few of those here.

Three-dimensional human figure models apparently arose independently from at least six different applications.

1. Crash simulation. Automobile and aircraft safety issues led to the development of sophisticated codes for linked mass deceleration studies. These programs generally ran in batch mode for long hours on mainframe computers. The results were tabulated, and in some cases converted to a form that could animate a simple 3D mannequin model [Fet82, Wil82, BOT79]. The application was characterized by non-interactive positioning and force-based motion computations with analysis of impact forces to affected body regions and subsequent injury assessment.

2. Motion analysis. Athletes, patients with psychomotor disabilities, actors, or animals were photographed in motion by one or more fixed, calibrated cameras. The two-dimensional information was correlated between views and reconstructed as timed 3D data points [RA90]. This

data could be filtered and differentiated to compute velocities, accelerations, torques and forces. Visualization of the original data validated the data collection process, but required human figure models. Often just wire-frames, they served in a support role for athletic performance improvement, biomechanical analysis, cartoon motion [TJ81], and training or physical therapy [Win90]. Related efforts substituted direct or active sensing devices for photographic processing [CCP80]. Presently, active motion sensing is used not only for performance analysis but gestural input for virtual environments (for example, [FMHR87, BBH$^+$90] and many others).

3. Workplace assessment. The earliest system with widespread use was SAMMIE [KSC81]. This problem domain is characterized by interactive body positioning requirements and analyses based on visual inspection of 3D computer graphics models. Fast interaction with wire-frame displays provided dynamic feedback to the workplace evaluator. Other modeling tools were developed, such as CAR II [HBD80], Combiman [BEK$^+$81], and Crew Chief [MKK$^+$88, EI91] to provide validated anthropometric or capability data for real populations.

4. Dance or movement notation. The specification of self-generated, purposive, aesthetically-pleasing, human movement has been the subject of numerous notational systems [Hut84]. Dance notations were considered as a viable, compact, computationally tractable mode of expression for human movement due to their refinement as symbolic motion descriptions [BS79]. An animation was to be the debugging tool to validate the correctness of a given notated score. The direct creation of movement through a notational or numeric interface was also considered [CCP80, CCP82, HE78].

5. Entertainment. People (or at least animate creatures) are the favorite subject of cartoons and movies. Two-dimensional animation techniques were the most widely used [Cat72, BW76, Lev77, Cat78]. In an effort to avoid rotoscoping live actors, early 3D modeling and animation techniques were developed at the University of Utah, Ohio State University, and the New York Institute of Technology [Wes73, Hac77, Stu84, Gom84, HS85a].

6. Motion understanding. There are deep connections between human motion and natural language. One of these attempted to produce a sort of narration of observed (synthetic) movement by characterizing changes in spatial location or orientation descriptions over time [Bad75]. More recently, the inverse direction has been more challenging, namely, producing motion from natural language descriptions or instructions [BWKE91, TST87].

Our earliest efforts were directed at language descriptions of object motion. Specifically, we created representations of 3D object motion and directional adverbials in such a way that image sequences of moving objects could be analyzed to produce English sentence motion descriptions [Bad75, Bad76]. We then extended the model to articulated figures, concentrating on graphically valid human figure models to aid the image understanding process [BOT79]. This effort led to the work of Joseph O'Rourke, who attempted model-driven analysis of human motion [OB80] using novel 3D constraint propagation and goal-directed image understanding.

To improve the motion understanding component we focused on motion representations specially designed for human movement [WSB78, BS79]. An in-depth study of several human movement notation systems (such as Labanotation [Hut70] and Eshkol-Wachmann [Hut84]) fostered our appreciation for the breadth and complexity of human activities. Our early attempts to re-formulate Labanotation in computational models reflected a need to cover at least the space of human (skeletal) motion. We investigated input systems for Labanotation [BS76, Hir77], although later they were discarded as a generally accessible means of conveying human movement information from animator to computer figure: there was simply too much overhead in learning the nuances and symbology of the notational system. Moreover, concurrent developments in three-dimensional interactive computer graphics offered more natural position and motion specification alternatives. The final blow to using Labanotation was its lack of dynamic information other than timing and crude "accent" and phrasing marks.

The movement representations that we developed from Labanotation, however, retained one critically important feature: goal-directedness for efficient motion specification. Given goals, processes had to be developed to satisfy them. A simulation paradigm was adopted and some of the special problems of human movement simulation were investigated [BSOW78, BOK80, KB82]. Others studied locomotion [CCP82, Zel82, GM85, Gir87, Bru88, BC89], while we concentrated on inverse kinematics for reach goals [KB82, Kor85]. We were especially anxious to manage multiple reach and motion goals that mutually affected many parts of the body. Solving this problem in particular led to later re-examination of constraint-based positioning and more general and robust algorithms to achieve multiple simultaneous goals [BMW87, ZB89]. Chapter 4 will discuss our current approach in detail.

Our study of movement notations also led to an appreciation of certain fundamental limitations most of them possessed: they were good at describing the changes or end results of a movement (*what* should be done), but were coarse or even non-specific when it came to indicating *how* a movement ought to be performed. The notator's justification was that the performer (for example, a dancer) was an *expert system* who knew from experience and training just how to do the notated motion. The transformation from notation into smooth, natural, expressive movements was part of the art. The exception to the nearly universal failure of notational systems to capture nuances of behavior was Effort-Shape notation [Del70, BwDL80]. We began a study of possible computational analogues to the purely descriptive semantics of that system. By 1986 a model of human movement emerged which integrated the kinematic and inverse kinematic approach with a dynamic, force-based model [Bad89]. Major contributions to dynamics-based animation were made by others, notably [AG85, AGL87, WB85, Wil86, Wil87, IC87, HH87, Hah88]. Recently we combined some of the characteristics of the dynamics approach – the use of physical torques at the body joints – with goal-directed behavior to achieve *strength guided motion* ([LWZB90] and Chapter 5).

While we were actively engaged in the study of motion representations, concurrent developments in interactive systems for the graphical manipulation of a computerized figure were being actively implemented at the University of Pennsylvania. Implementation and development has been a strong experimental component of our research, from the early positioning language based on Labanotation concepts [WSB78], to the next generation frame buffer-based system called *TEMPUS* [Kor85, BKK+85], to the direct manipulation of the figure with a 6-axis digitizer [BMB86], and finally to our present Silicon Graphics workstation-based system *Jack*[TM1] [PB88, PZB90] (Chapters 2 and 4).

As our experience with interactive graphical manipulation of a figure matured, we returned to the connections between language and motion we had begun in the mid-1970's. The manipulation of the figure for task analysis begged for more efficient means of specifying the task. So we began to investigate natural language control for task animation [Gan85, BG86, Kar87, Kar88, Kal90, KB90, KB91]. New representations for motion verbs and techniques for defining and especially *executing* their semantics were investigated. A simple domain of panel-type objects and their motions were studied by Jeff Gangel. Robin Karlin extended the semantics to certain temporal adverbials (such as repetitions and culminations) in a domain of kitchen-objects. Our present effort is exemplified here by the work of Jugal Kalita and Libby Levison. Kalita studied verbs of physical manipulation and used constraints in a fundamental fashion to determine generalized verb semantics. Levison makes explicit connections between a verb's semantic representation and the sorts of primitive behaviors and constraints known to be directly simulatable by the *Jack* animation system (Chapter 6).

Given that natural language or some other artificial language was to be used to describe tasks or processes, a suitable simulation methodology had to be adopted. In his HIRES system, Paul Fishwick investigated task and process simulation for human animation [Fis86, Fis88]. Output was produced by selecting from among pre-defined key postures. For example, an animation of the famous "Dining Philosophers" problem using five human figure models was produced by simulation of the petri net solution in the HIRES simulator. By 1989 we replaced HIRES by a new simulation system, YAPS, which incorporated temporal planning with imprecise specifications [KKB88], task interruption, and task time estimation based on human performance models [EBJ89, EB90, BWKE91] (Chapter 6).

This brings us to the present *Jack* system structure designed to accommo-

---

[1] *Jack* is a registered trademark of the University of Pennsylvania.

date as many of the historical applications as possible within an integrated and consistent software foundation. To begin to describe that, we need to review what human modeling capabilities are needed and what problem implementation choices we might make.

1.3 What is Currently Possible?

Since we wish to animate synthetic human figures primarily in the human factors engineering domain, we should decide what features are essential, desirable, optional, or unnecessary. Only by prioritizing the effort can such a large-scale undertaking be managed. Given priorities, implementation techniques and trade-offs may be investigated. Though we may often draw on existing knowledge and algorithms, there are many fundamental features which we may have to invent or evolve due to the specific structure of the human figure, characteristics of human behavior, timing demands of real-time interaction, or limitations of the display hardware. Accordingly, a variety of human figure modeling issues will be examined here to introduce and justify the choices we have made in our broad yet integrated effort.

The embodiment of our choices for human modeling is a software system called *Jack*. Designed to run on Silicon Graphics 4D workstations, *Jack* is used for the definition, manipulation, animation, and human factors performance analysis of virtual human figures. Built on a powerful representation for articulated figures, *Jack* offers the interactive user a simple, intuitive, and yet extremely capable interface into any three dimensional world. *Jack* incorporates sophisticated yet highly usable algorithms for anthropometric human figure generation, a flexible torso, multiple limb positioning under constraints, view assessment, reach space generation, and strength guided performance simulation of human figures. Of particular importance is a simulation level which allows access to *Jack* by high level task control, various knowledge bases, task definitions and natural language instructions. Thus human activities can be visualized from high level task understanding and planning as well as by interactive specification.

One can think of *Jack* as an experimental environment in which a number of useful general variables may be readily created, adjusted, or controlled: the workplace, the task, the human agent(s) and some responses of the workplace to internally or externally controlled actions. The results of specific instances of these input parameters are reported through computer graphics displays, textual information, and animations. Thus the field of view of a 50th percentile male while leaning over backwards in a tractor seat as far a possible may be directly visualized through the graphic display. If the figure is supposed to watch the corner of the bulldozer blade as it moves through its allowed motion, the human figure's gaze will follow in direct animation of the view.

In the following subsections, several desiderata are presented for human models. Under each, we summarize the major features – with justifications and benefits – of the *Jack* software. The detailed discussions of these features and their implementation constitute the bulk of the remaining chapters.

1.3.1 A Human Model must be Structured Like the Human Skeletal System

To build a biomechanically reasonable figure, the skeletal structure should resemble but need not copy that of humans. We can buffer the complexity of actual bone shapes, joint types and joint contact surfaces with requirements for interactive use and external motion approximations. For example, rotational joints are usually assumed to have a virtual center about which the adjacent body segments move. While such simplifications would not be appropriate for, say, knee prosthesis design, there appears to be little harm in variations on the order of a centimeter or so. Of course, there are situations where small departures from reality could affect the verisimilitude of the figure; accordingly we have concentrated on rather accurate models for the torso and shoulder complex. Many other software systems (or manual methods) presume a fixed shoulder joint but it is obvious that this is not true as the arm is elevated.

1. *Jack* has a fully linked body model including a 17 segment flexible torso with vertebral joint limits. In general, individual joints may have one, two, or three degrees of freedom (DOFs). Related groups of joints, such as the spine or the shoulder complex, may be manipulated as a unit. The result is reasonable biomechanical realism with only modest computational overhead.

2. The *Jack* shoulder mass joint center is posture-dependent. Accurate shoulder motion is modeled through an explicit dependency between arm position and clavicle rotation. The figure therefore presents appropriate shoulder and clavicle motions during positioning. The shoulder joint has spherical (globographic [EP87]) limits for improved motion range accuracy.

3. All joint rotations are subject to limits. During manipulation, rotations propagate when joint limits would be exceeded.

4. A fully articulated hand model is attached.

5. The foot is articulated enough to provide toe and heel flexibility. If more DOFs were required, they could be easily added.

1.3.2 A Human Model should Move or Respond Like a Human

Ideally, the motions presented by a simulated figure will be biomechanically valid. They should not only appear "human-like," but they should be validated against empirical data for real subjects under similar conditions. This goal is desirable but difficult to reach in a generalized motion model precisely because such a model must allow interpolation and extrapolation to situations other than those originally measured. Models are needed to provide reasonable interpretations of data that by necessity must be sampled rather coarsely, in specific situations, and with a collection of specific subjects. The closest we can get to the ideal is to provide generic mechanisms that incorporate whenever possible empirical data that a user believes to be valid up to the degree of error permitted for the task. Rather than hide such data, *Jack* takes the view of an open database where reasonable default human anthropometric, strength or performance data is provided, but user customizing is the rule rather than the exception.

1. *Jack* permits multiple figures to simultaneously inhabit an environment. Multi-person environments and operator interactions may be studied for interference, view, and coordinated tasks.

2. A number of active behaviors are defined for the figure and may be selected or disabled by the user. Among the most interesting is constraining the center of mass of the entire figure during manipulation. This allows automatic balance and weight-shifting while other tasks such as reaching, viewing, bending over, etc. are being performed. Spare cycles on the workstation are used inbetween human operator inputs to constantly monitor the active constraints and move the body joints towards their satisfaction.

3. People usually move in ways that conserve resources (except when they are deliberately trying to achieve optimum performance). If strength information as a function of body posture and joint position is available, that data may be used to predict certain end-effector motion paths under specified "comfort" conditions. Thus the exact motions involved in, say, lifting a weight are subservient to the strength model, comfort and fatigue parameters, and heuristics for selecting among various movement strategies. By avoiding "canned" or arbitrary (for example, straight line) motion paths, great flexibility in executing tasks is provided.

4. The *Jack* hand model has an automatic grip. This feature saves the user from the independent manipulation of large numbers of joints and DOFs. The user specifies a grip type and an optional site on the object to be grasped. When possible, the hand itself chooses a suitable approach direction. Though frictional forces are not modeled, the positioning task is greatly aided by the hand's skill. Once gripped, the object stays attached to the hand and moves along with it until explicitly freed by the user.

1.3.3 A Human Model should be Sized According to Permissible Human Dimensions

Effectively, there is no such thing as a "average" human. Statistically one must always prescribe a target population when talking about percentiles of size, weight, or stature. A person may be 50th percentile in stature, 75th percentile in weight, but 40th percentile in lower leg length. Human dimensional variability is enormous but not arbitrary. Within a given population, for example, 5th percentile legs might never be found on anybody with 95th percentile arms, even though the population allows such sizes individually. Moreover, dimensions are not just limited to lengths, stature, and weight, but include joint limits, moments of inertia for each body segment, muscle strengths, fatigue rates, and so on. For proper behaviors, one must be able to instantiate a properly sized figure with appropriately scaled attributes, preferably from a known population suitable for the required task analysis.

1. The *Jack* anthropometric database is not proprietary. All data is readily available and accessible. Consequently, it is easily customized to new populations or sets of individuals. Some databases are available, such as NASA astronaut trainees, Army soldiers, and Society of Automotive Engineers "standard people."

2. A database may consist of either population statistics or individuals. If populations, then percentile data points are expected in order to define body dimensions. If individuals, then explicit information for each person in the collection is separately stored. For example, the NASA astronaut trainees constitute an explicit list of individuals, while the Army soldier data is statistically derived.

3. Enough information about a human figure must be stored to permit body sizing, display, and motion. We use overall segment dimensions (length, width, thickness), joint limits, mass, moment of inertia, and strength. Geometric properties are used during graphical manipulation; physical properties aid active behaviors (balance), dynamic simulation, and strength guided motion.

4. With so many DOFs in a body and many useful physical attributes, there must be a convenient way of accessing, selecting, and modifying any data. *Jack* uses a spreadsheet-like interface to access anthropometry data. This paradigm permits simple access and data interdependencies: for example, changing leg length should change stature; changing population percentile should change mass distribution.

5. Seeing the results of changing body dimensions is important to understanding how different bodies fit, reach, and see in the same workplace. *Jack* allows interactive body sizing while the body itself is under active constraints. Changing a figure seated in a cockpit from 95th percentile to

5th percentile, for example, creates interesting changes in foot position, arm postures and view.

1.3.4 A Human Model should have a Human-Like Appearance

As we argued earlier, a human model's appearance has a lot to do with our perception of acceptable behavior. The more accurate the model, the better the motions ought to be. Providing a selection of body models is a convenient way to handle a spectrum of interactive analysis and animation requirements. For quick assessments, a human model with simplified appearance might be fine. If the skin surface is not totally realistic, the designer can move the view around to check for sufficient clearances, for example. When the completed analysis is shown to the boss, however, an accurate skin model might be used so that the robotic nature of the simpler model does not obscure the message. Looking better is often associated (in computer graphics) with being better.

1. The "standard" or default body model in *Jack* strikes a balance between detail and interactive manipulation speed. It appears solid, has a 17 segment flexible torso, has a reasonable shoulder/clavicle mass, has a full hand, and has a generic face. A hat is added to avoid modeling hairstyles. The figure is modeled by surface polygons to take advantage of the available workstation display capabilities.

2. There are times when more accurate skin surface models are needed. For that, computerized models of real people are used. These are derived from a database of biostereometrically-scanned bodies.

3. For extra realism, clothing is added to body segments by expanding and coloring the existing segment geometry. Besides the inherent desirability of having a virtual figure in a work environment appear to be dressed, clothing will also affect task performance if adjustments are made to joint limits or if collision tests are performed.

4. Facial features may be provided by graphical texture maps. By showing a specific face a particular individual may be installed in the scene, the figure may be uniquely identified throughout an animation, or generic gender may be conveyed. Moreover, if the face is animated, an entire communication channel is enabled.

1.3.5 A Human Model must Exist, Work, Act and React Within a 3D Virtual Environment

We do not live in Flatland [Abb53] and neither should virtual figures. Three-dimensional environment modeling is the hallmark of contemporary computer-aided design (CAD) systems. The workplace will frequently be constructed electronically for design, analysis, and manufacturing reasons; we merely add human factors analysis to the list. Design importation facilitates up-front analyses before commitment to production hardware. Since geometric models are readily constructed, we must be sure that our body models and interactive software are compatible with the vast majority of CAD modeling schemes so the two can work together in the same virtual space.

1. Since *Jack* manipulates surface polygon geometry, simple features are provided to interactively construct and edit the geometry of the virtual workplace. *Jack* is not intended as a substitute for a good CAD system, but CAD features are provided for convenience. For example, if a designer finds a problem with the imported workplace, the offending region can be immediately edited in *Jack*. When the changes prove acceptable, the designer can use the data values from *Jack* to modify the "real" model in the external CAD system. While not optimal, this avoids any tendency to migrate the working model into *Jack* and bypass the more generalized CAD features provided by most CAD systems.

2. Standardized geometric data transfer to and from *Jack* would be highly desirable, but the state of standards in geometric modeling still leaves some important gaps. For example, few CAD systems adequately model articulated objects. Currently, *Jack* imports models from several common CAD vendors through a less satisfactory scheme of explicit translators from external geometry files. This situation will change to a standard as soon as possible.

1.3.6   Use the Computer to Analyze Synthetic Behaviors

What would a real person do in a real environment? How can we get a virtual human to behave appropriately and report similar experiences? People are constantly managing multiple simultaneous constraints or tasks, for example, staying balanced while reaching to lift a box, or walking while carrying a cup of coffee. The essential parallelism of human motion demands an approach to behavior animation that does not just cope with parallelism but exploits it. We will be interested mostly in psychomotor and viewing behaviors; clearly auditory and cognitive tasks are worthy of inclusion but are not dealt with here.

1. *Jack* allows the user to specify, and the system maintains, multiple simultaneous position and orientation goals. For instance, a typical posture might involve reaching with two hands while looking at a target and staying balanced. There are constraints on the positions of the hands and the orientation of the eyes dictated by the task, and balance constraints required by gravity. Additionally, we might want the torso to remain upright or, if seated, for the pelvis to tilt to a more relaxed posture. There are too many possible human body configurations to manage every combination by specialized rules; our approach is to

use a global solution technique, *inverse kinematics*, to satisfy the given constraints subject to the inherent joint limits of the body.

2. While in a posture, the strength requirements of the figure may be displayed on screen. This interactive strength data display shows all torque loads along any selected chain of body segments. If a load is attached to an end-effector, for example, it permits the easy visualization of the distribution of that additional weight on the body.

3. What the figure is looking at is often a critical question in human factors analysis. In *Jack*, the direction of eye gaze is controlled through constraints to some environmental location or object site. If that site moves, the gaze will follow. Since eye movement will affect head orientation, the effect of gaze direction can propagate (because of joint limits) to the neck and torso and hence influence overall body posture.

4. In *Jack*, the user can see what the figure sees from an internal or external perspective. Internally, a separate graphics window may be opened which shows the view from the selected eye. The image appears naturally shaded and it moves as the figure's gaze is adjusted by direct manipulation or constraints. Concurrent changes to the environment and visible parts of the figure's own "self" are displayed in the view window. If field of view is critical, a *retinal projection* may be used where a polar projection displays workplace features based on their angle from the fovea. Although the image thereby appears distorted, the actual field of view may be superimposed to assess the range of foveal or peripheral perception. For the external perspective, a selected field of view is displayed as a translucent pair of view cones, one for each eye. The cones move with the eyes. Objects in view are shadowed by the translucent cones. Any overlapped region is clearly in the area of binocular vision.

5. It is not yet feasible to do real-time collision detection between all the moving objects in a complex environment. By various simplifications, however, sufficient capabilities may be presented. On fast displays with real-time viewing rotation (such as the Silicon Graphics workstations), the ability to rapidly change the view means that the user can quickly move about to check clearances. Another method used in *Jack* is to optionally project three orthogonal views of a figure and other selected objects onto back, side, and bottom planes. These three additional views give simultaneous contact and interference information and are used during interactive manipulations. Often, users will work with shaded images and detect collisions by noting when one object visually passes into another. The alternative to visual collision detection is direct object–object interference computation. Usually limited to a selected body segment and a convex object, this method is slower but guarantees to detect a collision even if it would be difficult to see.

6. Sometimes it is valuable to visualize the entire reachable space of an end-effector of the figure. Empirical data is sometimes available in the literature [NAS78, NAS87], but it is collected on specific subjects and does not readily extend to figures with differing anthropometry or joint limits. By constructing the reach space for a given figure in a given posture as a geometric object, the reach space may be viewed and objects may be readily classified as in or out of the reach space.

1.3.7 An Interactive Software Tool must be Designed for Usability

A system to build, move, and analyze virtual humans should be usable by mere mortals with a modest training period. Isolating the potential user community by requiring unusual artistic skills would be counter-productive to our wider purposes of aiding design engineers. Existing interaction paradigms (such as pop-up menus or command line completions) should be followed when they are the most efficacious for a particular task, but new techniques will be needed to manage and control three-dimensional articulated structures with standard graphical input tools. The interface should be simple yet powerful, comprehensive but easy to learn.

1. The *Jack* user interface is designed for fast response to multiple constraint situations. Real-time end-effector interactive dragging through arbitrary length joint chains means that the user can watch the figure respond to reach or movement tasks. The paradigm of manipulating one joint angle at a time is possible, but almost useless. The goal-directed behaviors provide an enormous benefit to the user in allowing the specification of *what* is to be done while constraint satisfaction handles the *how* through positioning interdependencies of the entire body structure. Dragging also permits quick experimentation with and manual optimization of postures.

2. By taking advantage of the Silicon Graphics display hardware, *Jack* shows the user shaded or wireframe displays during interaction for natural images and easy real-time visualization.

3. For the highest quality images, *Jack* provides its own multi-featured ray-tracing and radiosity programs.

4. Besides direct user input, *Jack* may be controlled through scripted commands (in the *Jack command language*) built in the course of interactive manipulation. This saves time and trouble in setting up complex situations, establishing a body posture, or trying a series of actions.

5. *Jack* also allows external control through operating system "sockets" to other programs, simulations, or real sensors, providing hooks into external data sources for virtual environments or networked remote systems

sharing a common virtual dataspace. *Jack* itself can share an environment with other *Jack*'s on the network. This could be used for novel cooperative workgroup applications.

6. The standard *Jack* user interface consists of just a three button mouse and keyboard. It is simple to learn and no special hardware devices are required unless a virtual environment setup is desired. The interaction paradigms in *Jack* include menu-driven or typed commands, on-line help, and command completion. It is easy to use after only a day or so of training.

7. The direct manipulation interface into three dimensions implemented in *Jack* is both highly efficient and natural to use. Depending only on the mouse and keyboard, it offers a friendly, kinesthetic correspondence between manually comfortable hand motions, on-screen displays, and three-dimensional consequences. Three dimensional cursors, rotation wheels, and orthogonal projections of the principal view provide excellent visual feedback to the user.

8. *Jack* provides multiple windows with independent camera views for complex analyses, multiple points of view, and internal and external eye views.

1.4 Manipulation, Animation, and Simulation

There are important distinctions between *manipulation*, *animation*, and *simulation*. Geometric manipulation is the process of interactive scene composition, or the interactive specification of positions and postures for geometric figures, usually on a trial and error basis. Manipulation usually involves movement of the figures, but the movement serves to assist in the control process and is generally not worth saving as a memorable motion sequence. Rather, the purpose of manipulation is to get the figures into a desired static posture, although the posture need not remain static afterwards. Manipulation is inherently real-time: objects move as a direct response to the actions of the user. In short, interactive manipulation is not necessarily choreography.

Animation, on the other hand, is choreography. In computer animation, the goal is to describe motion, and the animator usually imagines the desired motion before beginning the animation process. Of course, experimentation may lead to revisions, like an illustrator who erases lines in a drawing, but the computer does not serve so much to answer questions as to obey orders. Animators measure the success of a computer animation system in terms of how well it serves as a medium for expressing ideas.

Simulation is automated animation, and the concern is again with motion. The system generates the motion based on some kind of input from the user ahead of time. The input usually consists of objectives and rules for making decisions, and it is generally less specific than with animation. The user knows

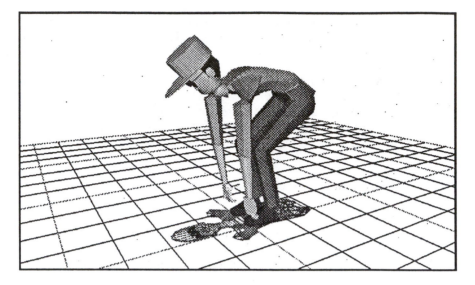

Figure 1.1: Is it the Motion or the Posture?

less about what motion should result. The job of the simulator is to predict what would happen under certain circumstances and inform the user of the results. Sometimes simulation can generate animation, as in the case of the animation of physics and natural phenomena. Simulation of human figures generally implies some modeling of human capabilities to deliberately off-load some of the low-level positioning overhead from the animator.

Animation and simulation have been studied extensively, but manipulation of articulated figures has not received the attention it deserves. Volumes of research discuss animation techniques and simulation algorithms, but most research directed at interactive manipulation deals either with the low-level input mechanisms of describing 3D translations and rotations, or with the numerical issues of real-time dynamics. For example, consider the task of bending a figure over to touch its toes (Fig. 1.1. Is the bending motion important, or is it just the final posture that is critical? In animation, it's the motion: the motion must look realistic. In simulation, the motion must *be* realistic. In manipulation, the finer points of the posture are critical. Is the figure balanced? Are the knees bent? Where is the head pointed? How are the feet oriented? The motion through which the manipulation system positions the figure is not important in itself. It serves only to assist the user in arriving at the posture.

1.5 What Did We Leave Out?

It is only fair that in this exposition we are clear about what our existing software does not do. There are choices to be made in any implementation, but the vastness of the human performance problem demands scope boundaries as well. There are fascinating problems remaining that we have not touched. Some of these problems are being examined now, but the early results are too premature to report. The activity in this field is amazing, and there will surely be advances in modeling, animation, and performance simulation reported each year.

A glance at the *Engineering Data Compendium* [BL88], for example, will quickly show how much information has been collected on human factors and simultaneously how little is available interactively on a computer. But even without much thought, we can place some bounds on this study.

- We have ignored auditory information processing, environmental factors (such as temperature and humidity), vibration sensitivity, and so on. While critical for harsh environments, we seek useful approximations to first order (geometric) problems to see if a figure can do the task in the absence of external signals, distress, or threats. The probable degradation of task performance may be established from intelligent (manual) search through existing publications. While it would be attractive to include such data, we have not begun to acquire or use it yet.

- We have bypassed super-accurate skin models because the enfleshment of a figure is so dependent on individual physiology, muscle tone, muscle/fat ratio, and gender. For the kinds of analyses done with whole body models, errors of a centimeter or so in skin surfaces are subordinate to anthropometric errors in locating true joint centers and joint geometry.

- We have avoided injury assessment, as that is another whole field developed from anatomy, crash studies, or national exertion standards. Of course, *Jack* could be used in conjunction with such systems, but we have not tried to connect them yet.

- Because we have taken a generalized view of human factors and restricted analyses to reach, fit, view, and strength, we have necessarily avoided any workplace-specific performance data. For example, action timings will be most accurate when measured with real subjects in a real environment. We have concentrated on measurements in environments prior to physical construction to save cost and possible personnel dangers.

- We have only touched on perceptual, reactive and cognitive issues. Many workers are engaged in control-theoretic activities: sensing the environment and reacting to maintain some desired state. We see this capability eventually driving the figure through the simulation interface, but at the present we have not modeled such situations. Instead we are investigating natural language instructions which generate an animation of the simulated agent's "artificial intelligence" understanding of the situation.

- Finally, we are leaving issues of learning for later study. There is much to be said for an agent who not only follows instructions but who also learns how to do similar (but not identical) actions in comparable situations in the future. Learning might first occur at the psychomotor level, for example, to figure out the best way to lift a heavy weight. Later, learning can extend to the task level: to repeat a variant of a previously successful plan when the overall goals are encountered again.

These issues are exciting, but we need to start with the basics and describe what exists today.

Chapter 2

Body Modeling

In order to manipulate and animate a human figure with computer graphics, a suitable figure must be *modeled*. This entails constructing a satisfactory surface skin for the overall human body shape, defining a skeletal structure which admits proper joint motions, adding clothing to improve the verisimilitude of analyses (as well as providing an appropriate measure of modesty), sizing body dimensions according to some target individual or population, and providing visualization tools to show physically-relevant body attributes such as torque loads and strength.

2.1 Geometric Body Modeling

In computer graphics, the designer gets a wide choice of representations for the surfaces or volumes of objects. We will briefly review current geometric modeling schemes with an emphasis on their relevance to human figures.

We classify geometric models into two broad categories: boundary schemes and volumetric schemes. In a boundary representation the surface of the object is approximated by or partitioned into (non-overlapping) 0-, 1-, or 2-dimensional primitives. We will examine in turn those representations relevant to human modeling: points and lines, polygons, and curved surface patches. In a volumetric representation the 3D volume of the object is decomposed into (possibly overlapping) primitive volumes. Under volumetric schemes we discuss voxels, constructive solid geometry, ellipsoids, cylinders, spheres, and potential functions.

2.1.1 Surface and Boundary Models

The simplest surface model is just a collection of 3D points or lines. Surfaces represented by points require a fairly dense distribution of points for accurate modeling. Clouds of points with depth shading were used until the early 1980's for human models on vector graphics displays. They took advantage of the display's speed and hierarchical transformations to produce the perceptual depth effect triggered by moving points [Joh76] (for example, [GM86]).

A related technique to retain display speed while offering more shape information is to use parallel rings or strips of points. This technique is used in *LifeForms*™[1] [Lif91, Cal91]. Artistically positioned "sketch lines" were used in one of the earliest human figure models [Fet82] and subsequently in a Mick Jagger music video, "Hard Woman" from Digital Productions.

Polygons

Polygonal (polyhedral) models are one of the most commonly encountered representations in computer graphics. The models are defined as networks of polygons forming 3D polyhedra. Each polygon (primitive) consists of some connected vertex, edge, and face structure. The polygons are sized, shaped, and positioned so that they completely tile the required surface at some resolution. Polygon models are relatively simple to define, manipulate, and display. They are the most common models processed by workstation hardware and commercial graphics software. In general, polygons are best at modeling objects meant to have flat surfaces, though with a large enough number of polygons quite intricate and complex objects can be represented. "Large enough" may mean hundreds of thousands of polygons!

All viable *interactive* human figure models are done with polygons, primarily because the polygon is the primitive easiest to manage for a modern workstation such as the Silicon Graphics machines. With real-time smooth shading, polygon models of moderate complexity (several hundred polygons) can look acceptably human-like; accurate skin models require thousands. A realistic face alone may require two or three thousand polygons if it is to be animated and if the polygons are the only source of detail.

Polygon models are too numerous to cite extensively. Ones with an interesting level of detail have been used in Mannequin software from Biomechanics Corporation of America [Pot91], various movies such as "Tony de Peltrie" from the University of Montreal [Emm85], and detailed synthetic actor models of Marilyn Monroe and Humphrey Bogart from Daniel Thalmann and Nadia Magnenat-Thalmann [MTT90, MTT91b]. They even model details of skin deformation by applying physical forces to polygon meshs [GMTT89, MTT91b].

The polygon models used in *Jack* are polygonal with two different levels of detail. The normal models have a few hundred polygons. More accurate models obtained from actual scans of real bodies have several thousand polygons. (See Section 2.1.3.)

Curved Surfaces

Since polygons are good at representing flat surfaces, considerable effort has been expended determining mathematical formulations for true curved surfaces. Most curved surface object models are formed by one or more para-

---

[1]LifeForms is a registered trademark of Kinetic Effects, Inc.

metric functions of two variables (bivariate functions). Each curved surface is called a patch; patches may be joined along their boundary edges into more complex surfaces. Usually patches are defined by low order polynomials (typically cubics) giving the patch easily computed mathematical properties such as well-defined surface normals and tangents, and computable continuity conditions between edge-adjacent patches. The shape of a patch is derived from control points or tangent vectors; there are both approximating and interpolating types. The former take the approximate shape of the control vertices; the latter must pass through them. There are numerous formulations of curved surfaces, including: Bezier, Hermite, bi-cubic, B-spline, Beta-spline, and rational polynomial [Far88, BBB87].

Various human figure models have been constructed from curved patches, but display algorithm constraints make these figures awkward for real-time manipulation. They are excellent for animation. provided that sufficient care is taken to model joint connections. This is a good example of where increased realism in the body segments demands additional effort in smoothing and bending joint areas properly. Curved surface models were used in a gymnastic piece [NHK86] and the Academy Award-winning "Tin Toy" [GP88].

2.1.2 Volume and CSG Models

The volume and CSG models divide the world into three-dimensional chunks. The models may be composed of non-intersecting elements within a spatial partition, such as voxels or oct-trees, or created from (possibly overlapping) combinations of inherently 3D primitive volumes.

Voxel Models

The first volumetric model we examine is the voxel model. Here space is completely filled by a tessellation of cubes or parallelopipeds called voxels (volume elements). Usually there is a density or other numerical value associated with each voxel. Storing a high resolution tessellation is expensive in space but simple in data structure (just a large 3D array of values). Usually some storage optimization schemes are required for detailed work (1K x 1K x 1K spaces). Special techniques are needed to compute surface normals and shading to suppress the boxiness of the raw voxel primitive. Voxel data is commonly obtained in the medical domain; it is highly regarded for diagnostic purposes as the 3D model does not speculate on additional data (say by surface fitting) nor suppress any of the original data however convoluted.

Voxel models are the basis for much of the scientific visualization work in biomedical imaging [FLP89]. The possible detail for human models is only limited by the resolution of the sensor. Accurate bone joint shapes may be visualized, as well as the details of internal and external physiological features. These methods have not yet found direct application in the human factors domain, since biomechanical rather than anatomical issues are usually addressed. Real-time display of voxel images is also difficult, requiring either low resolution image sets or special hardware [GRB+85].

Constructive Solid Geometry

One of the most efficient and powerful modeling techniques is constructive solid geometry (CSG). Unlike the voxel models, there is no requirement to regularly tessellate the entire space. Moreover, the primitive objects are not limited to (uniform) cubes; rather there are any number of simple primitives such as cube, sphere, cylinder, cone, half-space, etc. Each primitive is transformed or deformed and positioned in space. Combinations of primitives or of previously combined objects are created by the Boolean operations. An object therefore exists as a tree structure which is "evaluated" during rendering or measurement.

CSG has been used to great advantage in modeling machined parts, but has not been seriously used for human body modeling. Besides the mechanical look created, real-time display is not possible unless the CSG primitives are polygonized into surfaces. When the set of primitives is restricted in one way or other, however, some useful or interesting human models have been built.

Single Primitive Systems

The generality of the constructive solid geometry method – with its multiplicity of primitive objects and expensive and slow ray-tracing display method – is frequently reduced to gain efficiency in model construction, avoid Boolean combinations other than union, and increase display speed. The idea is to restrict primitives to one type then design manipulation and display algorithms to take advantage of the uniformity of the representation. Voxels might be considered such a special case, where the primitives are all coordinate axis aligned and integrally positioned cubes. Other schemes are possible, for example, using ellipsoids, cylinders, superquadrics, or spheres.

Ellipsoids have been used to model cartoon-like figures [HE78, HE82]. They are good for elongated, symmetric, rounded objects. Unfortunately, the shaded display algorithm is nearly the same as the general ray-tracing process.

Cylinders have also been used to model elongated, symmetric objects. Elliptic cylinders were used in an early human modeling system [Wil82]. These primitives suffer from joint connection problems and rather poor representations of actual body segment cross-sections.

Superquadrics are a mathematical generalization of spheres which include an interesting class of shapes within a single framework: spheres, ellipsoids, and objects which arbitrarily closely look like prisms, cylinders, and stars. Simple parameters control the shape so that deformations through members of the class are simple and natural. Superquadrics are primarily used to model man-made objects, but when overlapped can give the appearance of faces and figures [Pen86].

Spheres as a single primitive form an intriguing class. Spheres have a simplicity of geometry that rivals that of simple points: just add a radius.

There are two methods of rendering spheres. Normally they are drawn as regular 3D objects. A human modeled this way tends to look like a large bumpy molecule. Alternatively, spheres may be treated like "scales" on the modeled object; in this case a sphere is rendered as a flat shaded disk. With sufficient density of overlapping spheres, the result is a smoothly shaded solid which models curved volumes rather well. A naturalistic human figure was done this way in our earlier TEMPUS system [BB78, BKK$^+$85, SEL84]. We stopped using this method as we could not adequately control the sphere/disk overlaps during animation and newer workstation display technology favored polygons.

Potential Functions

An interesting generalization of spheres which solves some major modeling problems is to consider the volume as a potential function with a center and a field function that decreases monotonically (by an exponential or polynomial function) from the center outward. There is no "radius" or size of the potential function; rather, the size or surface is determined by setting a threshold value for the field. What makes this more interesting is that potential functions act like energy sources: adjacent potential functions have overlapping fields and the resultant value at a point in space is in fact the sum of the fields active at that point. Thus adjacent fields blend smoothly, unlike the "creases" that are obtained with fixed radius spheres [Bli82]. Recently, directional dependence and selective field summation across models have been added to create "soft" models that blend with themselves but not with other modeled objects in the environment [WMW86, NHK$^+$85]. Potential functions were originally used to model molecules, since atoms exhibit exactly this form of field behavior, but the models have an amazing naturalistic "look" and have been used to great effect in modeling organic forms including human and animal figures [NHK$^+$85, BS91]. The principal disadvantages to potential functions lie in properly generating the numerous overlapping functions and very slow display times. They remain an interesting possibility for highly realistic models in the future.

2.1.3 The Principal Body Models Used

[2]The default polyhedral human figure in *Jack* is composed of 69 segments, 68 joints, 136 DOFs, and 1183 polygons (including cap and glasses). The appearance is a compromise between realism and display speed. No one is likely to mistake the figure for a real person; on the other hand, the movements and speed of control are good enough to convey a suitably responsive attitude. The stylized face, hat, and glasses lend a bit of character and actually assist in the perception of the forward-facing direction.

For more accurate human bodies, we have adapted a database of actual body scans of 89 subjects (31 males and 58 females) supplied by Kathleen

---

[2]Pei-Hwa Ho.

Robinette of Wright-Patterson Air Force Base and used with her permission. The original data came in contours, that is, slices of the body in the transverse plane [GQO+89]. Each body segment was supplied as a separate set of contours. A polygon tiling program was used to transform the contours of each body segment into a surface representation.

In order to represent the human body as an articulated figure we needed to first compute the proper joint centers to connect the segments together. Joint center locations were computed through the coordinates of anthropometric landmarks provided with the contour data.

Real humans are not symmetrical around the sagittal plane: our left half is not identical to our right half. This was the case with the contour data. For consistency, rather than accuracy, we used the right half of the body data to construct a left half and then put them together. We also sliced the upper torso to take advantage of the seventeen segment spine model (Section 2.3). The resulting human body model has thirty-nine segments and about 18,700 polygons compared to the 290 slices in the original data.

2.2   Representing Articulated Figures

Underneath the skin of a human body model is a representation of the skeleton. This skeletal representation serves to define the moving parts of the figure. Although it is possible to model each of the bones in the human body and encode in the model how they move relative to each other, for most types of geometric analyses it is sufficient to model the body segments in terms of their lengths and dimensions, and the joints in terms of simple rotations. There are some more complex joint groups such as the shoulder and spine where inherent dependencies across several joints require more careful and sophisticated modeling.

The increasing interest in recent years in object-oriented systems is largely due to the realization that the design of a system must begin with a deep understanding of the objects it manipulates. This seems particularly true in a geometric modeling system, where the word "object" takes on many of its less abstract connotations. It has long been an adage in the user interface software community that a system with a poorly designed basic structure cannot be repaired by improving the interface, and likewise that a well designed system lends itself easily to an elegant interface.

This section describes **Peabody**, which represents articulated *figures* composed of *segments* connected by *joints*. The **Peabody** data structure has a companion language and an interactive interface in *Jack* for specifying and creating articulated figures. The data structure itself maintains geometric information about segment dimensions and joint angles, but it also provides a highly efficient mechanism for computing, storing, and accessing various kinds of geometric information. One of the principal tasks requested of **Peabody** is to map segment dimensions and joint angles into global coordinates for end effectors.

Peabody was designed with several criteria in mind:

- It should be general purpose. It should be able to represent many types of figures of tree-structured topology. It should not be hard coded to represent a specific type of figure, such as a human figure or a particular robot manipulator.

- It should have a well developed notion of articulation. Rather than concentrating on representations for primitive geometric shapes, **Peabody** addresses how such shapes can be connected together and how they behave relative to each other.

- It should represent tree-structured objects through a hierarchy. The inverse kinematics positioning algorithm can calculate and maintain the information necessary to simulate closed loops.

- It should be easy to use. The external user view of the figures should be logical, clear, and easy to understand. Understanding the figures should not require any knowledge of the internal implementation, and it should not require any advanced knowledge of robotics or mechanics.

2.2.1 Background

Kinematic Notations in Robotics

The most common kinematic representation in robotics is the notation of Denevit and Hartenberg [Pau81, DH55]. This representation derives a set of parameters for describing a linkage based on measurements between the axes of a robot manipulator. The notation defines four parameters that measure the offset between subsequent coordinate frames embedded in the links, or segments: 1) the angle of rotation for a rotational joint or distance of translation for a prismatic joint; 2) the length of the link, or the distance between the axes at each end of a link along the common normal; 3) the lateral offset of the link, or the distance along the length of the axis between subsequent common normals; and 4) the twist of the link, or the angle between neighboring axes. The notation prescribes a formal procedure for assigning the coordinate systems to the links in a unique way.

The objective behind these kinematic notations in robotics is to develop a standard representation that all researchers can use in the analysis and description of manipulators. There are several types of manipulators that are extremely common in the robotics research community. The adoption of a standard representation would greatly simplify the process of analyzing and implementing robotics algorithms since so many algorithms are described in the literature using these manipulators.

Animation Systems

Computer graphics and animation literature seldom addresses syntactic, or even semantic, issues in representations for mechanisms, except as background for some other discussion of an animation technique or system.

Most interactive animation systems such as GRAMPS [OO81], TWIXT [Gom84], and BBOP [Stu84, Ste83], as well as commercial animation packages such as Alias [Ali90] and Wavefront [Wav89] only provide a mechanism of attaching one object to another. In this way, the user can construct hierarchies. When the user manipulates one object, its child objects follow, but there is no real notion of articulation. The attachments simply state that the origin of the child object is relative to the origin of the parent.

Many animation systems are non-interactive and are based on scripts that provide a hierarchy only through a programming language interface. Examples of such systems are ANIMA-II [Hac77], ASAS [Rey82] and MIRA-3D [MTT85]. In this kind of system, the hierarchy is hard-coded into the script, possibly through an interaction loop. A hierarchy designed in this way is very limited, except in the hands of a talented programmer/animator who can write into the animation a notion of behavior.

Physically-Based Modeling Systems

Physically based modeling systems such as that of Witkin, Fleisher, and Barr [WFB87] and Barzel and Barr [BB88] view the world as objects and constraints. Constraints connect objects together through desired geometric relationships or keep them in place. Otherwise, they float in space under the appropriate laws of physics. There is no notion of articulation other than constraints. This forces the burden of maintaining object positions entirely to the algorithms that do the positioning. For simple objects, this is conceptually pleasing, although for complex objects it is computationally difficult. If a system represents joints like the elbow as a constraint, the constraint must have a very high weighting factor in order to ensure that it never separates, requiring very small time steps in the simulation. This may also complicate the user's view of objects such as robots or human figures, which are inherently articulated. We believe it is important to differentiate the relationship between body segments at the elbow and the relationship between a hand and a steering wheel.

2.2.2   The Terminology of Peabody

Peabody uses the term *environment* to refer to the entire world of geometric objects. The environment consists of individual *figures*, each of which is a collection of *segments*. The segments are the basic building blocks of the environment. Each segment has a geometry. It represents a single physical object or part, which has shape and mass but no movable components. The geometry of each segment is represented by a *psurf*, which is generally a polyhedron or a polygonal mesh but can be of a more general nature.

The term *figure* applies not only to articulated, jointed figures such as a human body: any single "object" is a figure. It need not have moving parts. A figure may have only a single segment, such as a coffee cup, or it may be composed of several segments connected by *joints,* such as a robot. Sometimes the term "object" denotes any part of the **Peabody** environment.

Joints connect segments through attachment frames called *sites.* A site is a local coordinate frame relative to the coordinate frame of its segment. Each segment can have several sites. Joints connect sites on different segments within the same figure. Sites need not lie on the surface of a segment. A site is a coordinate frame that has an orientation as well as a position. Each site has a *location* that is the homogeneous transform that describes its placement relative to the base coordinate frame of its segment.

Segments do not have specific dimensions, such as the length, offset, and twist of Denevit and Hartenberg notation, because the origin can lie anywhere on the segment. The location of the axes of the joints that connect the segment are phrased in terms of this origin, rather than the other way around. The measurement of quantities such as length is complicated, because segments may have several joints connected to them, and none of these joints is designated in the definition as the "parent."

Joints may have several DOFs, which are rotational and translational axes. Each axis and its corresponding angle form a single rotation or translation, and the product of the transform at each DOF defines the transform across the joint, defining the placement of the sites, and thus the segments, that the joint connects.

The directionality of a joint is important because it defines the order in which the DOF transforms are concatenated. Because these transforms are not commutative, it is essential that the order is well-defined. This is an especially important feature of **Peabody**, since it is sometimes convenient to define the direction of the joint in a way different from the way the joint occurs in the figure hierarchy. An example of this is the human knee. Although it may be useful to structure the hierarchy of a human body with the root at the foot, it is also appealing to have the joints at both knees defined in the same manner.

2.2.3   The Peabody Hierarchy

Peabody avoids imposing a predefined hierarchy on the figures by encouraging the user to think of figures as collections of segments and joints, none with special importance. However, there must exist an underlying hierarchy because **Peabody** is not equipped to handle closed-loop mechanisms. (Closed loop structures are managed through the constraint satisfaction mechanism.) The structure of the **Peabody** tree is defined by designating one site on the figure as the *root.* The root site roughly corresponds to the origin of the figure, and it provides a handle by which to specify the location of the figure. Viewing the figure as a tree, the root of the figure is the root of the tree. The root site of a figure may change from time to time, depending upon the desired behavior of the figure.

This means there are two representations for the hierarchy, one internal and one external. There are many advantages to having a dual representation of the hierarchy. First, it allows the hierarchy to be inverted on the fly. Most models have a natural order to their hierarchy, emanating from a logical origin, but this hierarchy and origin may or may not correspond to how a model is placed in the environment and used.

The choice of the figure root is particularly important to the inverse kinematics algorithm, since the algorithm operates on chains of joints within the figure. At least one point on the figure must remain fixed in space. Because the internal representation of the hierarchy is separate, the user maintains a consistent view of the transform across a joint, regardless of how the figure is rooted.

The example below illustrates the **Peabody** hierarchy. Each segment has its base coordinate frame in the middle and an arc leading to each of its sites. The transform along this arc is the site's location. Each site may have several joints branching out from it, connecting it downwards in the tree to sites on other segments.

```
figure table {
    segment leg {
        psurf = "leg.pss";
        attribute = plum;
        site base->location = trans(0.00cm,0.00cm,0.00cm);
        site top->location = trans(5.00cm,75.00cm,5.00cm);
    }
    segment leg0 {
        psurf = "leg.pss";
        attribute = springgreen;
        site base->location = trans(0.00cm,0.00cm,0.00cm);
        site top->location = trans(5.00cm,75.00cm,5.00cm);
    }
    segment leg1 {
        psurf = "leg.pss";
        attribute = darkslategray;
        site base->location = trans(0.00cm,0.00cm,0.00cm);
        site top->location = trans(5.00cm,75.00cm,5.00cm);
    }
    segment leg2 {
        psurf = "leg.pss";
        attribute = darkfirebrick;
        site base->location = trans(0.00cm,0.00cm,0.00cm);
        site top->location = trans(5.00cm,75.00cm,5.00cm);
    }
    segment top {
        psurf = "cube.pss" * scale(1.00,0.10,2.00);
        site base->location = trans(0.00cm,0.00cm,0.00cm);
        site leg0->location = trans(95.00cm,0.00cm,5.00cm);
        site leg2->location = trans(5.00cm,0.00cm,5.00cm);
```

```
            site leg3->location = trans(95.00cm,0.00cm,195.00cm);
            site leg4->location = trans(5.00cm,0.00cm,195.00cm);
        }
        joint leg1 {
            connect top.leg3 to leg1.top;
            type = R(z);
        }
        joint leg2 {
            connect top.leg2 to leg0.top;
            type = R(z);
        }
        joint leg3 {
            connect top.leg4 to leg2.top;
            type = R(z);
        }
        joint leg4 {
            connect top.leg0 to leg.top;
            type = R(z);
        }
        root = top.base;
        location = trans(0.00cm,75.00cm,0.00cm);
    }
```

2.2.4 Computing Global Coordinate Transforms

The root site for the figure is the one at the top of the tree, and its global location is taken as given, that is, not dependent on any other element of the environment. The root, the site locations, and the joint displacements uniquely determine the global location of every site and segment in the tree in terms of a product of transforms from the root downward.

The computation of the coordinate transforms for each segment and site in the downward traversal of the tree requires inverting the site locations that connect the segment to other segments lower in the tree. It may also require inverting joint displacements if the joint is oriented upwards in the tree. Computationally, this is not expensive because the inverse of a homogeneous transform is easy to compute, through a transpose and a dot product.

2.2.5 Dependent Joints

[3]The human figure can be abstracted as an object which is to be instantiated (into a certain pose) by any specification of all the joint angles. While any pose can be represented by a set of joint angles, it is not always possible to supply a full and reasonable set of angles. Often, for example, there is a

---

[3] Jianmin Zhao.

natural grouping of joints such as the torso or shoulder mass that typically work together. Arbitrary (admissible) joint angles for the joints in the group may not represent a legitimate posture: they are functionally dependent on each other.

Conceptually, these dependencies compromise the notion of the joint and joint angle and blur the boundary of the object definition. It seems that not all joints are created equal. Rather than have a system which tries to cope with every joint the same way, we take a more practical approach. We use a *joint group* concept in **Peabody** to accommodate joint dependency so that the relationship is coded into the object definition rather than the application program.

A joint group is a set of joints which are controlled as one entity. Internal joint angles are not visible outside of the group: they are driven by the group driver. The driver is nothing but a mapping from a number of parameters (counterparts of joint angles of the independent joint) to joint angles of its constituent joints. Those independent parameters will be called *group angles*. Similar to the joint angles of the independent joint, the group angles of the joint group are subject to linear constraints of the form

$$\sum_{i=1}^{n} a_i \theta_i \leq b_i \qquad\qquad (2.1)$$

where θ's are group angles and n is the number of θ's, or number of DOFs of the joint group. There may be many such constraints for each group.

There can be many applications of the joint group. Forearm pronation and supination change the segment geometry, so one way to manage that within the geometry constraints of psurfs is to divide the forearm into a number of nearly cylindrical sub-segments. As the wrist moves, its rotation is transmitted to the forearm segments such that distal sub-segments rotate more than proximal ones. The segment adjacent to the elbow does not pronate or supinate at all. Fingers could be managed in a similar fashion by distributing the desired orientation of the fingertip over the three joints in the finger chain. The most interesting examples, though, involve the torso and the shoulder. We address these cases in the next sections.

2.3   A Flexible Torso Model

[4]Human figure models have been studied in computer graphics almost since the introduction of the medium. Through the last dozen years or so, the structure, flexibility, and fidelity of human models has increased dramatically: from the wire-frame stick figure, through simple polyhedral models, to curved surfaces, and even finite element models. Computer graphics modelers have tried to maximize detail and realism while maintaining a reasonable overall display cost. The same issue pertains to control: improving motion realism

---

[4]Gary Monheit.

requires a great number of DOFs in the body linkage, and such redundancy strains effective and intuitively useful control methods. We can either simplify control by simplifying the model, thereby risking unrealistic movements; or complicate control with a complex model and hope the resulting motions appear more natural. The recent history of computer animation of human figures is focused on the quest to move the technology from the former situation towards the latter while simultaneously forcing the control complexity into algorithms rather than skilled manual manipulation.

This point of view motivates our efforts in human figure modeling and animation, as well as those of several other groups. Though notable algorithms for greater animation power have addressed kinematics, dynamics, inverse kinematics, available torque, global optimization, locomotion, deformation, and gestural and directional control, the human models themselves tended to be rather simplified versions of real human flexibility. In the early 1980's we warned that increased realism in the models would demand ever more accurate and complicated motion control; now that the control regimes are improving, we must return to the human models and ask if we must re-evaluate their structure to take advantage of algorithmic improvements. When we considered this question, we determined that a more accurate model of the human spine and torso would be essential to further realism in human motion.

Although many models have appeared to have a flexible torso, they have been computer constructions of the surface shape manipulated by skilled animators [Emm85]. We needed a torso that was suitable for animation, but also satisfied our requirements for anthropometric scalability. Thus a single model of fixed proportions is unacceptable as human body types manifest considerable differences. (A similar type of flexible figure is found in snakes [Mil88, Mil91], but the anthropometry issues do not arise. Moreover, this snake animation is dynamics-based; humans do not need to locomote by wiggling their torsos and so a kinematics model was deemed adequate.) Zeltzer and Stredney's "George" skeleton model has a detailed vertebral column, but it is not articulated nor is it bent during kinematic animation [Zel82]. Limited neck vertebral motion in the saggital plane was simulated by Willmert [Wil82]. Various body models attempt a spine with a 3D curve but shape and control it in a *ad hoc* fashion.

If the spine were realistically modeled, then the torso, a vessel connected and totally dependent on the spine, could then be viewed and manipulated interactively. So we undertook the development of a far more satisfactory and highly flexible vertebral model of the spine and its associated torso shape.

The conceptual model of the spinal column is derived from medical data and heuristics related to human kinesiology. The spine is a collection of vertebrae connected by ligaments, small muscles, vertebral joints (called processes), and intervertebral discs [BBA88]. Nature has designed the spine for support of the body's weight, stability of the torso, flexibility of motion, and protection of the spinal cord [AM71, Hol82].

The spine moves as a column of vertebrae connected by dependent joints, meaning that it is impossible to isolate movement of one vertebral joint from the surrounding vertebrae [Lou83]. Muscle groups of the head, neck, abdomen and back initiate the movement of the spine, and the interconnecting ligaments allow the movement of neighboring vertebrae [BBA88, Wel71].

2.3.1 Motion of the Spine

Anatomy of the Vertebrae and Disc

The spinal column consists of 33 vertebrae organized into 5 regions [BBA88]: cervical, thoracic, lumbar, sacral, and coccyx.

The vertebrae are labeled by medical convention in vertical descending order: C1–C7, T1–T12, L1–L5, and S1–S5. Which regions should be considered part of the torso? The cervical spine lies within the neck. The sacrum and coccyx contain vertebrae that are fixed through fusion [AM71]. Since the mobile part of the torso includes the 12 thoracic and 5 lumbar vertebrae, all together 17 vertebrae and 18 joints of movement are included in the torso model.

Each vertebra is uniquely sized and shaped, but all vertebrae contain a columnar body and an arch. The body is relatively large and cylindrical, supporting most of the weight of the entire spine. The vertebral bodies increase gradually in size from the cervical to the lumbar region [AM71].

The arch supports seven processes: four articular, two transverse, and one spinous [AM71]. The processes are bony protrusions on the vertebra that aid and limit the vertebral motion. The transverse and spinous processes serve as levers for both muscles and ligaments [BBA88]. The articular processes provide a joint facet for the joint between successive vertebral arches. These processes, due to their geometry, cause the vertebrae to rotate with 3 DOFs. Ligaments and small muscles span successive vertebral processes. They give the spinal column its stability. Because of this strong interconnectivity, spinal movement is modeled as interdependent movements of neighboring joints.

Vertebrae are each separated by intervertebral discs. The disc has 3 parts [Lou83]:

- **nucleus pulposus** - the sphere in the center, consisting of 85% water

- **annulus fibrosus** - the fibers running as concentric cylinders around the nucleus

- **cartilaginous plates** - a thin wall separating the disc from the vertebral body.

The disc changes shape as the neighboring vertebrae bend. But, since the nucleus is 85% water, there is very little compression. The disc can bulge out spherically, as force is applied to the columnar body above or below. Therefore, overall the disc does not function as a spring, but as a deformable cylindrical separation between vertebrae, supporting the theory that the vertebrae do not slide, but rotate around an axis [Lou83].

Range of Movement of Each Vertebra

Vertebral movement is limited by the relative size of the disks, the attached ligaments, and the shape and slant of the processes and facet joints. Statistics for joint limits between each successive vertebra have been recorded and compiled [Lou83]. Also, the spine has a natural shape at rest position. The initial joint position of each vertebra is input to the model.

The range of movement of each region of the spine is different. For instance, the optimum movement of the lumbar region is flexion or extension. The thoracic area easily moves laterally, while flexion/extension in the sagittal plane is limited. The cervical area is very flexible for both axial twisting and lateral bending. The joint limits for each region affect how much that joint is able to participate in any given movement. The posture of the torso is a result of the specialization of the spinal regions [Wil75].

Effect of the Surrounding Ligaments and Muscles

The vertebrae are interconnected by a complex web of ligaments and muscles. If the force initiated by a muscle group is applied at one joint, the joint moves and the neighboring joints also move to a lesser degree. Some joints farther away might not be affected by the initiator joint's movement.

It is possible to deactivate joints that are not initiating the movement. This action is achieved by simultaneous contractions of extensor and flexor muscles around the spinal column [Wil75]. Depending on the force of these resisting muscles, the joints on or near the joint closest to the resistor will move less than they would if the resisting force had not been applied. The final position of the spine is a function of the initiator force, the resisting muscle, and the amount of resistance.

2.3.2 Input Parameters

The spine is modeled as a black box with an initial state, input parameters, and an output state [MB91]. To initiate movement of the spine, several input parameters are introduced. These parameters are:

joint range FROM and TO: Within the total number of joints in the spine, any non-empty contiguous subset of vertebral joints may be specified by two joint indices. These joints indicate which part of the spine is active in movement. For example, the user specifies movement in the range between T5 and T10. All other joints are frozen in the movement.

initiator joint: The joint where movement begins, usually the joint with greatest motion.

resistor joint: The joint that resists the movement. This may be equated to a muscle that contracts and tries to keep part of the spine immobile.

resistance: The amount of resistance provided by the resistor joint.

spine target position: This is a 3D vector describing the target position
   after rotation around the x, y, and z axis. The target position is the
   sum of all joint position vectors in the spine after movement succeeds.

zero interpolation: A value of "yes" indicates that movement is interpolated through the joint rest position. A value of "no" indicates that only
   the joint limits are used to interpolate movement.

2.3.3   Spine Target Position

The joint between each vertebra has three degrees of rotation. The spine will
move toward the target position by rotating around the three possible axes
[Lou83]:

ROTATION OF THE SPINE		
flexion/extension	Forward/backward bending	Rotation around x axis
axial rotation	Twisting	Rotation around y axis
lateral bending	Side bending	Rotation around z axis

The position of the flexion rotational axis for each vertebral joint has
been measured from cadavers, and is not equidistant to the two adjacent
vertebrae, but is closer to the bottom vertebra [Lou83]. The origin of the axis
of movement determines how the vertebrae move. When the torso is modeled
on the spine, the axis also directly determines how the torso changes shape.

Elongation and compression are absent from the model. The hydrophilic
intervertebral disc, when submitted to prolonged compression induces a slight
decrease in height due to fluid leakage. Conversely, after a long period of rest
or zero-gravity, the spine elongates by maximum filling of the nucleus pulposus
(at the center of the disc) [Lou83]. Dehydration during a day's activity can
result in a loss of height of 2 cm in an adult person. In any short duration
of movement the disc is essentially incompressible, and therefore elongation
is imperceptible [Hol81].

Shearing or sliding (translational movements) of the vertebrae would lead
to variation in the intervertebral separation. This would not be allowed by
the mechanics of the intervertebral disc [Lou83]. Therefore, the assumption
is made that for normal activities the three degrees of rotational movement
are the only ones possible for each vertebral joint.

2.3.4   Spine Database

Any human figure can have a wide variety of torso shapes. Also, each person
has a different degree of flexibility and range of movement. In order to model
the position and shape changes of an individual's spine, a database has been
designed for creating a unique set of features for the spine and torso. Medical
data is the source of the database elements of an average person [Lou83].
The database consists of the size of each vertebra in the x, y, z dimension,

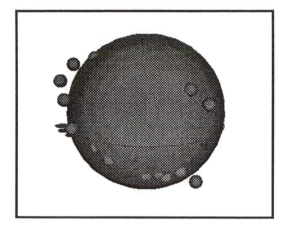

Figure 2.1: Spherical Trajectory of the Shoulder.

the intervertebral disc size, the joint limits (3 rotations with 2 limits per rotation), and the joint rest (initial) position. In Section 4.2.3 we will see how spine movement is realized.

2.4 Shoulder Complex

[5]It is well known that the movement of the humerus (the upper arm) is not a matter of simple articulation as most computer graphics models would have it. The movement is caused by articulations of several joints – glenohumeral joint, claviscapular joint and sternoclavicular joint. Collectively, they are called the *shoulder complex* [EP87, ET89].

In *Jack*, the shoulder complex is simplified with two joints – one connecting the sternum to the clavicle and the other connecting the clavicle to the humerus [GQO[+]89]. We call the former joint the *clavicle joint* and the latter the *shoulder joint*. This simplification implies that the rotational center of the humerus lies on a spatial sphere when the upper arm moves. It turns out that it is very close to empirical data collected with a 6-D sensor attached to the external midpoint between the dorsal and ventral side of the right upper arm [Mau91]. The z-axis of the sensor was along the longitudinal axis of the upper arm with the positive z axis direction pointing proximally, and the negative y-axis pointing into the upper arm. The sensor was placed 10 inches from the shoulder (the extremal point of the humerus).

From the experimental data the trajectory of the shoulder can be easily computed. We fitted the trajectory by the sphere which yields minimum average residual error. The result is quite satisfactory: the radius of the sphere is 6.05cm, and the average error (the distance from the trajectory point to the sphere) is 0.16cm. (Figure 2.1). Notice that the radius of the

---

[5] Jianmin Zhao.

Figure 2.2: A Neutral Human Figure.

sphere is not the same as the dimension of the clavicle. This is due to the
fact that the shoulder complex has indeed three joints instead of two. The
net result can be modeled by two joints, however, if we put the center of the
clavicle joint inbetween the two clavicle extremes.

In our applications we feel that two joints are adequate to model the
shoulder complex. So, we modeled the shoulder complex by grouping these
two joints into a joint group. Now we need to define the group angles and the
way they drive the internal joint angles.

2.4.1   Primitive Arm Motions

It will be convenient to have the group angles of the shoulder complex describe
the arm's motion in a natural way. To focus on this motion, we assume
that the elbow, the wrist and all joints down to fingers are fixed. What are
the arm's primitive motions? Mathematically, any three independent arm's
motions will suffice. But careful selection will pay off in positioning ease.

The arm's motion can be decomposed into two parts: spherical and twisting motions. The motion which moves the vector from the proximal end to
the distal end of the upper arm is called spherical motion, and the motion
which leaves this vector unchanged is called twisting.

In a neutral body stance, consider a coordinate system where the z axis
points vertically downward, the x axis points towards the front, and the y
axis points to the right. If we place the starting end of the vector from
the proximal end to the distal end of the upper arm at the origin of the
coordinate system, the terminating end will stay on a sphere with the center
at the origin when the arm moves. The spherical motion can be further
decomposed into two motions: one which moves the arm vector along the
longitude of the sphere (elevation), and another which moves the vector along

the latitude (abduction). To describe the current status of the arm vector, we need a convention for zero elevation or abduction. Let us define the amount of elevation as the unsigned angle ϕ between z axis and the arm vector and, for the left arm, the amount of abduction as the signed angle θ between the $-y$ axis and the projection of the arm vector on the xy plane. The positive abduction is defined when the absolute angle from $-y$ to the projection is less than $180°$. Joint limits can be specified in terms of these spherical or "globographic" limiting angles [EP87].

2.4.2 Allocation of Elevation and Abduction

Naturally, the joint group shoulder complex will have elevation, abduction and twist as its group angles. They will be realized by internal joints — the clavicle and the shoulder joints. The amounts of elevation and abduction of the arm are allocated to the shoulder joint and the clavicle joint, while the twist is allocated to the shoulder joint alone.

According to clinical data, Otani gave a formula for distributing elevation and abduction to the shoulder and clavicle [Ota89]:

$$\phi_c = \cos(\theta)\beta_1 + (1 - \cos(\theta))\beta_2 - 90 \tag{2.2}$$

$$\theta_c = 0.2\,\theta \tag{2.3}$$

$$\phi_s = \phi - \phi_c \tag{2.4}$$

$$\theta_s = \theta - \theta_c \tag{2.5}$$

where ϕ and θ are total elevation and abduction of the shoulder complex, subscripts "c" and "s" stand for the portions carried by the clavicle and shoulder joints, respectively, and

$$\beta_1 = \begin{cases} 0.2514\phi + 91.076 & \text{for } 0 \leq \phi \leq 131.4 \\ -0.035\phi + 128.7 & \text{for } \phi > 131.4 \end{cases} \tag{2.6}$$

$$\beta_2 = \begin{cases} 0.21066\phi + 92.348 & \text{for } 0 \leq \phi \leq 130.0 \\ 120.0 & \text{for } \phi > 130.0 \end{cases} \tag{2.7}$$

2.4.3 Implementation of Shoulder Complex

In Peabody,

$$R(x, y, z) \tag{2.8}$$

is used to denote a generic rotation about the axis (x, y, z). Since we need rotations about some coordinate axis, let

$$R_x(\omega) \tag{2.9}$$

represent the rotation about x axis by ω degrees. Analogous notation will be used for the y and z axes.

Peabody uses row vector convention. So a string of rotations, when read from the right, can be interpreted as applying the first rotation (the rightmost one), then applying the next one about the rotated reference frame, and so on. When read from the left, it should be interpreted as applying successive rotations about the fixed starting frame.

With respect to the standing reference frame the spherical motion can be described as

$$R(1, 0, 0) * R(0, 0, 1), \tag{2.10}$$

that is, to achieve elevation and abduction of amounts ϕ and θ, the arm can rotate about the x axis by ϕ, followed by rotating about the unrotated y axis by θ. This is just spherical coordinates which designate a point on a sphere. The first problem we shall encounter is the singularity inherent to the spherical coordinate system.

Dealing with Singularities of Spherical Coordinates

As is known, the spherical coordinates have two singularities: when the elevation is 0 or 180°, it represents the pole (south pole for 0 or north pole for 180) no matter what the longitude (abduction amount) is. To see how this would affect the description of the spherical motion of the arm, let us do a small experiment. Starting with your left arm hanging down at your side, elevate your arm by 90°, then abduct by 90°, and finally elevate by −90°. Now see where your hand is. You will find that your hand comes back but with an axial twist. Where does this twist come from? It means that the pair of so defined elevation and abduction motions are not independent from twist. As long as elevation is zero, the arm vector would not change. This is nothing but a twist, as our decomposition of spherical motion and twisting motion intended. The final coordinates are (0, 90), since the last elevation cancels the first one and leaves the "abduction" there. To compensate for this unwanted twist, we untwist the arm by the amount that the "abduction" would induce before the shoulder leaves the zero elevation. Therefore, we need a joint of three cascaded rotations as follows,

$$R(0, 0, 1) * R(1, 0, 0) * R(0, 0, 1) \tag{2.11}$$

Let τ, ϕ and θ be desired twist, elevation and abduction, respectively. Then the joint angles (or displacement, in **Peabody** language) should be

$$(\tau - \theta, \phi, \theta). \tag{2.12}$$

The values in (2.12) are the amount of rotation about each of the corresponding axes in (2.11). The minus θ term in the first joint angle is to compensate for the unwanted twist induced by the abduction θ (so realized). As a matter of fact, the amount of twist is a relative quantity. It is meaningful only if we have zero twist assumed for any direction of the arm. So (2.12) should be

$$(\tau_0 + \tau - \theta, \phi, \theta), \tag{2.13}$$

where τ_0 is a function of (ϕ, θ), which defines the zero twist for each (ϕ, θ). Function τ_0 should be such that

$$\tau_0(0, \theta) = \text{constant}, \tag{2.14}$$

since $(0, \theta)$ denotes the same direction of the arm regardless of the value of θ. Now elevation by $90°$, followed by abduction of $90°$, and then elevation of $-90°$ would wind up with

$$(\tau_0 - 90, 0, 90).$$

Since $R_x(0) = $ identity matrix, the final matrix $R_z(\tau_0 - 90) * R_x(0) * R_z(90)$ would be equal to $R_z(\tau_0)$, which is exactly the starting configuration without twisting.

Now let us take care of the other singular point, that is, when $\phi = 180°$. At this point, $R_x(180) \neq$ identity. But we have

$$R_x(180) * R_z(\theta) = R_z(-\theta) * R_x(180).$$

To deal with this singularity, we require that

$$\tau_0(180, \theta) = 2\theta + \text{constant} \tag{2.15}$$

to compensate for unwanted twist induced by "abduction" θ. When $\phi = 180°$,

$$R_z(\tau_0(180, \theta) + \tau - \theta) * R_x(180) * R_z(\theta) \tag{2.16}$$

$$
\begin{aligned}
&= & R_z(\tau_0(180, \theta) + \tau - \theta) * R_z(-\theta) * R_x(180) \\
&= & R_z(\tau_0(180, \theta) + \tau - 2\theta) * R_x(180).
\end{aligned}
$$

(2.15) guarantees that that the final configuration is independent of the abduction by θ.

Combining (2.14) with (2.15), a possible choice of τ_0 could be

$$\tau_0(\phi, \theta) = \frac{\phi}{90}\theta. \tag{2.17}$$

This is the choice in our current implementation. To achieve more natural zero twist definition, we need to fine tune τ_0. One possibility is shown in Section 4.1.2 based on [Hut70] and [BOK80]. But (2.14) and (2.15) are required to deal with the singularity due to the spherical coordinate system.

Dealing with Hierarchical Nature of Connection

So far, we have focused on the shoulder joint. However, as we argued, the shoulder complex will consist of two joints – shoulder and clavicle joints. The total amount of elevation and abduction will be distributed to shoulder and clavicle joint according to the formula in Section 2.4.2.

In the *Jack* human figure model, the clavicle joint has the form

$$R(1, 0, 0) * R(0, 1, 0), \tag{2.18}$$

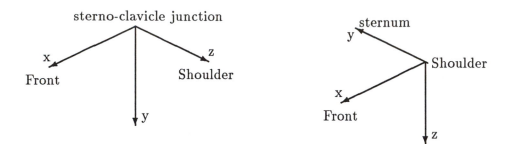

Figure 2.3: Site Orientations at Clavicle and Shoulder Joints.

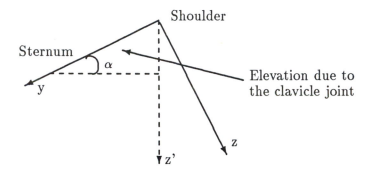

Figure 2.4: Tilted Shoulder Frame.

since the site orientation at the clavicle joint is a little bit different from that at the shoulder joint (Figure 2.3). We do not need to worry about the singularity problem here as we did with the shoulder joint because the arm, which the shoulder complex drives, is not aligned with the center of this joint. The amount of elevation and abduction of the clavicle is given in (2.2 ∼ 2.5). The clavicle is closer to the (normal) root of the human figure than the shoulder. This means that the global (relative to the neutral torso) orientation of the site at the shoulder joint will be altered by the movement of the clavicle: the z axis of the site at the shoulder would no longer point vertically downward. This causes the trajectory of the hand drawn by "abduction" to no longer be on the horizontal plane. Notice that the x axis will always be horizontal, and hence the meaning of elevation is not challenged. To protect "abduction" against this alteration, we need to do a transformation of the site coordinates.

After some movement of the clavicle, the shoulder reference frame is tilted as shown in Figure 2.4. (The Figure displays only the plane $x = 0$. The x axis does not show up in the Figure, but should be understood by the right-hand principle.) The tilted abduction is due to the tilted z axis. The "correct" abduction should be the rotation about the dotted z' axis. This axis is not constant due to variable clavicle elevation, but the **Peabody** language requires a constant axis. To circumvent this restriction, we can perform a transformation of coordinates. The rotation axis described in (x, y', z') is simply $R(0,0,1)$. The matrix representation of a rotation in a different coordinate system is just a similarity transformation of the coordinate transformation matrix. Let vectors in (x, y', z') be primed. The transformation of coordinates is

$$v = R_x(\alpha)v' \qquad (2.19)$$

where α is the amount of elevation allocated to the clavicle joint. The rotation about z' axis by ω represented in (x, y', z') is $R_{z'}(\omega)$ but, when represented in the old coordinate frame (x, y, z), it would be

$$R_x(\alpha)R_z(\omega)R_x(-\alpha). \qquad (2.20)$$

Substituting this for the second $R(0,0,1)$ in the shoulder joint cascaded rotations (2.11), we get

$$R(0,0,1) * R(1,0,0) * R(1,0,0) * R(0,0,1) * R(1,0,0).$$

We do not need to substitute for the first $R(0,0,1)$ in (2.11), because it is there for twist and to compensate for unwanted twist caused by the abduction allocated to the shoulder joint. Two contiguous rotations about the x axis can be combined into one. The final form of the shoulder joint becomes

$$R(0,0,1) * R(1,0,0) * R(0,0,1) * R(1,0,0). \qquad (2.21)$$

Let τ be the amount of twist and the notations of elevation and abduction be as in Section 2.4.2. The joint angles for the clavicle take values

$$(\theta_c, \phi_c) \qquad (2.22)$$

with respect to (2.18), and the joint angles for the shoulder take values

$$(\tau + (\frac{\phi}{90} - 1)\theta_s, \phi, \theta_s, -\phi_c). \qquad (2.23)$$

with regard to (2.21). It is not difficult to verify that the hand orientation does not depend on the abduction allocated to the shoulder joint, θ_s, when the total elevation, ϕ, is 0 or 180°.

2.5   Clothing Models

[6]In most workplace environments we have encountered, clothed figures are the norm and would be expected by the designer. Adding clothing to a human

---

[6]Eunyoung Koh.

figure improves its graphical appearance and realism. Clothes modeling can be done in many ways ranging from very simple to more realistic but complicated. The simplest clothing technique is to change the attributes of certain segments of the body figure; for example, by modifying the colors of the pelvis and upper leg segments we get the effect of a body wearing short pants. This is not quite as silly as it sounds, because the body segment geometry can be created with a clothed rather than bare-skinned shape. The best but more complicated approach is to drape and attach clothing over a body to simulate the intricate properties of garments.

Besides improving realism, there is a practical human factors aspect to clothing. Clothing constrains movement by restricting the joint angle limits. Preliminary attempts to analyze this problem use collision detection over a geometric clothes model.

2.5.1   Geometric Modeling of Clothes

Rigid clothing models are created by designing special segment psurfs. Thus a shirt or jacket would have, say, five parts: one for the torso, and two for each limb segment. Clothing exists independently of a given figure model as a library of objects which can be selectively placed on a model at user determined sites. This database is modifiable through typical geometric editing commands. A clothing item is positioned by matching key points on the clothing to key points on the body segments. A global deformation algorithm [SP86] can be used to fit the clothing piece correctly on the segment.

One apparent problem with geometrically modeled clothing occurs when the human figure moves joints. Since the clothing model is not deformable, there are gaps between segments. (This is in fact true even without clothing if the figure is modeled with polyhedral meshes. As the geometry is carried on the segment, it inherits the geometric transformation without any compensation for the interaction of material, flesh or clothes, at the joint.) Extra work is necessary to alleviate the joint gap problem. A gap filling algorithm has been developed to make up these gaps when animating. It connects the boundaries of two adjacent segments by generating spline surfaces using the tangent information of the two segments at the boundaries.

As an initial attempt to develop geometric models of clothes, a sweatshirt and pants were designed (Plate 2). Each segment of a clothing item is a psurf whose geometry and position are closely related to a corresponding body segment. The following is a step by step procedure for geometric clothes design.

1. Determine the size of clothes:

   In conventional clothing design, circumferences are measured at certain positions of the body in order to determine the clothing size. In our approach, the maximum segment breadth in two orthogonal directions are measured instead of circumferences.

   The following list shows the positions at which the maximum breadths are measured and lists their corresponding slices from the accurate biostereometric bodies (Section 2.1.3).

   - For trousers

waist	the 6th slice of lower_torso
hip	the 9th slice of hip_flap
upper leg	the first slice of upper_leg
lower leg	the last (24th) slice of lower_leg

   - For a sweatshirt

neck	the first slice of upper_torso
chest	the 6th slice of upper_torso
breast	the 12th slice of upper_torso
waist	the first slice of lower_torso
upper arm	the 8th slice of upper_arm
lower arm	the last (16th) slice of lower_arm

   Also, a measure of the length from the neck to the bottom of the shirt is provided to determine the length of the shirt. These sizes are specified in advance for each article of clothing.

2. Create psurfs:

   The geometry of each segment is determined by a set of body slices. A new set of slices for clothing is constructed by sculpturing the body slices depending on the shape of the segment and the specified sizes in the previous step. The fundamental idea in the construction is to pick a few thick slices and duplicate them appropriately along the segment after scaling. Scaling is done by linear interpolation so that the scaled slices may match with the specified maximum breadth sizes at the positions designated.

   The completed surface definition of a clothes segment can be obtained by tiling the slices. Tiling is performed by generating rectangles from the data points which define two adjacent slices.

3. Attach clothes segments to human body:

   Each clothes segment can be attached to the corresponding body segment by a joint which is located at the upper part of that segment.

The clothing shape can be easily modified by changing the slice definition of the clothes. For example, folded sleeves, short sleeves, and short pants can be simulated by simple modification or deletion of slices.

2.5.2   Draping Model

The most realistic clothing can be created by simulating the support and draping of pattern pieces of arbitrary shape. Wrinkling, folding, and the effects of gravity are displayed through a relaxation method or a finite element method. Pattern pieces may also be stitched at seams and draped simultaneously. Pattern pieces of different lengths may be sewn together, resulting in an oversewing effect.

The draping of the pattern pieces is done on a figure in a static posture. Interference testing is done in the draping algorithm to make sure that the pattern pieces slide over the surface of the figure without penetrating the surface (Plate 3).

There are several methods to simulate the draping of a square piece of cloth, isolated from other cloth, which are based on a relaxation method. Feynman [Fey86] uses a formula which minimizes the energy of a cloth and tries to simulate the shape of thin flexible membranes under the influence of force fields and rigid bodies. The local minimum of the cloth is found by moving each of the grid points in turn toward a position which decreases the energy of the cloth. The energy expression of a cloth is described as:

$$E_{total}(S) = k_s s(S) - k_b b(S) - k_g g(S)$$

where $s(S), b(S), g(S)$ represent the effects of strain, bending, and gravity. The parameters k_s, k_b, k_g control the relative strengths of these three effects: a large k_s means the cloth is difficult to stretch; a large k_b means the cloth is stiff and resists bending; and a large k_g means the cloth is heavy.

Relaxing a single point is the process of moving it so that the energy of the cloth of which it is a part is decreased. The method used to relax a single point first finds the direction in which the point would most like to move: the direction of the negative gradient of the energy as a function of position. Then it moves the single point in that direction so that its energy is minimized.

Feynman suggests using a multigrid method to speed up the relaxation sweeping process. However, it must be used carefully to avoid distortion. He also introduces fixed points in order to forbid the cloth to move into a solid.

Weil [Wei86] considered the problem of hanging a piece of cloth by fixing some constraint locations of the cloth. The cloth is represented as a rectangular grid (u, v) of 3D coordinates (x, y, z). His method is a two phase algorithm. The first part approximates the surface within the convex hull in (u, v) space of the constraint points; that is, all the interior points are placed on catenaries. The second phase uses an iterative relaxation process to minimize maximum displacement of all the points in the grid up to a given tolerance.

Terzopoulos, Platt, Barr and Fleisher [TPBF87] use elasticity theory to describe the behavior of a deformable object. The model responds in a natural way to applied forces, constraints, and impenetrable obstacles. The equations of motion governing the dynamics of the deformable bodies under the influence of applied forces is given by

$$\frac{\partial}{\partial t}(\mu\frac{\partial r}{\partial t}) + \gamma\frac{\partial r}{\partial t} + \frac{\delta\mathcal{E}(\nabla)}{\delta\nabla} = f(r,t),$$

where $r(a,t)$ is the position of the particle a at time t, $\mu(a)$ is the mass density of the body at a, $\gamma(a)$ is the damping density, and $f(r,t)$ represents the net externally applied forces. $\mathcal{E}(\nabla)$ is a functional which measures the net instantaneous potential energy of the elastic deformation of the body.

To create animation with this model, the motion equation is solved numerically, integrating through time. This model is active in the sense that it responds to forces and interacts with objects.

2.6 The Anthropometry Database

[7]While animation research may be content with demonstrating action on a convincing human form, there is often only a single carefully structured figure involved. Its body dimensions may be estimated or obtained by measurement of a specific individual. In contrast, engineering human factors applications have long been concerned with construction of valid ranges of human forms based on empirically measured populations such as aircraft pilots, flight attendants, or astronaut trainees. These engineering applications recognized the need for a variety of accurately scaled body dimensions to facilitate reach and fit analysis [Fet82, HBD80, KSC81, Doo82]. Unfortunately, most of these systems are either proprietary, hard-wired to some particular population, non-interactive, or otherwise difficult to use with contemporary graphical systems. *Jack*, however, permits an open and accessible database for human dimensional data. Interactive access is provided through a novel spreadsheet-like interface.

2.6.1 Anthropometry Issues

Anthropometry, the science of human body measurement, has been an area of interest throughout history [LRM88]:

> In his authoritative book "A History of the Study of Human Growth," Professor Tanner writes that the ancient Greeks, as well as sculptors and painters of the Renaissance, measured the human body to estimate body proportions and, thus, reproduce life–like images of varying sizes. Interest in absolute size developed later in the 17th and 18th centuries out of military concerns. The European armies preferred taller soldiers, and recruiting officers became anthropometrists. Interest in scientific study of growth and in the

---

[7]Marc Grosso, Susanna Wei.

relative importance of nature versus nurture in explaining human
variability has been pronounced since the 19th century.

The vast majority of work in "modern" anthropometry has been done by
anthropologists who were studying the effects of some environmental factor
on some population. While there are studies dating back to the mid– to late–
1800's, more recent studies covering groups of adults (i.e. populations) from
around the world are summarized in the *Anthropometry Source Book* [NAS78].
Its two volumes have become one of the foundation sources for contemporary
anthropometry.

Anthropometric studies differ greatly in the number and kind of measurements selected. They all report a statistical analysis of the values of each
measurement, giving at least a median with standard deviation and the maximum and minimum values. The studies typically report the above values
along with intermediate values at selected percentiles of the population, typ-
ically 1st, 5th, 25th, 50th, 75th, 95th and 99th, since body size data does not
vary linearly with percentile.

Some of the data found in these studies was used in the *NASA Man-
Systems Integration Manual* [NAS87], as the basis for the estimated measurements for male and female astronauts in the year 2000, using the body
dimensions of American males and Japanese females. It is felt that these
populations provide the maximum range in body sizes in the developed world
today since the American male is among the largest of males and the Japanese
female is the smallest of females. There is a growth rate factor which is used
to adjust the values for projection to the year 2000.

The measurements selected for inclusion in the *NASA Man-Systems Integration Manual* were chosen to meet the various needs of NASA and were
not intended to be a complete set of measurements for all purposes or for all
possible users. These measurements were publicly available, however, and detailed enough to satisfy many ergonomic analysis requirements. They served
as the basis for the human figure model we developed but are are not complete
enough to totally describe it [GQO+89, GQB89]. Some needed measurements
and data are missing; though most of the missing values can be found in the
Anthropometry Source Book, there were a number of measurements required
for our model which were not easy to track down. Where this occurred, intelligent estimates have been made based upon data values from closely related
measurements (possibly from a different population) or by calculating the
values from other measurements. In no case were the undefined values set
arbitrarily.

2.6.2   Implementation of Anthropometric Scaling

Each body segment or structure having associated geometry contains length,
width, and depth (or thickness) attributes[8]. Therefore, we require a minimum

---

[8] We presently ignore segment shape changes though we realize their importance for
realistic animation.

of seventy–two (72) measurements to describe the physical dimensions of our human figure.

Psurfs describe the shape of each segment. Anthropometric scaling modifies the segment dimensions as well as any associated psurfs. It is very simple to change to alternative polygon models, e.g. to the detailed contour bodies, to vary detail in the segment while preserving the correct anthropometric scale. Each psurf for the various segments is stored in a normalized format where the z (length) dimension ranges from 0 to $+1$, and the x (depth) and y (width) dimensions range from -1 to $+1$. In order to display these psurfs, using either real measurements for a person or percentile measurements for some specified population, the psurfs must be scaled.

Body definition files containing the desired values can be created (or modified) by manually entering the body part names and their values in the proper format, but this is clumsy and rarely used. A superior approach uses the Spreadsheet Anthropometry Scaling System (**SASS**) which will be discussed in detail in Section 2.7.

2.6.3 Joints and Joint Limits

There are three different types of human body joints [TA75]: Fibrous, Cartilaginous, and Synovial. Of these three we are only concerned with the synovial joints (joints with joint cavities). The synovial joints are categorized based upon the shape of the articulating surface of the joint. There are seven sub–types of synovial joints found in the human body [MB77, TA75]. These subtypes are:

- Monaxial (or uni–axial) joints (1 DOF)

  a. Hinge joints. A convex surface of one bone fits in a concave surface of another bone. This joint allows movement in only one plane, usually extension and flexion, similar to that of a door hinge. Examples are the elbow joint, knee joint, ankle joint, and interphalangeal joints (joints in the toes and fingers).

  b. Pivot joint. A rounded, pointed, or conical surface of one bone articulates with a shallow depression in another bone. The primary motion of this joint sub–type is rotation. Examples are shown by the supination and pronation of the palms, atlas–axis joint (Alanto–Axial joints located at the very top of the spine), and radioulnar joint (between radius and ulna in forearm).

- Bi–axial joints (2 DOFs)

  a. Condyloid joints. These are the joints like those at the heads of the metacarpals (hand bones), i.e. the knuckles, which is the best example of this type of joint.

   b. Ellipsoidal joints. The oval–shaped condyle (end) of one bone fits
      into the elliptical cavity of another bone. This type of joint permits
      side–to–side and back–and–forth movements (in the principal axes
      of the ellipse). Examples are shown by the flexion and extension
      and abduction and adduction of the wrist (radiocarpal) joint.

- Tri–axial (or multi–axial) joints (3 DOFs)

   a. Saddle joint. Both bones in this joint are saddle–shaped, that
      is convex in one direction and concave in the other. This type of
      joint is essentially a modified ellipsoidal joint and has more freedom
      of movement. Saddle joints allow side–to–side and back–and–forth
      movements as well as rotation. An example is the joint between the
      trapezium and metacarpal bones of the thumb (carpometacarpal
      joint of the thumb).

   b. Ball and socket joints. A ball–like surface of one bone fits into a
      cup–like depression of another bone. These joints permit flexion–
      extension, abduction–adduction, and rotation. Examples are the
      hip and shoulder joints.

   c. Gliding (or plane) joints. Bones involved have flat or nearly flat
      articulating surfaces. Movement can occur in almost any plane,
      with side–to–side and back–and–forth movements the most com-
      mon. The movements are always slight. Examples of this type of
      joint can be found between the carpal (wrist) bones (intercarpal
      joints), between the tarsal bones (foot/ankle) (intertarsal joints),
      between the sacrum (lower end of the spine) and ilium (a hip bone)
      (the sacro–iliac joint), between the sternum (breast bone) and clav-
      icle (collar bone), between the scapula (shoulder blade) and clav-
      icle, between the individual vertebral arches, at the heads and at
      the tubercles of the ribs, and at the front ends of the costal (rib)
      cartilages.

Each joint in the human body has a range of motion over which it will allow movement to occur. A joint's range of motion is determined by a number
of factors including joint type, muscle size at the joint, muscle tension (tonus)
for the muscles at the joint (i.e. fitness of the person), ligament stretchabil-
ity or give, amount of fatigue, and training adaptations for the joint. The
term flexibility is frequently used to describe the influence that each of the
components listed above has on joint movement.

Joint range of motion, described in terms of angles, is measured in degrees
for each DOF, that is, each plane in which movement is allowed at a joint.
When a joint has more than one DOF, the range of motion at the joint for each
DOF may be variable because one DOF may influence the others. Also, for
joints which are influenced by muscles crossing two joints (as in some muscles
of the thigh, for example) there may be a two joint dependency on the joint
limit.

Jack incorporates upper and lower joint limits for every single DOF joint. For two DOF joints, independent limits for each DOF are used. But the shoulder is treated as a three DOF system with spherical joint limits and a function that relates the default upper arm orientation to the upper arm position (Section 2.4). *Jack* respects these joint limits during both interactive positioning and inverse kinematic reaching.

2.6.4 Mass

As dynamic simulations achieve ever more realistic animation, mass information becomes essential. Fortunately, along with stature, mass is among the most common body measures taken. There have been a number of studies which have determined that each of the various body segments contributes a certain percentage of the total body mass; this percentage determines the mass of each individual segment. The mass percentages used are average percentile values for a fit male population as would be found in the NASA male crewmember trainees. The distribution may very well differ for the average general population or a population which is skewed toward either the small/light weight (like horse racing jockeys) or large/heavy weight (like American Football lineman). The segment mass percentages are also likely to be different for female subjects.

2.6.5 Moment of Inertia

The concept of moment of inertia is important when attempting to describe the dynamic behavior of a human figure. These values are needed when determining the motion of a figure under the influence of forces (both external and internal), moments, and instantaneous transfers of momentum (i.e. collisions). When considering human figure modeling the common forces and moments effecting the human figure include:

1. gravity: a force acting at the center of mass of each segment with a magnitude proportional to the segment's mass.

2. internal forces generated by muscles: forces actually acting at some insertion point along the length of the segment but modeled as a driving moment applied at the joint.

3. reaction forces generated by the figure's surroundings: for example, the normal forces and friction forces applied to the figure's hand by the surface it is leaning on.

4. external forces: for example, weights lifted by the figure, levers the figure attempts to pull, etc.

5. collisions: usually approximated as an instantaneous change in velocity of the point on the figure being struck.

2.6.6   Strength

Human strength capabilities have been found crucial for more realistic and
natural human motions (Section 5.3). Human strength (maximum torques) is
defined as muscle group strengths and is stored on a joint DOF basis. Modeling strength this way allows different people to possess different capacities
in different muscle groups. Thus, the strength differences between two people
– such as a dancer and a pianist – can be readily modeled and illustrated.
Each DOF of a joint has two joint movements which are associated with two
different muscle groups. For example, an elbow joint is modeled to have one
DOF because it can only rotate around one axis. Its rotational movements are
flexion and extension, corresponding to the flexor and extensor muscle groups.
Therefore, strength data of flexion and extension are stored for an elbow joint.
Each muscle group strength is modeled as a function of body position, anthropometry, gender, handedness, fatigue, and other strength parameters [AHN62,
Lau76, NAS78, AGR+81, AGR+82, Imr83, CA84, HJER86, MS86, NAS87].
In terms of body position, we choose a more generalized model that takes the
effects of adjacent joint angles into consideration [Sch72]. For example, the
muscle group strengths of a shoulder joint are modeled to be functions not
only of the shoulder angles but also of the elbow angle.

2.7   The Anthropometry Spreadsheet

[9]Given the large number of data items needed for anthropometric body sizing,
a spreadsheet–like format was a natural choice for the user interface. We called
it **SASS**: the Spreadsheet Anthropometry Scaling System.

   SASS was originally developed with one idea in mind, i.e., generating
the dimensions of each segment of a human figure based upon population
supplied as input. The human model used by the current version of SASS
consists of thirty-one segments (body structures), of which twenty-four have
a geometrical representation. For each of those twenty-four segments, there
are three dimensions which are required, namely, length, width, and thickness.
This means that at least these seventy-two measurements should be available.

   The psurf geometry of each segment must be scaled by real measurements
for a person, or percentile measurements for some specifiable population.
SASS generates figure files with the appropriate description of the segment
dimensions and joint limits, so that *Jack* can display the resulting figure.

   SASS uses population statistic data to create generic human figures. Al-
ternately, **SASS** has a built-in database that stores anthropometric data for
(real) individuals and provides an interactive query system for database access.

   SASS allows flexible interactive access to all variables needed to size a
human figure described structurally by a **Peabody** body file. The **SASS**
screens, as shown in Fig. 2.5 and more diagrammatically in Fig. 2.6, are

---

[9]Richard Quach, Francisco Azuola, Welton Becket, Susanna Wei.

POPULATION:	Natick Air Pilots Data					
FIGURE TYPE:	Contour Body	STRENGTH TYPE:	ISOMETRIC			
GENDER: Male	SOMA: 15%	MOTION SPEED:	0.00m/sec			
MASS: 91.56kg	97.35%	HANDEDNESS:	Right			
STATURE: 189.92cm	97.35%	TRAINING LEVEL:	0			
GROUP PERCENTILE:	50.00%	FATIGUE LEVEL:	0			

Segments (Unit: cm)	Width (x)		Thickness (y)		Length (z)	
	Values	(%)	Values	(%)	Values	(%)
0) bottom_head	7.65	50.00%	9.95	50.00%	23.12	97.94%
1) neck	6.03	50.00%	6.03	50.00%	10.85	40.42%
2) upper_torso	16.56	50.00%	12.51	50.00%	40.99	1.00%
3) center_torso	16.10	50.00%	11.55	50.00%	4.47	30.69%
4) lower_torso	17.40	50.00%	12.35	50.00%	15.41	1.50%
5) r_upper_arm	5.32	50.00%	5.32	50.00%	34.32	91.44%
6) l_upper_arm	5.32	50.00%	5.32	50.00%	34.32	91.44%
7) r_lower_arm	4.76	50.00%	4.76	50.00%	26.82	89.97%
8) l_lower_arm	4.76	50.00%	4.76	50.00%	26.82	89.97%
9) r_upper_leg	8.39	50.00%	9.45	50.00%	41.54	84.47%
10) l_upper_leg	8.39	50.00%	9.45	50.00%	41.54	84.47%
11) r_lower_leg	5.99	50.00%	5.99	50.00%	43.41	89.18%
12) l_lower_leg	5.99	50.00%	5.99	50.00%	43.41	89.18%
13) r_foot	9.05	50.00%	5.00	93.23%	6.94	50.00%
14) l_foot	9.05	50.00%	5.00	93.23%	6.94	50.00%
15) r_hand	4.51	50.00%	1.65	50.00%	10.90	50.00%
16) l_hand	4.51	50.00%	1.65	50.00%	10.90	50.00%
17) r_clavicle	10.03	50.00%	0.51	50.00%	1.02	50.00%
18) l_clavicle	10.03	50.00%	0.51	50.00%	1.02	50.00%
19) r_eye	1.11	50.00%	1.38	50.00%	2.22	50.00%
20) l_eye	1.11	50.00%	1.38	50.00%	2.22	50.00%
21) eye_loc	9.80	50.00%	1.55	50.00%	11.77	50.00%
22) ball_r_foot	3.55	50.00%	5.00	50.00%	6.00	50.00%
23) ball_l_foot	3.55	50.00%	5.00	50.00%	6.00	50.00%
24) knuck_r_hand	4.51	50.00%	1.65	50.00%	0.53	50.00%

Press LEFT Mouse Button to select items

Figure 2.5: Sample Display From SASS.

divided into different sections including anthropometric group selection, global data, command menu, local data.

Data that may be accessed is organized into anthropometric "groups". The current version can handle four groups: segment girth, joint limits, segment center of mass, and strength.

The global data section of the spreadsheet is intended to allow a "whole body" view of the current figure parameters. Currently, the six items considered for any human figure are: **population, sex, figure type, mass, stature,** and **overall percentile.** It is important to realize that since **SASS** is a relational spreadsheet, modifying any data in this section will affect the values of the individual segments. For example, changing the figure's percentile will cause the data to be scaled in other appropriate segments contributing to stature.

The data section is used for the display of individual segment data and their corresponding percentiles. The leftmost column is reserved for the segment names, while the other six columns are used for the data and percentile display. The segment name column cannot be modified. The data is read in from the selected population input file.

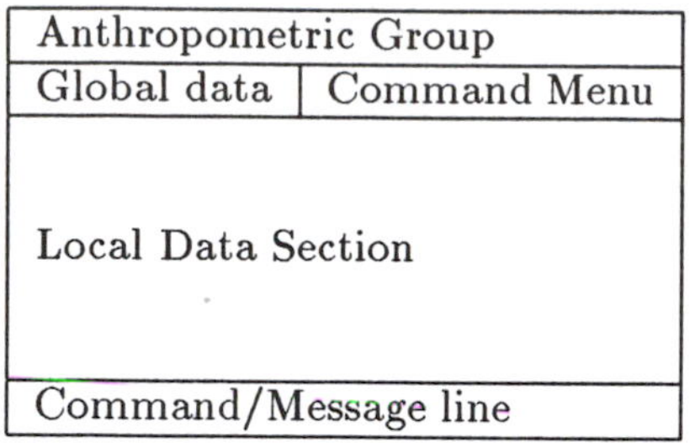

```
+---------------------------------------+
| Anthropometric Group                  |
|---------------------------------------|
| Global data  | Command Menu           |
|---------------------------------------|
|                                       |
|                                       |
| Local Data Section                    |
|                                       |
|                                       |
|---------------------------------------|
| Command/Message line                  |
+---------------------------------------+
```

Figure 2.6: SASS Screen Layout.

Data and its corresponding percentile is modified by simply moving the locator device to the desired cell and pressing on a button. Changing any segment percentile will change its corresponding dimension. **SASS** keeps a current measurement unit type for each group (**in, cm, deg, rad**). Unit conversion is performed when necessary.

2.7.1   Interactive Access Anthropometric Database

An anthropometric database stores attribute data for a specific set of individuals rather than a population. Each person has associated groups of anthropometric data: girth (segment dimensions), joint limit, center of mass, and strength. Each group of anthropometric data is stored in a separate relation.

In the application of a task simulation, it is very important to find an individual with the requisite anthropometric characteristics such as body dimensions, joint limits, and strength. **SASS** provides a query system using pop-up menus to allow the user to select the people with the desired characteristics from the anthropometric database. Therefore, the user does not need to know the database structure nor its query language.

The user can query on different anthropometric characteristics separately or in combination using operations *and, or, greater than, equal to, less than,* etc. For example, the user can inquire about people with the desired strength capabilities alone, or query about individuals with the required strength capabilities, body dimensions, joint limits, and center of masses together. The individuals that satisfy the query and their global data are stored in a list called the *query list*. After examining the global information in the query list, the user can choose all or some of these individuals and store them in the selected list. The detailed anthropometric data of each individual in the selected list can be displayed on the anthropometric spreadsheet. If desired, the user can also create the **Peabody** structure files for those selected individuals by using the *SASS* command Create Figure.

2.7.2 SASS and the Body Hierarchy

Our first version of **SASS** handled segments by gathering them in a simple list. This was good enough to represent any number of segments, but presented some inconveniences in defining relations among the segments. In a substantial modification, the structure was changed to a hierarchical tree. At the bottom of the tree the leaves correspond to the segments. The internal nodes correspond to conceptual body parts composed of sets of actual body segments, for example, the "arm" consists of the upper arm, lower arm, and hand segments. Thus concepts such as the "length of the arm" can be well-defined. A figure can be defined as a collection of body parts, joined together by joints. Each body part, in turn, can be defined as a collection of body segments connected by joints.

2.7.3 The Rule System for Segment Scaling

The introduction of the body part hierarchy permits **SASS** to determine and use attributes of body parts as well as individual segments. For example, **SASS** defines a rule for computing the height of an individual as the sum of the segments' lengths in a path that goes from head to feet. For those segments in the path, the rule allows varying their lengths if the stature changes and, vice versa, to change the stature if the length of any of the segments in the path changes. There is an alternate rule that keeps the stature fixed and adjusts the segments' lengths accordingly, if the length of one of them varies. Another rule includes changing the mass according to the stature and, conversely, changing the stature according to a specific mass value.

The underlying criterion for doing the stature changes is a linear one. The segments in the stature path are head, neck, upper torso, center torso, lower torso, upper leg, lower leg, and feet. The length of each of these segments, except for the feet, is computed as the length in the z coordinate. For the feet, the length is the y coordinate (since for the feet, the z coordinate is the longitudinal dimension). The thickness and width of the segments are not affected by these changes, for there is no rule to decide the effects of stature changes in these parameters. The updating process must be done carefully, for it might happen that modifying the length of a given segment violates the range of possible stature values admitted by the current population or conversely, if the stature is changed, it might not be satisfiable by variations in the segment lengths.

The other case considers fixed stature. The idea is to adjust the segments' lengths along the stature path if the length of one of them varies, such that the global length (stature) remains constant. While this might appear easy to do at first, it is not a trivial matter. Recall that segment dimensions are based on population percentile data suitably interpolated and are therefore restricted to legitimate ranges. Furthermore, the stature itself is restricted by a "real" set of values (for each of the percentiles). When the user specifies a particular change in the length (or other dimension) of a given segment, the underlying rule attempts to satisfy the constraint of fixed stature, that is, it tries to keep the stature value constant. For example, assume the length of the head has decreased. To keep the stature fixed, the lengths of the other segments in the stature path must vary in the opposite way. Currently, the modification is done in a linear fashion since there are no rules to define this otherwise. But it might be the case that in the updating process one of the segment's dimensions (length) cannot be satisfied, that is, the resulting dimension is out of the range established by the $5 - 95^{th}$ percentile values. In this situation, the rule sets the length to its closest limit (5th or 95th percentile value) and tries to satisfy the requirement of fixed stature by modifying the remaining segments in the path. Notice that there is a possibility that the stature cannot be kept constant. There is one more step involved in the updating process for fixed stature: if the stature is varied by the user the segments change correspondingly if possible.

It is important to understand the back and forth process that goes on between body parts and segments. If the overall body is supposed to be 50th percentile, the body parts need not all be 50th percentile. In fact, we do not have a rule yet to specify the percentile of the body parts (segment-wise) for a given global body percentile. That information must come from multi-variate analysis of population data. So we must be able to change dimensions of the body parts or segments to comply with all the possible *valid* compositions of a 50th percentile body. If the stature is modified, then a new global percentile is computed. For that new global percentile, we have a specific rule telling us what the possible compositions are. Unfortunately, the compositions are not unique since they depend on the population data used. To illustrate this, suppose we have the following (partial) composition set percentiles: feet 30%, legs 45%, torso 60%, head 40%,... for a 50th percentile body. Then suppose we want to change the stature in such a way that the resulting body percentile is 60th percentile, and the analogous (partial) composition set is (feet 40%, legs 56%, torso 50%, head 40%,...). Then we scale the objects in the stature path (which are those listed in the composition sets) to comply with this second composition set. But we must be sure that there is no conflict in doing so; for instance, the feet might be able only to grow from 30% to a 40% under the given population. In general, different populations will have different compositions.

In this example, the compositions were stated at the body part level. There must be an equivalent composition at the segment level: the segment version of the composition for the 50th percentile figure is, for instance, upper leg (45%, lower leg 60%) assuming legs decompose in two pieces. But what if the compositions, even though being based on a particular population data, are not available for all the possible percentiles? We would have to use a fixed composition or else interpolate compositions (if it is sound to do that) and make sure a given segment's length is not violated (according to its percentile range) when trying to go from a composition for the 50th percentile figure to that of the 60th.

Anthropometrists who argue against the cavalier usage of percentiles in characterizing body size distributions would seem to be on pretty safe ground. Since the only obvious alternative involving enumerating all the individuals in a database we are stuck with the population statistics available. As multi-variate population dimension distribution data becomes available, **SASS** will be ready to utilize it for proper figure creation.

2.7.4   Figure Creation

SASS can produce a file containing the scaling of a figure which *Jack* then interprets to create the figure file. Scaling files offer a particular benefit over direct creation of the figure in **SASS**. Consider the situation in which the *Jack* user wants to determine the percentile ranges of a figure that can satisfy a given task, that is, the problem of finding the specific figure percentile (or range) that can fit in a particular workplace. One can attempt to read each of the possible figure files out of *Jack* libraries and try to keep the figure in the desired position. The other, more sensible, option is not to load different figure files, but instead, to load different scaling files. Then the same figure can be scaled using all these different files to find the one that best suits the given environment. This is faster and more appealing to the user.

2.7.5   Figure Scaling

The scales in the figure scaling file are obtained directly from the dimensions of the body segments or parts. Thus, this scaling file represents the dimensions specified in the (population's) girth file, for a given figure percentile. If there were only one scale factor for each dimension of a segment, there would be some scaling mismatches towards the ends of the segments. This is in fact a major problem, especially for the low resolution polyhedral body model. For instance, the scaled upper leg appears to be too thick and too wide, in comparison to the lower leg. The same problem occurs with the upper arm and the lower arm. The scaling of the pelvis of the simple polyhedral body seems to be too wide and thick, while the torso appears to be too narrow and short. There are various solutions to these problems. The simplest one is to adapt the data to the model by modifying the scaling factors to obtain a good (looking) figure scaling. There are no strict rules for this, though. The rule we use is to consider body lines as second order continuous curves. There are no abrupt changes from one body part to the next one (assuming no deformations). Thus we approximate (in a rather arbitrary way) the scaling factors to achieve this continuity. The largest discrepancies are the ones mentioned above. Other minor ones are the scaled neck being too wide and hands being too narrow. In general, the scaling factors are not changed by more than 10% in the simple polyhedral *Jack* figure.

The scaling factors generated by **SASS** are mapped into the contour body with almost no modifications necessary (for the contour figure case, adjustments are done to the torso, legs, arms, and hands). These adjustments do not go over 5% of the actual values. Again, one must keep in mind that even though the contour model is a more accurate representation of the human body, it is not a perfect one. Moreover, we must remember that the **SASS** scaling factors file is created based on a given population and the figure resulting from that scaling might not completely match a real human being (for suppose that the population's average torso length is greater than the torso length of a given individual and the population's average leg length is smaller than that of the same individual, then we end up with a not so real scaling for the contour model). Thus, even though we have assumed some adjustments are required, it is still necessary to prove if this is the right way to proceed. So far, the criterion that prevails is to display a good-looking (well proportioned) human figure.

2.8   Strength and Torque Display

[10]Human strength information has applications in a variety of fields. In physical education, it can be used to classify participants for specific activities or to search for a body position or motion which will improve an athlete's performance; in medicine, it can be used as an indicator for a muscular injury or disease; and in ergonomics and human factors, it can be used to guide the design of workspace or equipment to reduce work related injuries, and to help in personnel selections to increase work efficiency [MKK+88, McD89, Eva88, CA84]. Human strength information can also be used in a human task simulation environment to define the load or exertion capabilities of each agent and, hence, decide whether a given task can be completed in a task simulation [EBJ89].

To convey the multi-dimensional characteristics of strength data, we use special data display methods that use human figures together with two or three dimensional graphics. Various forms of *strength box* and *strength bar* displays allow visualization of strength parameters, give a dynamic changing view of the effects of parameters on strength, and show safe and forbidden regions in terms of different strength capabilities of individuals or populations [WB92].

We define strength (maximum torque) to be the maximum achievable joint torque. It is modeled as muscle group strength and is stored on a joint DOF basis in the human figure model. Each DOF of a joint has two joint movements which are associated with two different muscle groups. For example, an elbow is modeled to have one DOF. It can only rotate around one axis; its rotational movements are flexion and extension which correspond to the flexor and extensor muscle groups. Therefore, strength information of flexion and extension is stored for an elbow joint. Each muscle group strength is modeled as a function of body position, anthropometry, gender, handedness, fatigue, and other strength parameters [AHN62, AGR+81, NAS87, HJER86, Imr83, Lau76, NAS78].

---

[10]Susanna Wei

2.8.1 Goals of Strength Data Display

Strength depends on a set of parameters. To properly display these parameters, one should use a multi-parameter system that can convey the meaning of these parameters as well as their values. Unfortunately, existing multi-dimensional display methods [And60, Ber83, GFS71, Har75, And72, Che73, KH81] are unsuitable in presenting the human body-specific semantics of strength parameters. They are also visually ineffective in displaying strength data because they fail to tie the parameters to the body properties they describe. We prefer to define multi-dimensional graphing methods which use the body itself as a context for the parameter display.

Strength data displays show the current force and torque capabilities of a figure in a given posture or motion. A good strength data display should show the direction and magnitude of forces and torques. Since strength depends on many parameters, for example, body posture, body size, gender, fatigue, training, and handedness, it is useful to observe interactively how the change of each parameter affects strength. Finally, a strength data display should show the comparative capabilities of different individuals or populations.

2.8.2 Design of Strength Data Displays

An effective strength data display conveys the meaning of the parameters and their values [Eva85, CBR, EC86, EPE88, MKK+88]. To design displays that can portray the multi-dimensional nature of strength effectively, we use the human figure as a context [Wei90].

The *Jack* strength data display system evaluates the strength fields in the current figure's body definition file. The strength data for the people who are related (in the database sense) to the given figure displayed on the screen can be obtained by querying the strength database. For example, suppose Fred is a NASA crewman. The required joint strength data for Fred can be calculated from the equations stored in the strength fields of Fred's body definition file. However, any strength data for other people in the NASA crewmen population must be queried from the strength database. If end effector forces are not stored in the strength database, they can be calculated.

Strength Box Display

Six orthogonally intersecting rods are used to show the end effector forces in different directions at a given body posture. They can also be used to show muscle group strengths of a three DOFs joint at a given body configuration. The direction of the given force (or strength) is shown by the position and the orientation of the rod. It is also indicated by the text at the side of rods. The length of each strength rod shows the magnitude of the force/strength value at a given direction of movement. As the body configuration changes, the rod lengths are changed to reflect changing strength.

The strength rods in Figure 2.7 show the hand forces at **up, down, left, right, push,** and **pull** directions of the displayed human figure at the currently displayed body configuration. The internal box represents average female strength while the outer box represents average male strength given the same posture. The length of the interior segment of the rod represents the average strength value of females and the length of the exterior segment of the rod indicates the difference between the female and male average strengths. Thus, the average male strength is represented by the length of the whole rod. The box itself is used to show the boundary of the maximum forces of the range of motions in six different directions. The length of the red line attached to the end of each rod shows the difference between the maximum force and the force of the current body position shown on the screen at a given direction. The resulting display of the strength rods and the box is called the *strength box* display. The user can find the body configuration associated with the maximum force for the entire range of motions at a given direction by interactively adjusting the body posture until the end of the given rod touches the corresponding edge of the box.

This strength box display can be modified in many ways to show other strength or force data. For example, it can be changed to display data for a one or two DOF joint or to show the effects of different parameters:

- Two collinear rods can be used to display the strength data for a one DOF joint, and four coplanar rods can be used to display the strength data of a two DOF joint.

- Each rod can be divided into one or more segments by using two different colors to show the comparative muscle group strength of a strength parameter that has one or more values, respectively. This is shown for a male/female comparison in Figure 2.7. Strengths corresponding to dominant and nondominant hands can also be shown in this fashion. A three-segment rod can be used to show strengths of three different percentiles of a population.

- A two-segment rod can be modified to show the maximum strength and required torque of a joint. For a given load applied at an end effector, we can calculate the required torque via static force analysis at each joint in the active joint chain.

- A trace can be incorporated in the strength display to show the movement path of an end effector. Two different trace colors can be used to show the safe region where the maximum strength (of all joints) is greater than the required torque (green), and the forbidden region where the maximum strength (of at least one joint) is less than the required torque (red). (Figure 2.8). The number "20 lbs." written on the cube at the end effector is a reminder of the current load.

The strength box display is mainly designed to show the strengths for a "single" joint or the forces of "one" end effector. Although it can also be used to display strengths for more than one joint by showing them in two or

Figure 2.7: Strength Box Display of Hand Forces for Males and Females of a Population.

more strength box displays, it may not be easy to compare the values across different boxes. To effectively display strengths for more than one joint or end effector, we use the strength bar display.

Strength Bar Display

The *strength bar* display is used to show forces of end effectors or strengths of joints in a given body chain. Figure 2.8 illustrates a strength bar display that shows the maximum muscle group strengths and required torques of joints in the highlighted body chain when the hand is holding a load of 20 lbs. If the maximum muscle group strength is greater than the corresponding required torque, the interior segment of a bar shows the required torque in red. Otherwise, the interior segment of a bar shows the maximum muscle group strength in green. The exterior segment of a bar is always used to show the difference between the maximum strength and the required torque. If the maximum strength is greater than the required torque, the exterior segment is shown in green, otherwise it is shown in red. The bar (joint) with the required torque exceeding the maximum strength can be indicated by

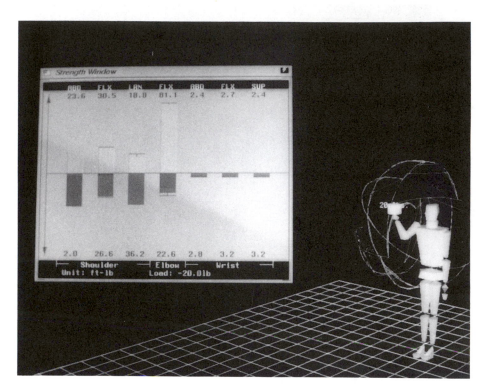

Figure 2.8: Strength Bar Display for Maximum Strengths and Required Torques.

highlighting. A one-segment bar in green indicates that the required torque is zero; the length of the green bar shows the value of the maximum strength. Similarly, a one-segment bar in purple indicates that the required torque is equal to the maximum strength.

The strength bar display can also be modified to show strength or force data in different applications. We list some simple extensions in the following.

- Similar to a rod in the strength box display, each bar in the display can also be divided into a number of segments by using various colors to show strengths corresponding to different values of a parameter.

- Multiple viewports can be used to display the strengths associated with different values of a parameter. For example, we can use two viewports to show the strength bar displays for the dominant and non-dominant hand of a given individual. Comparing strength values from different strength bar displays is as easy as comparing strength values within a strength bar display because the 2D screen location of the display does not affect the visual length of each bar.

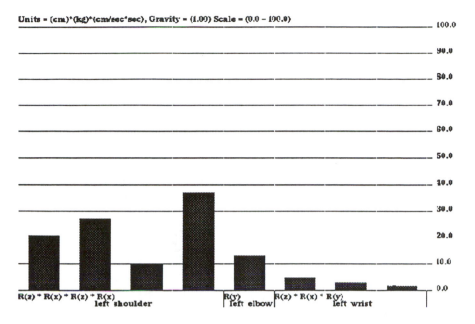

Figure 2.9: Torques Computed by Static Analysis.

The strength bar display can be used to show strengths of any number of joints in a body chain. It gives a very clear view of the simultaneous effects of the body configuration on several muscle group strengths. It also shows the safe and forbidden regions of each joint in a body chain. This display method does not depend on a particular strength model: it only shows whatever data is currently available for the figure.

Whole body strength and torque display

[11]Using static analysis, torques throughout the body may be computed given any posture and any loading condition. The strength bar display can show the individual joint torques (Figure 2.9). If suitable strength data for each muscle group is available, then whole body loading may be assessed.

Of course, with so many joints the interpretation of multiple graphs becomes difficult. To alleviate this problem we map the strength or torque data directly onto the contour body (Figure 2.10)[12]. The mapping interpolates a given value at a joint onto the adjacent contour body polygon vertices. A parameter controls how far from the joint the mapped color will propagate. A typical color scale is based on mapping zero torque load to white and maximum strength to blue. Reacted torques exceeding the joint's maximum strength are colored red. Since only one attribute can be selected for

---

[11]Hyeongseok Ko, Susanna Wei, Michael Kwon
[12]This will also work for the simpler polyhedral body but is much less interesting.

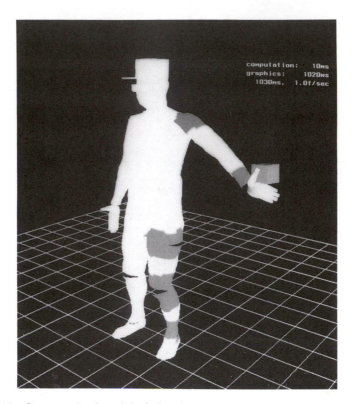

Figure 2.10: Contour Body with Color Coded Segments Representing Torque Load.

a given value at a joint onto the adjacent contour body polygon vertices. A parameter controls how far from the joint the mapped color will propagate. A typical color scale is based on mapping zero torque load to white and maximum strength to blue. Reacted torques exceeding the joint's maximum strength are colored red. Since only one attribute can be selected for a joint, the maximum load at multiple DOFs is used to select the color. As the mapping and color interpolation across each polygon take advantage of the Silicon Graphics workstation display speed, the visualization may even be interactively observed as the posture and loads change.

Chapter 3

Spatial Interaction

This chapter describes the basic architecture of the *Jack* interactive system. The primary tools available to the *Jack* user involve direct manipulation of the displayed objects and figures on the screen. With articulated figures, movement of one part will naturally affect the position of other parts. Constraints are used to specify these relationships, and an inverse kinematics algorithm is used to achieve constraint satisfaction. As a consequence of user actions, certain global postural manipulations of the entire human figure are performed by the system. This chapter presents the direct spatial manipulations offered in *Jack* and shows how constraints are defined and maintained. One particular application of the body constraints is included: the generation of the reachable workspace of a chain of joints.

3.1 Direct Manipulation

3D direct manipulation is a technique for controlling positions and orientations of geometric objects in a 3D environment in a non-numerical, visual way. It uses the visual structure as a handle on a geometric object. Direct manipulation techniques derive their input from pointing devices and provide a good correspondence between the movement of the physical device and the resulting movement of the object that the device controls. This is *kinesthetic correspondence*. Much research demonstrates the value of kinesthetically appropriate feedback [Bie87, BLP78, Sch83]. An example of this correspondence in a mouse-based translation operation is that if the user moves the mouse to the left, the object moves in such a way that its image on the screen moves to the left as well. The lack of kinesthetic feedback can make a manipulation system very difficult to use, akin to drawing while looking at your hand through a set of inverting mirrors. Providing this correspondence in two dimensions is fairly straightforward, but in three dimensions it is considerably more complicated.

The advantage of the direct manipulation paradigm is that it is intuitive:

it should always be clear to the user how to move the input device to cause
the object to move in a desired direction. It focuses the user's attention on
the object, and gives the user the impression of manipulating the object itself.

3.1.1   Translation

Several techniques have been developed for describing three dimensional transformations with a two dimensional input device such as a mouse or tablet.
Nielson and Olson [NO87] describe a technique for mapping the motion of
a two dimensional mouse cursor to three dimensional translations based on
the orientation of the projection of a world space coordinate triad onto the
screen. This technique uses a one-button mouse, and it compares the 2D
displacement of the mouse cursor to the screen projection of the six world coordinate axes and causes a differential movement in world space along the axis
whose projection is closest to the mouse movement. For example, if the view
is positioned such that the world coordinate x axis points left, then moving
the mouse to the left will cause a $+x$ translation. This provides good kinesthetic correspondence, but it has problems if two of the axes project onto the
screen close to one another, since it will not be able to distinguish between
the two. In other words, it is highly dependent on the view.

3.1.2   Rotation

Rotations are considerably more complex, but several techniques have been
developed with varying degrees of success. The most naive technique is to simply use horizontal and vertical mouse movements to control the world space
euler angles that define the orientation of an object. This technique provides little kinesthetic feedback because there is no natural correspondence
between the movements of the mouse and the rotation of the object. A better
approach, described by Chen et al [CMS88], is to make the rotation angles either parallel or perpendicular to the viewing direction. This makes the object
rotate relative to the graphics window, providing much greater kinesthetic
feedback.

The problem with screen-space transformations is that it is impossible to
make movements around either the global or local axes. In an integrated
geometric environment, it is more common to move objects relative to either
the global or local coordinate frame, rather than along axes aligned with the
screen. For example, the simple task of raising an object vertically requires
translating along the global y axis. Unless the view in the graphics window is
perfectly horizontal, the vertical direction in screen coordinates is not exactly
vertical. As another example, the task of moving a hand forward may require
moving along an axis aligned with the body, not the screen.

Evans, Tanner, and Wein [ETW81] describe a rotation technique that
suggests a turntable on which objects sit. Movements of the mouse in circles
around the origin of the turntable cause the turntable, and thus the object,

to rotate. There must also be a way of positioning the turntable underneath the object.

Chen, Mountford, and Sellen [CMS88] also describe a technique originally developed by Evans, Tanner, and Wein [ETW81] known commonly as the *virtual sphere*. This technique simulates the effect of a trackball centered around the object's origin. You "grab" the trackball with the mouse and rotate it much as you would rotate a physical trackball with a single finger. The virtual sphere is an efficient technique for certain operations, as Chen et al verify experimentally. However, since the rotation is not confined to a specific axis, it can be difficult to rotate around a particular axis. It is nearly impossible to make precise rotations around global coordinate axes.

Chen et al describe an experimental comparison between several techniques for 3D rotation. The subjects were asked to rotate a geometric object, in the shape of a house, to align it with a similar object in a random orientation. They were measured for both speed and accuracy. The techniques evaluated included several angle-based rotations with and without kinesthetic correspondence, and the virtual sphere. The studies generally showed that the virtual sphere was the best, out-performing the others in both precision and speed.

The virtual sphere is good at "tumbling" objects, when the path of their rotation is not important. This may be the case for objects floating in space. However, in an integrated modeling environment, the technique has some limitations because it does not allow constrained movement. Because of its free-form nature, it is very difficult to rotate an object around a single axis at a time, global or local, which is often required. For example, to turn around a human being standing on the floor requires rotating only around the vertical axis. With the virtual sphere, it is nearly impossible to rotate precisely around only one axis at a time.

An improvement over the virtual sphere is proposed by Shoemake [Sho92]. His "ArcBall" approach uses the visual correspondence between arcs on a hemisphere and 3D quaternions to define simultaneously both a rotation angle and axis. Any 2D screen point input has a well-defined rotational value. The ArcBall appears best for tumbling objects, but a constrained axis formulation is essentially similar to the *Jack* local rotation operation described below.

3.1.3 Integrated Systems

Bier's *snap-dragging* technique [Bie86, Bie87, Bie90] simulates gravity between objects and takes advantage of surface geometry to constrain and control object movements. The user first positions *jacks* in space using a 3D cursor called the *skitter*. The jacks are coordinate frames that serve as anchors for other operations. The skitter slides along faces and edges, controlled by the mouse or through dials. The technique determines the position and orientation of the visible surface beneath the mouse in order to control the position and orientation of the skitter. Jacks can be placed with the skitter and then used to specify rotation axes or end-points for angles.

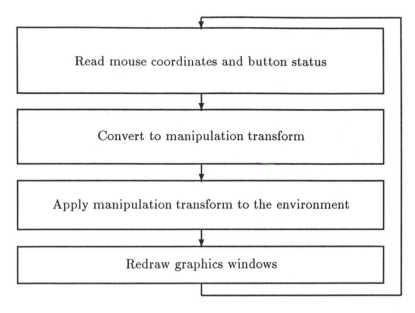

Figure 3.1: The manipulation loop.

This technique exploits the geometric structure of the objects, but it provides little help for manipulating positions and orientations in the absence of geometry. This means that the technique does not work especially well for manipulating points in open space as is often required.

3.1.4   The Jack Direct Manipulation Operator

The 3D direct manipulation mechanism in *Jack* interactively describes a global homogeneous transform. Internally, this is called the *manipulation transform*. There are many different commands in *Jack* that require the user to enter three-dimensional translational and rotational quantities. Each command may interpret the transform in its own way, possibly mapping it to a local coordinate system.

The user manipulates this transform through the 3-button mouse, together with the SHIFT and CONTROL keys on the keyboard. The keys alter the interpretation of the mouse buttons. Each mouse button corresponds to an axis in space, using a mapping scheme described below. The direct manipulation mechanism can alter the manipulation transform based on the selected axis by rotating around it, translating along it, or translating in a plane perpendicular to the axis. This characterizes the three primitive types of direct manipulation: linear translation, planar translation, and rotation [PB88]. The manipulation procedure is a loop, shown in Figure 3.1, that continues until the user terminates it.

The *Jack* user interface is modal: each manipulation command places *Jack* in a mode where the mouse buttons and keyboard keys are interpreted

SHIFT	CONTROL	mouse buttons	action
		left	linear transl along global x axis
		middle	linear transl along global y axis
		right	linear transl along global y axis
		left and middle	planar transl in global xy plane
		left and right	planar transl in global xz plane
		middle and right	planar transl in global yz plane
	CONTROL	left	rotation around global y axis
	CONTROL	middle	rotation around global y axis
	CONTROL	right	rotation around global z axis
SHIFT		left	linear transl along local x axis
SHIFT		middle	linear transl along local y axis
SHIFT		right	linear transl along local y axis
SHIFT		left and middle	planar transl in local xy plane
SHIFT		left and right	planar transl in local xz plane
SHIFT		middle and right	planar transl in local yz plane
SHIFT	CONTROL	left	rotation around local y axis
SHIFT	CONTROL	middle	rotation around local y axis
SHIFT	CONTROL	right	rotation around local z axis

Table 3.1: Axis mappings for manipulation.

as instructions to move the transform in question. How the movement is interpreted depends upon the command. This mode is terminated by hitting the ESCAPE key. While in the manipulation mode, the mouse buttons and keys behave as described below.

The user interface for the manipulation operation encodes by default the left, middle, and right mouse buttons to control translations along the x, y, and z axes, respectively, of the global coordinate frame. When the user presses down any mouse button, it enables translation along that axis. When the user presses two mouse buttons, translation is enabled in the plane spanned by those two axes. With this technique, it is not possible to translate along three axes simultaneously, so pressing three buttons at once has no effect.

Rotation is signified by holding down the CONTROL key. In this case, the mouse buttons are interpreted as rotations around the x, y, and z axes of the global coordinate. Only one rotation button may be selected at once.

The user can change the axes of translation and rotation to the local coordinate frame of the manipulation transform by holding down the SHIFT key. The CONTROL key still signifies rotation, but the rotational axes are local to the manipulation transform instead of the global axes. Table 3.1 summarizes how the state of the keys and mouse buttons translates into the transform axis.

Jack relies on a set of graphical icons to inform the user about the axes of translation and rotation. The manipulation transform is drawn as a labeled six-axis coordinate frame. The translation icon is a transparent arrow. The rotation icon is a spoked wheel. Each icon is overlaid against the objects themselves, but since they are transparent, they do not intrude too severely.

The Mouse Line

The translation and rotation of the manipulation transform is determined interactively by the ray in the world coordinates that is cast through the location on the screen where the mouse cursor lies. This line in space is referred to internally as the *mouse line*, and it can be easily computed by an inversion of the viewing transform. The mouse line serves as a *probe* into the environment with which to move the manipulation transform. This notion of a probe is useful in describing the implementation, although it is not one that is visible to the user. The user has the feel of moving the object itself.

Linear and angular displacements are computed by intersecting the mouse line with lines and planes defined by the origin of the manipulation transform and the translation or rotation axis using a scheme described below.

Linear Translation

As described above, linear translation takes place when the user presses one mouse button. The mouse may move anywhere on the screen, but the translation is restricted to the particular axis, determined by which mouse button was pressed. This axis projects to a line on the screen. The translation icon illustrates this line, and it also instructs the user to move the mouse in that direction on the screen. Ideally, the user moves the mouse exactly along this line, but in practice the mouse will not follow the line precisely. The position of the manipulation transform is the point along the translational axis that is nearest to the mouse line. Figure 3.2 shows the translation icon.

Planar Translation

Planar translation is actually somewhat simpler than linear translation because its two DOFs more closely match those of the mouse. The plane of translation passes through the origin of the manipulation transform, and is spanned by the two axes defined by the selected mouse buttons. The technique is to intersect the mouse line with the plane of translation and supply the point of intersection as the origin of the manipulation transform. This means that the object automatically goes to the location in the plane that lies underneath the mouse cursor. Figure 3.3 shows the planar translation icon.

The user can translate in the global or local xy, xz, or yz planes, but in practice the linear and planar translation techniques provide a comfortable pattern of use involving only planar translation in the xz plane. This is the horizontal plane, and it is the most intuitive to visualize. The user can comfortably translate objects in the horizontal plane using planar translation, and then raise and lower them using linear translation along the y axis.

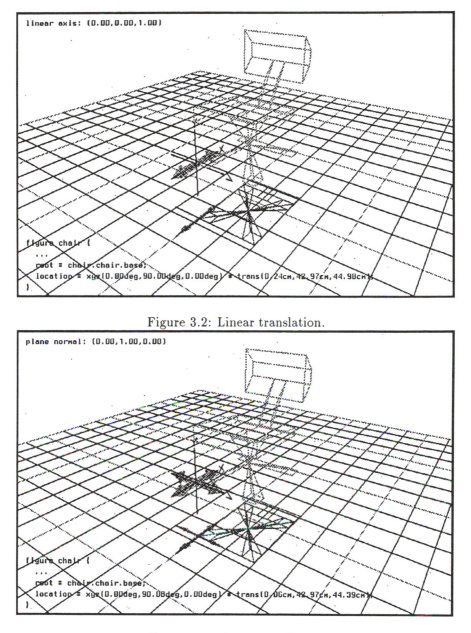

Figure 3.2: Linear translation.

Figure 3.3: Planar translation.

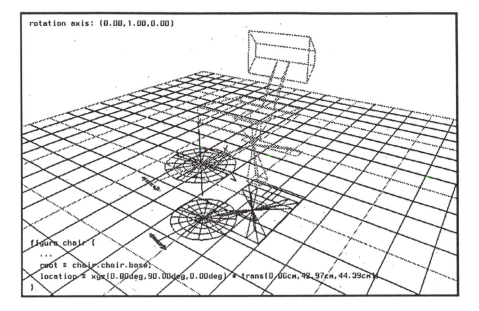

Figure 3.4: Rotation.

Rotation

The user interface for rotation requires the user to move the mouse around in circles on its pad. This is similar in some ways to the turntable technique of [ETW81] described earlier, except that the turntable used a rotation angle in screen coordinates, not world coordinates, making the angular displacement independent of the viewing direction. The *Jack* operator provides a more direct feel over the rotation because it gives the sense of actually holding on to the wheel.

The three mouse buttons are encoded as rotation around the x, y, and z axes. When the user presses down on a button, a wheel is displayed at the origin of the manipulation transform describing the rotational axis. This wheel lies in the plane in which the rotation is to take place, with the origin of the wheel at the rotational axis. Then a vector is drawn from the current intersection point between the plane and the mouse line. This vector forms an extended *spoke* of the wheel, and as the user moves the mouse around in this plane, *Jack* computes a new spoke and then measures the angular distance between it and the original spoke. This determines the angle of rotation. The sensation that the user gets is one of twisting a crank by moving the mouse around in circles on the screen. Figure 3.4 shows the rotation wheel icon.

If the rotation involves a **Peabody** joint with joint limits, the inadmissible sector of the rotation wheel is colored red. Mouse movements will cause the wheel to rotate beyond its limits, but the rotated segment will not move past the limit. Thus the semantics of the user's interaction are consistent with the free rotation case, yet object behavior is natural.

3.2 Manipulation with Constraints

The term "constraint" has many meanings and applications. Some researchers use it to mean a very low level concept. Isaacs and Cohen [IC87] use the term to mean essentially any kinematic control over a joint or group of joints during dynamic simulation. The constraint removes DOFs from the system in a straightforward way. Witkin and Kass [WK88] and Girard [Gir91] use the term to mean a global optimization criterion, such as minimum expended energy. Sometimes, the term means an desired relationship, which in computer graphics usually implies a geometric one. This is the case of Nelson's Juno system [Nel85]. Many researchers use the term to mean specifically a desired *spatial* relationship, that is, goals for reference points. This is usually the meaning in physically based modeling, as in the dynamic constraints of Barzel and Barr [BB88].

Constraints that mean geometric goals may be interpreted with an additional temporal component. Most constraint-based systems like those just mentioned feature the ability to vary the effect of constraints over time. Given this, it is rather nebulous whether the temporal component is a part of the constraint definition. We feel that it is better to view a constraint instantaneously as a static entity, although its parameters can be changed over time by some means external to the constraint itself.

3.2.1 Postural Control using Constraints

Most formulations of positioning algorithms in robotics and computer animation are principally concerned with motion — smooth motion. In robotics, this is necessary because jerky motion could damage a manipulator. In animation, jerky motion looks bad. For postural control the motion is not as important because the static posture is the principal objective. This means that for interactive postural control, it may be possible to entertain options which are not available to robotics and animation.

In particular, the requirements for postural control are, first, that the technique accommodate massively redundant figures, and second, that it perform fast enough for interactive manipulation, even with complex, highly constrained figures. The third concern is that it generate smooth movement. The interactive postural control process consists of placing the figure in a sequence of postures closely spaced in time and space, giving the illusion of motion for purposes of assisting in the postural specification process.

We use inverse kinematics for posture determination [ZB89]. It dispenses with physical interpretations and solves a minimization problem for pure functions using a nonlinear programming algorithm. The approach uses a variable-metric optimization technique. The function it minimizes is a defined through a linear combination of kinematic constraints as defined below. The objective function describes positions, not velocities. This approach essentially treats the figure a purely geometric entity rather than a physical one. It does not take into account overtly the figure's mass and inertia, though we will see that it can be used to control the center of mass. Our implementation of inverse kinematics is highly efficient and is capable of controlling a complex figure model with large numbers of constraints.

The approach that we advocate for defining postures is somewhat similar to the energy constraints of Witkin, Fleischer, and Barr [WFB87], although there are some important distinctions. Their approach models connections between objects using energy functions. The energy functions do not measure mechanical energy, but are simply constructed to have zeros at the proper locations and have smooth gradients so that the object can follow the gradient towards the solution. This provides the animation of the solution process. The user interface of Witkin, Fleischer, and Barr's system allows the user to specify these energy functions and turn them on. This causes a sudden increase in energy and thus causes the model to begin descending in the direction of the gradient of the energy function. One drawback of this approach is that the timestep of the iterative process must be sufficiently small to ensure convergence. This is particularly a problem in the case of articulated figures. Witkin, Fleischer, and Barr's formulation of the gradient descent algorithm does not permit jointed mechanisms, so they must model joints as constraints. The joints must have a very steep energy function to ensure that they never come apart. This means that the timestep must be very small, making the system of equations very stiff.

Another problem with Witkin, Fleischer, and Barr's approach, from a higher level point of view, is that the user's notion of time is embedded in the algorithm. The energy function defines the path of the end effectors towards their ultimate destinations because the gradient of the energy function determines the direction of movement. We remove the notion of time from the numerical process and put it in a higher level control scheme. This control scheme decides on discrete locations for the goals for end effector reference points, closely spaced in space and time — the user's notion of time. The inverse kinematics algorithm solves an instantaneous positioning problem. The control scheme has two components, the interactive manipulation previously discussed and the behaviors described in Chapter 4.

The inverse kinematics procedure itself has no notion of time. It uses the joint angles of the **Peabody** figures as the variables of optimization. This means that the search step can be significantly larger, and thus the convergence is faster. The control scheme guides the movement in cartesian space, rather than in the space of the energy function. It is still convenient to interpret the positioning criteria as a potential energy function, but the control scheme ensures that the figure is always very near a state of equilibrium.

Using the example of a human arm reaching for a switch, the technique of Witkin, Fleischer, and Barr would model the reach by defining an energy function with a zero when the hand is on the switch, that is, a constraint for the hand to lie at the switch. If the arm begins by the side of the body, the arm would see a sudden increase in energy when the constraint becomes active and would immediately begin to move in a way to minimize the energy. This would cause the hand to begin to move towards the switch. The velocity would be controlled through the intensity of the potential energy function.

Using inverse kinematics, the higher level control scheme computes successive locations for the hand, starting at its current location and progressing towards the switch. The number of steps and the spacing between them is not the domain of the inverse kinematics algorithm but of the control scheme. A kinematic constraint describes the position of the hand and the algorithm's parameters at each time step. The inverse kinematics algorithm is invoked at each time step to place the hand at the desired location.

3.2.2 Constraints for Inverse Kinematics

The *Jack* notion of a kinematic *constraint* defines a *goal* coordinate frame, an *end effector* coordinate frame, a *set of joints* which control the end effector, and an *objective function* which measures the distance between the goal and the end effector. The set of joints is usually defined in terms of a *starting joint*, and the joint set then consists of the chain of joints between the starting joint and the end effector. We can think of individual constraints as defining a potential energy, measured by the objective function, much like that of Witkin, Fleischer, and Barr. The constraint is satisfied when the objective function is minimized, although the function need not be zero. The potential energy of several constraints is a weighted sum of the energies from the individual constraints.

The objective function of a constraint has separate position and orientation components. The potential energy of the constraint is a weighted combination of the two, according to the constraint's *position/orientation weight*. The weight may specify one or the other, or a blending of the two. Our inverse kinematics procedure provides the following objective types [ZB89]:

point The point-to-point distance between the end effector and the goal.

line The point-to-line distance between the end effector and a line defined in the goal coordinate frame.

plane The point-to-plane distance between the end effector and a plane defined in the goal coordinate frame.

frame The orientational difference between the end effector frame and the goal frame. This measures all three orientational DOFs.

direction The orientational difference between a vector defined in the end effector frame and a vector defined in the coordinate frame of the goal.

aim A combined position/orientation function designed to "aim" a reference vector in the coordinate frame of the end effector towards the position of the goal. This is used mostly for eye and camera positioning, but it could also be used, for example, to point a gun. This should never be done in the presence of multiple human figures, of course, particularly children.

3.2.3 Features of Constraints

Each constraint in *Jack* has its own set of joint variables, so the control of each constraint can be localized to particular parts of the figure. Since the joint angles are the variables of optimization, this means that the algorithm operates on chains of joints, ultimately terminated at the root of the figure hierarchy. This implies that the root of the figure remains fixed during the positioning process. This makes the placement of the figure root particularly important. One of the major components of **Peabody** is that the actual definition of a figure does not include the figure root. Instead, the root is a dynamic property which can be changed from time to time. Since the inverse kinematics algorithm operates on chains emanating from the root, the inverse kinematics algorithm cannot change the location of the root.

Our inverse kinematics algorithm works very well provided that it doesn't have to search too far for a solution, although it will converge from any starting point. The farther it has to search, the more likely it is to produce large changes in the joint angles. In geometric terms, this means that the goals should never be too far away from their end effectors, lest the interior segments of the joint chains move too far. This also relieves the problem of getting trapped in a local minimum because hopefully the higher level control strategy which is specifying the goal positions will do so in a way to lead the figure away from such conditions.

The elegance of the potential energy approach, like that of Witkin, Fleischer, and Barr, is that the constraints can be overlapped. This means that it is acceptable to over-constrain the figure. The posture which the algorithm achieves in this case yields the minimum energy state according to the weighting factors between the constraints. This provides a way of resolving the redundancies in a massively redundant figure: use lots of constraints, and don't worry too much about whether the constraints specify conflicting information.

3.2.4 Inverse Kinematics and the Center of Mass

The center of mass of an object is one of its most important landmarks because it defines the focal point for forces and torques acting on it. The center of mass of an articulated figure such as a human figure is particularly significant because its location relative to the feet defines the state of balance. This is critical for human figures, because so many aspects of the movement of a human figure are dictated by the need to maintain balance. The center of mass of is, of course, a dynamic property, but it is possible to manipulate it in a purely kinematic way and thus produce some of the effects of dynamic simulation without the extra cost.

Methods of Maintaining Balance

One approach to maintaining balance of an articulated figure is to root the figure through its center of mass. The center of mass is a dynamic feature of a figure, so rooting the figure through the center of mass means that each time the figure moves, the center of mass must be recomputed and the figure's location updated so that the center of mass remains at the same global location.

This approach works, but it does not give good control over the elevation of the center of mass, since the center of mass is effectively constrained to a constant elevation as well as location in the horizontal plane. The figure appears to dangle as if suspended from its waist with its feet reaching out for the floor. This is particularly true during an operation in which the center of mass normally goes down, such as bending over. In order for the balance behavior to function naturally, the elevation of the center of mass must be allowed to float up and down as required by the movement of the feet. This is more appropriately handled through a constraint.

Kinematic Constraints on the Center of Mass

Balancing a figure is achieved by constraining the center of mass to remain directly above a point in the support polygon. The constraint designates a single point as the balance point rather than using the entire support polygon because this gives control over the placement of the point within the polygon. This allows the figure's weight to shift side to side or forward and backward, without moving the feet.

Jack associates the center of mass logically with the lower torso region of the human figure, and it uses this as the end effector of the constraint, with the ankle, knee, and hip joints of the dominant leg as the constraint variables. During the constraint satisfaction process at each interactive iteration, the center of mass is not recomputed. Since the center of mass belongs logically to the lower torso, its position relative to the torso remains fixed as the inverse kinematics algorithm positions the ankle, knee, and hip so that the previously computed center of mass point lies above the balance point. There are generally other constraints active at the same time, along with other postural adjustments, so that several parts of the figure assume different postures during the process.

After the constraints are solved, *Jack* recomputes the center of mass. It will generally lie in a different location because of the postural adjustments, indicating that the figure is not balanced as it should be. Therefore, the constraints must be solved again, and the the process repeated until the balance condition is satisfied. In this case the structure of the human figure helps. Most of the postural adjustments take place on the first iteration, so on subsequent iterations the changes in the center of mass relative to the rest of the body are quite minor. *Jack* measures the distance that the center of mass changes from one iteration to the next, and it accepts the posture when the change is below a certain threshold. Although it is difficult to guarantee the convergence theoretically, in practice it seldom takes more than two iterations to achieve balance.

3.2.5 Interactive Methodology

There are several possibilities for overcoming the problems with redundancies and local minima. One is to incorporate more information into the objective function, modeling such factors as strength, comfort, and agent preference (Section 5.3). This is an important addition, although it adds significantly to the computational complexity of the constraint solving procedure. *Jack*'s technique is to provide the positional input to the inverse kinematics algorithm with the 3D direct manipulation system. *Jack* allows the user to interactively "drag" goal positions and have the end effector follow[PZB90]. In this case, the geometric information obtained by the mouse at each iteration of the manipulation process is applied to the goal position of a constraint, and the inverse kinematics algorithm is called to solve the constraints before the graphics windows are redrawn. Alternatively, the user can move a figure which has end effectors constrained to other objects. Each case causes a relative displacement between the end effector and the goal.

Interactive Dragging

This dragging mechanism is a modified version of the basic direct manipulation scheme described in Section 3.1. After selecting the parameters of the constraint, the manipulation procedure works as shown in Figure 3.5. The inverse kinematics procedure is invoked at every iteration during the interactive manipulation.

This is a very effective and efficient tool for manipulation for several reasons. Because of the incremental nature of the interactive manipulation process, the goals never move very far from one iteration to the next, as necessary. The algorithm still suffers from problems of local minima, but since the user can drag the end effector around in space in a well-defined and easy to control way, it is relatively easy to overcome these problems by stretching the figure into temporary intermediate configurations to get one part of the figure positioned correctly, and then dragging the end effector itself into the final desired position. This takes advantage of the user's abilities, because local minima can be easy for the user to see but difficult for the system to detect and avoid.

A common example of this dragging technique involves the elbow. The user may initially position the hand at the proper place in space but then find that the elbow is too high. If this is the case, the user can extend the hand outwards to drag the elbow into the correct general region and then drag the hand back to the proper location.

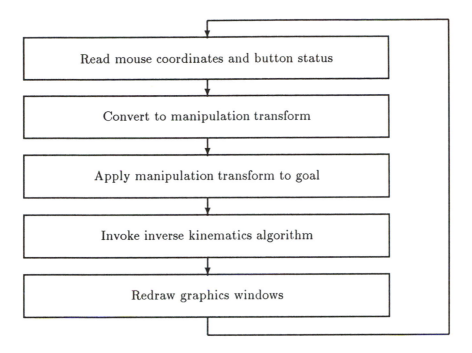

Figure 3.5: Interactive Dragging.

Interactive Twisting

Another effective feature of the direct manipulation interface is the use of orientation constraints, particularly the weighted combination of position and orientation. In this case, the orientation of the goal is significant as well as the position, so the user may manipulate segments in the interior of the joint chain by twisting the orientation of the goal and thus the end effector. This is especially helpful because of the difficulty the user encounters in visualizing and numerically describing rotations which will achieve a desired orientation. The above example of the elbow position may be handled this way, too. By twisting the desired orientation of the hand, the interior of the arm can be rotated up and down while the hand remains in the same location. This achieves in real-time a generalization of the "elbow circle" positioning scheme implemented by Korein [Kor85].

This raises an interface issue concerning the relationship between the actual orientation of the end effector coordinate frame and the manipulation transform. The manipulation technique described in Section 3.1 allows the user to translate and rotate a 6D quantity which now guides the position and orientation of the end effector. We noted, however, that this technique is not so good at choreographing smooth movements through space. The movement trajectory generated by the technique consists of intermittent seg-

Figure 3.6: The Orientation Constraint Icon.

ments of straight-line translations and rotations. As the user translates the manipulation transform, its orientation remains fixed, and vice versa. Is this appropriate behavior for the end effector as well?

If the end effector is sensitive to orientation, then translating the manipulation transform means that the end effector will translate *but will try keep the same global orientation.* Typically, the user can quickly arrive at a goal position for the end effector which is not achievable.

Positional differences are easy to visualize; orientational differences are not. It is easy to manipulate a positional goal which is outside of the reachable space of the end effector. We can intuitively think of a spring or rubber band pulling the end effector towards the goal. Orientational differences are much harder to visualize. Even though it may be easy to conceptualize "rotational springs," in practice is it very difficult to apply that intuition to the geometric model. If the goal is very far outside of the reachable space of the end effector along *angular dimensions*, all correspondence between the orientation of the goal and the end effector gets quickly lost. *Jack* illustrates orientational differences through rotation *fans*, shown in Figure 3.6, which are icons to illustrate how an object must rotate to achieve a desired orientation, but no amount of graphical feedback can help when the differences are large. Therefore, it is absolutely essential that the orientation of the goal – the manipulation transform — not deviate too far from the end effector.

Jack solves this problem through an orientation *offset* to the goal which can be adjusted during the manipulation process. This offset is a relative transform which is applied to the manipulation transform to rotate it into the true orientation of the goal as supplied to the inverse kinematics algorithm. The end effector dragging mechanism resets this offset each time a translation or rotation is completed during the manipulation process, that is, each time a mouse button comes up and the movement stops. This means that each time the user begins to rotate or translate the goal, the manipulation transform starts out from the current orientation of the end effector. This prevents the user from getting lost in the orientation difference.

This simulates the effect of a spring-loaded crank which applies a torque to an object, but only as long as the user holds down the mouse button. When the mouse button comes up, the torque disappears so that it doesn't continue to have a undesirable effect. This lets the user control the goal through a ratcheting technique of applying short bursts of rotation.

Manipulation with Constraints

The nature of the 3D direct manipulation mechanism allows the user to interactively manipulate only a single element at a time, although most positioning tasks involve several parts of the figure, such as both feet, both hands, etc. In addition to interactively dragging a single end effector, there may be any number of other kinematic constraints. These constraints are persistent relationships to be enforced as the figure is manipulated using any of the other manipulation tools. By first defining multiple constraints and then manipulating the figure, either directly or with the dragging mechanism, it is possible to control the figure's posture in a complex way.

This mechanism involves another slight modification to the direct manipulation loop, shown in Figure 3.7. Step #4 may cause the end effectors to move away from their goal positions. The inverse kinematics algorithm in step #5 repositions the joints so the goals are satisfied.

3.3 Inverse Kinematic Positioning

[1]Having modeled the articulated figure with segments and joints we need to deal with the issue of how to manipulate it. There are two basic problems: given all joint angles, how to compute the spatial configuration and, conversely, given a certain posture, what values should be assigned to joint angles. The first problem, forward kinematics, is simply a matter of straightforward transformation matrix multiplication [FvDFH90]. The second, inverse kinematic problem, is much harder to solve.

Inverse kinematics is extremely important in computer animation, since the spatial appearance, rather than the joint angles, interest an animator. A good interactive manipulation environment such as *Jack* may simply hide the numerical values of the joint angles from the user. In such an environment, where the user is concerned only with spatial configuration, the joint angles can become merely an internal representation. The transformation from the

---

[1] Jianmin Zhao.

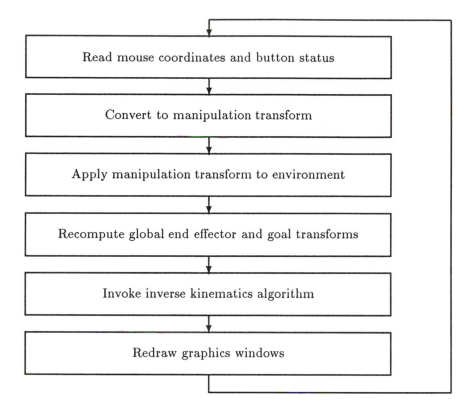

Figure 3.7: Manipulation with Constraints.

spatial configuration into the joint angles is carried out by the inverse kinematic computation so an efficient implementation is most desirable.

Inverse kinematics for determining mechanism motion is a common technique in mechanical engineering, particularly in robot research [Pau81]. In robots, however, redundant DOFs are usually avoided. Moreover, the computation is usually carried out on particular linkage systems [KH83, KTV+90]. In contrast, an interesting object in the computer animation domain – the human body – has many redundant DOFs when viewed as a kinematic mechanism. Therefore a means for specifying and solving underconstrained positioning of tree-like articulated figures is needed.

We first studied methods for kinematic chain positioning, especially in the context of joint limits and redundant DOFs [KB82, Kor85]. Later we tried position constraints to specify spatial configurations of articulated figures [BMW87]. A simple recursive solver computed joint angles of articulated figures satisfying multiple point-to-point position constraints.

About the same time, Girard and Maciejewski used the pseudo-inverse of the Jacobian matrix to solve spatial constraints [GM85]. The main formula is

$$\Delta\theta = J^+\Delta\mathbf{r}$$

where $\Delta\theta$ is the increment of the joint angle vector, $\Delta\mathbf{r}$ is the increment of the spatial vector and J^+ is the pseudo-inverse of the Jacobian $\partial\mathbf{r}/\partial\theta$. For a large step size the method is actually the well-known Newton-Raphson method, which is not globally convergent and often needs some special handling (e.g., hybrid methods [Pow70]). On the other hand, for a sufficiently small step size, as Girard and Maciejewski suggested, excessive iterations are required. The inverse operation is normally very expensive; moreover, they did not deal with joint limits.

Witkin *et al* used energy constraints for positioning [WFB87]. The energy function they adopted is the sum of all constraints including ones for position and orientation. Constraints are satisfied if and only if the energy function is zero. Their method of solving the constraint is to integrate the differential equation:

$$d\theta(t)/dt = -\nabla E(\theta)$$

where θ is the parameter (e.g., joint angle) vector, E is the energy function of θ, and ∇ is the gradient operator. Clearly, if $\theta(t)$ is the integral with some initial condition, $E(\theta(t))$ monotonically decreases with time t. This integral not only gives a final configuration which satisfies the constraint in terms of θ, but also a possible motion from the initial configuration which is driven by the conservative force derived from the gradient of the energy function.

Instead of associating energy functions with constraints, Barzel and Barr introduced deviation functions such that a constraint is met if and only if the deviation function vanishes $(= 0)$ [BB88]. They have presented various constraints, such as point-to-point, point-to-nail, etc., and their associated deviation functions. A set of dynamic differential equations are constructed to control the way by which the deviations vanish (e.g., exponentially in a certain amount of time). Constraint forces are solved which, along with other external forces, drive geometric models to achieve constraints. They dealt with rigid bodies which may be related by various constraints. Witkin and Welch [WW90] used a dynamic method on nonrigid bodies. In all these approaches articulated figure joints would be considered as point-to-point constraints, which are added to the system as algebraic equations. It is not unusual to have several dozen joints in an highly articulated figure, which would add to the number of constraint equations appreciably. Besides, a joint is meant to be an absolute constraint. In another words, it should not compete with other constraints which relate a point in a segment of the figure with a point in the space. This competition often gives rise to numerical instability. So these methods seem inappropriate to the highly articulated figure.

Although the energy or dynamics methods may be used to solve the spatial constraint problem, they are also concerned with computing plausible (dynamically-valid) paths. For articulated figure positioning, the additional work involved in path determination is not so critical. So, we first focus on a more elementary version of the problem — to position the articulated figure into desired pose — hoping that the solution can be found much faster and more robustly, and joint angles limits can be dealt with effectively. We will see later in Chapter 5 how more natural motions may be generated by considering human strength models and collision avoidance.

3.3.1   Constraints as a Nonlinear Programming Problem

A spatial constraint involves two parts. The part on the figure is called the end-effector and its counterpart in the space is called the goal. A constraint is a demand that the end-effector be placed at the goal. Since a goal always implies a related end-effector, we may sometimes take goals as synonymous for constraints.

As is done with energy constraints, we create a function with each goal such that its value, when applied to the end effector, represents the "distance" of the end-effector from the goal. This distance need not be only Euclidean distance. Let us call this function "potential," because it is a scalar function of spatial position or vectors. The vector field generated by the negation of the gradient of the function could be interpreted as a force field toward the goal. Depending on the goal types, an end-effector on a segment can be a point, a vector, a set of two vectors, or a combination of them, in the local coordinate system of the segment. Let P denote the potential function associated with a goal and e the "location" of the end-effector. The constraint is satisfied if and only if $P(\mathbf{e})$ vanishes. Clearly the end-effector is a function of the vector of all joint angles.

A single constraint may not be sufficient to specify a pose. For example, in addition to the position of the hand, the placement of the elbow is often desired. In positioning two arms, we may need to keep the torso in some orientation. The function associated with these conjunctively combined goals is defined as a weighted sum:

$$G(\theta) = \sum_{i=1}^{m} w_i G_i(\theta) \tag{3.1}$$

where m is the number of goals combined, and

$$G_i(\theta) = P_i(\mathbf{e}_i(\theta)) \tag{3.2}$$

where the subscript i refers to the ith goal, and w_is are weights on respective constraints.

Sometimes, goals may need be combined disjunctively. In other words, the combined goal is achieved if and only if either constituent goal is achieved. For example, the interior of a convex polyhedron is the conjunction of inner half-spaces defined by its surrounding faces, while the exterior is the disjunction of those opposite half-spaces. Obstacle avoidance is a situation where constraining an end-effector to the outside of a volume is useful. The function associated with the disjunctively combined goal is defined as

$$G(\theta) = \min_{i \in \{1, \dots m\}} G_i(\theta) \tag{3.3}$$

By definition of the function G, the overall constraint is met if and only if G vanishes. Due to the physical constraint of the figure and the redundancy of DOFs, there may not be θ such that $G(\theta) = 0$, or there may be many such θ's. Therefore we attempt to find a θ, subject to constraints on joint angles, which minimizes the function G. Although constraints on joint angles may be complicated, linear constraints suffice in most situations. Typical constraints are represented as a lower limit and an upper limit for each joint angle. Therefore we formulate our problem as a nonlinear programming problem subject to linear constraints, i.e.,

$$\begin{cases} \min G(\theta) \\ s.t. \quad \mathbf{a}_i^T \theta = b_i, i = 1, 2, \dots, l \\ \quad\quad \mathbf{a}_i^T \theta \le b_i, i = l+1, l+2, \dots, k \end{cases} \tag{3.4}$$

where $\mathbf{a}_i, i = 1, 2, \dots, k$ are column vectors whose dimension is the total number of DOFs. The equality constraints allow for linear relations among the joint angles. The lower limit l^i and upper limit u^i on θ^i, the ith joint angle, contribute to the set of inequality constraints on θ :

$$\begin{aligned} -\theta^i &\le -l^i \\ \theta^i &\le u^i \ . \end{aligned}$$

3.3.2 Solving the Nonlinear Programming Problem

There are many algorithms to solve problem (3.4). One efficient algorithm is based on Davidon's variable metric method with BFGS (Broyden, Fletcher, Goldfarb, Shanno) rank-two update formula [Fle70, Gol70, Sha70]. Rosen's projection method is used to handle the linear constraints on variables [Ros60, Gol69]. No matter what algorithm we choose, efficiency requires computation of the gradient as well as the value of the objective function when θ is given. So first we develop an efficient way to compute the gradient of, as well as the value of, the objective function $G(\theta)$ for figures with tree-like data structure and various sorts of goals.

Single Constraints

Since the human figure has a tree-like structure, an end-effector of a constraint depends only on those joints which lie along the path from the root of the figure tree to the distal segment containing the end-effector [BMW87]. Call this path the *constraint chain*. The constraint chain is illustrated in Figure 3.8. For simplicity, we assume each joint in Figure 3.8 has only one DOF. A joint with multiple DOFs can be decomposed conceptually into several joints with each having one DOF, i.e., zero distance from one joint to another is allowed.

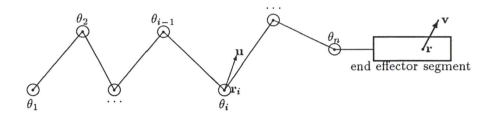

Figure 3.8: Constraint Chain.

The length of the constraint chain is the total number of joints along the chain; in Figure 3.8, it is n.

This module is to compute $G_i(\theta)$, as defined in equation (3.2) and its gradient for a single constraint chain and its corresponding goal. In this section, we only consider a single chain, so the subscript i is dropped.

Notice that

$$G(\theta) = P(e(\theta)) \tag{3.5}$$

and

$$
\begin{aligned}
g(\theta) &= \nabla_\theta G \\
&= \left(\frac{\partial e}{\partial \theta}\right)^T \nabla_e P
\end{aligned}
\tag{3.6}
$$

where $\frac{\partial e}{\partial \theta}$ is the Jacobian matrix of the vector function $e(\theta)$, i.e.,

$$\frac{\partial e}{\partial \theta} = \left(\begin{array}{cccc} \frac{\partial e}{\partial \theta^1} & \frac{\partial e}{\partial \theta^2} & \cdots & \frac{\partial e}{\partial \theta^n} \end{array}\right).$$

These expressions suggest that end-effectors and goals can be abstracted as functions $e(\cdot)$ and $P(\cdot)$ which, by pair, constitute constraints. The range of the function e depends on the type of the constraint, but it must be equal to the domain of its respective P function, which measures the distance of the current end-effector to the goal. For the sake of numerical efficiency, we require that those functions be differentiable.

By virtue of equations (3.5) and (3.6), two sub-modules, end-effector and goal modules, can be built separately. Note that the goal potential P does not depend on the figure model. Only the end-effector function e does.

End-effectors

This module is the only one which depends on the model of the articulated figure. It turns out that it is easy to compute e and $\frac{\partial e}{\partial \theta}$, under our assumption of rigidity of segments, for many useful types of constraint.

We only consider constraints where end-effectors are points (for positions) or vectors (for orientations) on distal segments. So e consists of either a position vector **r**, one or two unit vectors attached on the distal segment **v**'s, or a combination of them (see Figure 3.8). Because all the joints of the human body are revolute joints, we discuss here only revolute joints. (Translational joints are simpler and can be treated similarly.)

Let the ith joint angle along the chain be θ^i, the axis of this joint be **u** (a unit vector), and the position vector of the ith joint be $\mathbf{r}_i$. The vectors **r** and **v** can be easily computed with cascaded multiplication of transformation matrices. The derivative can be computed as follows [Whi72]:

$$\frac{\partial \mathbf{r}}{\partial \theta^i} = \mathbf{u} \times (\mathbf{r} - \mathbf{r}_i) \tag{3.7}$$

$$\frac{\partial \mathbf{v}}{\partial \theta^i} = \mathbf{u} \times \mathbf{v} \ . \tag{3.8}$$

These formulas are enough for the types of goals we have considered. The particular forms of e will be explained with particular goals, since they must match the arguments of the goal potential $P(\cdot)$.

Goal Types

We have implemented several useful, as well as simple, types of goals (or constraints).

Position Goal. The goal is a point **p** in 3D space. The end-effector is, correspondingly, a point **r** which sits on the distal segment of the constraint chain, but it is not necessarily a leaf segment in the figure tree (see Figure 3.8). The potential function is:

$$P(\mathbf{r}) = (\mathbf{p} - \mathbf{r})^2 \tag{3.9}$$

where p is the parameter of the function, and the gradient is:

$$\nabla_{\mathbf{r}} P(\mathbf{r}) = 2(\mathbf{r} - \mathbf{p}) \ . \tag{3.10}$$

Orientation Goal. The orientation in the space is determined by two orthonormal vectors. So the goal is defined by a pair of orthonormal vectors, say,

$$\{\mathbf{x}_g, \mathbf{y}_g\} \ .$$

Accordingly, the end effector is a pair of orthonormal vectors

$$\{\mathbf{x}_e, \mathbf{y}_e\}$$

attached on the distal segment of the constraint chain.

The potential function could be:

$$P(\mathbf{x}_e, \mathbf{y}_e) = (\mathbf{x}_g - \mathbf{x}_e)^2 + (\mathbf{y}_g - \mathbf{y}_e)^2 \ .$$

In combination with a positional goal, this function implies that one length unit is as important as about one radian in angle. To enforce one length unit compatible with d degrees in angle, we need to multiply the previous P by c_d such that

$$\frac{1}{c_d} = \frac{2\pi}{360}d$$

i. e. ,

$$c_d = 360/(2\pi d) \ . \tag{3.11}$$

To be more general, our potential function is then

$$P(\mathbf{x}_e, \mathbf{y}_e) = c_{dx}^2(\mathbf{x}_g - \mathbf{x}_e)^2 + c_{dy}^2(\mathbf{y}_g - \mathbf{y}_e)^2 \ . \tag{3.12}$$

The gradient is

$$\nabla_{\mathbf{x}_e} P(\mathbf{x}_e, \mathbf{y}_e) = 2c_{dx}^2(\mathbf{x}_e - \mathbf{x}_g) \tag{3.13}$$
$$\nabla_{\mathbf{y}_e} P(\mathbf{x}_e, \mathbf{y}_e) = 2c_{dy}^2(\mathbf{y}_e - \mathbf{y}_g) \ . \tag{3.14}$$

Any direction, such as y, could be suppressed by setting c_{dy} to 0. This is useful, for example, to constrain a person holding a cup of water while attaining other constraints.

Position/Orientation Goals. Position and orientation goals can be treated separately, but sometimes it is convenient to combine them together as a single goal. The potential function for position/orientation goal is just the weighted sum of respectively goals:

$$P(\mathbf{r}, \mathbf{x}_e, \mathbf{y}_e) = w_p(\mathbf{p} - \mathbf{r})^2 + w_o c_{dx}^2(\mathbf{x}_g - \mathbf{x}_e)^2 + w_o c_{dy}^2(\mathbf{y}_g - \mathbf{y}_e)^2 \tag{3.15}$$

where w_p and w_o are weights put on position and orientation respectively such that

$$w_p + w_o = 1 \ .$$

The gradients $\nabla_{\mathbf{r}} P, \nabla_{\mathbf{x}_e} P$ and $\nabla_{\mathbf{y}_e} P$ are obvious from above.

Aiming-at Goals. The goal is a point $\mathbf{p}$ in the space, but the end-effector is a vector $\mathbf{v}$ attached to the distal segment at $\mathbf{r}$ (see Figure 3.8). The goal is attained if the vector $\mathbf{v}$ points toward the point $\mathbf{p}$. This is useful, for example, when we want to make the head face toward a certain point.

The potential function is:

$$P(\mathbf{r}, \mathbf{v}) = c_d^2 \left(\frac{\mathbf{p} - \mathbf{r}}{\|\mathbf{p} - \mathbf{r}\|} - \mathbf{v}\right)^2 \tag{3.16}$$

where c_d is defined in (3.11) and $\| \cdot \|$ denotes the norm operation. The gradient is:

$$\nabla_{\mathbf{r}} P(\mathbf{r}, \mathbf{v}) = 2c_d^2(\|\mathbf{p} - \mathbf{r}\|^2\mathbf{v} - (\mathbf{p} - \mathbf{r})\cdot\mathbf{v}\,(\mathbf{p} - \mathbf{r}))/\|\mathbf{p} - \mathbf{r}\|^3 \tag{3.17}$$
$$\nabla_{\mathbf{v}} P(\mathbf{r}, \mathbf{v}) = -2c_d^2\left(\frac{\mathbf{p} - \mathbf{r}}{\|\mathbf{p} - \mathbf{r}\|} - \mathbf{v}\right) \ . \tag{3.18}$$

Line Goals. The goal is a line and the end-effector is a point **r**. The goal is to force the point to go along the line. Let the line be defined by point **p** and unit vector ν such that the parametric equation of the line is

$$\mathbf{p} + t\nu \ .$$

The potential function is:

$$P(\mathbf{r}) = ((\mathbf{p} - \mathbf{r}) - (\mathbf{p} - \mathbf{r}){\cdot}\nu\,\nu)^2 \tag{3.19}$$

and the gradient is:

$$\nabla_{\mathbf{r}}P(\mathbf{r}) = 2(\nu{\cdot}(\mathbf{p} - \mathbf{r})\,\nu - (\mathbf{p} - \mathbf{r})) \ . \tag{3.20}$$

Plane Goals. The goal is a plane and the end-effector is a point **r**. The point must be forced to lie on the plane. Let a point on the plane be **p** and the normal of the plane be ν. The potential function is:

$$P(\mathbf{r}) = ((\mathbf{p} - \mathbf{r}){\cdot}\nu)^2 \tag{3.21}$$

and the gradient is:

$$\nabla_{\mathbf{r}}P(\mathbf{r}) = -2\nu{\cdot}(\mathbf{p} - \mathbf{r})\,\nu \ . \tag{3.22}$$

Half-space Goals. The goal is one side of a plane and the end-effector is a point **r**. The point is constrained to lie to one side of the plane. Let a point on the plane be **p** and the normal of the plane be ν which points to the half space the goal defines. The potential function is:

$$P(\mathbf{r}) = \begin{cases} 0 & \text{if } (\mathbf{p} - \mathbf{r}){\cdot}\nu < 0 \\ ((\mathbf{p} - \mathbf{r}){\cdot}\nu)^2 & \text{otherwise} \end{cases} \tag{3.23}$$

and the gradient is:

$$\nabla_{\mathbf{r}}P(\mathbf{r}) = \begin{cases} 0 & \text{if } (\mathbf{p} - \mathbf{r}){\cdot}\nu < 0 \\ -2\nu{\cdot}(\mathbf{p} - \mathbf{r})\,\nu & \text{otherwise} \end{cases} \ . \tag{3.24}$$

As the number of joint angles n along the chain grows, the computational complexity of G and $\mathbf{g}$ is linear for the listed goal types, since the end-effector module needs $O(n)$ time and the goal module needs $O(1)$ time.

3.3.3 Assembling Multiple Constraints

In the single constraint module, we consider only those joint angles which lie on the constraint chain. To make our constraint system useful, multiple constraints would be combined to one constraint, as in equations (3.1) or (3.3). The arguments in these formulas, the vector θ, may involve joint angles along many paths in the figure tree. In other words, with respect to this

θ the gradient of G_i in (3.1) or (3.3) contains many zeros. For the sake of computational efficiency and program modularity, we choose not to pass the overall index of joint angles to the single constraint module.

Suppose there are m constraints. The ith constraint involves n_i joint angles, whereas the combined constraint involves n joint angles. Notice that this n is not simply the summation of n_is, since one joint angle may be involved in several chains. The relationship between the index used in the ith constraint chain and the overall index is represented by the mapping

$$M_i : \{1, 2, \ldots, n_i\} \longrightarrow \{1, 2, \ldots, n\} \ ; \tag{3.25}$$

the jth joint angle in the ith constraint chain corresponds to the $M_i(j)$th joint angle in the overall index system.

Let θ_i denote the vector formed by the joint angles along the ith constraint chain. For disjunctively combined goals with G defined in (3.3) , one can always focus on the goal with minimal $G_i(\theta_i)$ at each iteration. So this is nothing but a collection of goals.

This module is designed for conjunctively combined goals with G defined in (3.1). The evaluation of G is simply a summation of the individual G_i. To compute the overall gradient

$$\begin{aligned} g &= (\ g^1 \quad g^2 \quad \cdots \quad g^n \ )^T \\ &= \nabla_\theta G(\theta) \end{aligned}$$

by using the outputs of the single constraint module

$$\begin{aligned} g_i(\theta_i) &= (\ g_i^1 \quad g_i^2 \quad \cdots \quad g_i^{n_i} \ )^T \\ &= \nabla_{\theta_i} G_i(\theta_i) \ , \end{aligned}$$

we only need to do

1. $g^j \leftarrow 0$, for $j = 1, 2, \ldots, n$

2. For $i = 1$ to m do
   $g^{M_i(j)} \leftarrow g^{M_i(j)} + w_i g_i^j$, for $j = 1, 2, \ldots, n_i$.

From above one can see that all the G_i and their gradients g_i can be computed in parallel.

We assumed in Section 3.3.2 that the constraint chain went from the root of the figure tree to the distal segment. It is possible and sometimes useful that the chain go from a specified joint which is nearer to the root than the distal segment is. Then we must take care of those joints which affect an end-effector, but are not in the constraint chain. For example, suppose that the torso is the root of the figure, one constraint chain is from the right shoulder to the right hand, and the other is from the torso to the left hand. Although the torso is not assigned to the end-effector right hand, it will affect the right hand when it moves the left one. The system should add joints from the torso to the left shoulder to the constraint chain for the right hand [BOK80].

Constraints may exist in a hierarchy. With multiple constraints, there may be one (or more) constraint(s) which consists of several constraints disjunctively combined. In general, a logic formula which contains conjunctive and disjunctive connectors can be implemented. For example, the exterior of a convex polyhedron can be defined as the union of the outside half-space of all of its surrounding faces. This can be used to avoid obstacles: we may want the hand to get somewhere while keeping the elbow away from the obstacle. This does not solve *segment* obstacle avoidance, however.

Joints can be locked or added to the constraint chain for a particular task.

3.3.4 Stiffness of Individual Degrees of Freedom

A nonlinear programming algorithm which utilizes gradient information has a property that, given the same termination tolerance, a variable would undergo more displacement if the value of the objective function changes more due to the unit increment of that variable. This property can be used to control the stiffness of each DOF by assigning a scaling factor to each joint angle. These scaling factors change the unit of each joint angle.

For example, if the standard unit of joint angles is a radian, and 0.5 is assigned to a particular joint angle, which is to take half of the radian as the unit of that joint angle, then this joint angle will be more reluctant to move. One unit of change in this joint angle will have half of the effect on the end-effector as it would without that scaling factor. This makes the effect of other joint angles more apparent.

3.3.5 An Example

Jack contains an implementation of this multiple spatial constraint solver as a basic tool for the interactive manipulation of articulated figures. Constraints can be of any types listed above, or can be sets of simple constraints disjunctively combined. Users may create various constraints, any of which can be moved interactively, and the achieving configuration is solved and observed in real-time.

The pose in Figure 3.9 is achieved by using 6 constraints. Two Position/Orientation goals are used for two hands to hold the tube, where one direction of the orientation is suppressed so that only normals of the hand and the tube are aligned. Two Plane goals are used to constrain two elbows on two side planes. To have the person look down towards the end of the tube, we used two goals – a Line goal was used to constrain the view point on the central axis of the tube; an Aiming-at goal was used to point the view vector towards the end of the tube. In all, 22 DOFs are involved. To encourage forward bending, we set the rigidities of the lateral bending and axial rotation of the torso to a mid-range (0.5) value. Starting from an upright neutral position and moving from the waist, the solution took only 2 seconds on a Silicon Graphics Personal Iris (4D-25TG), not one of the faster machines of its type.

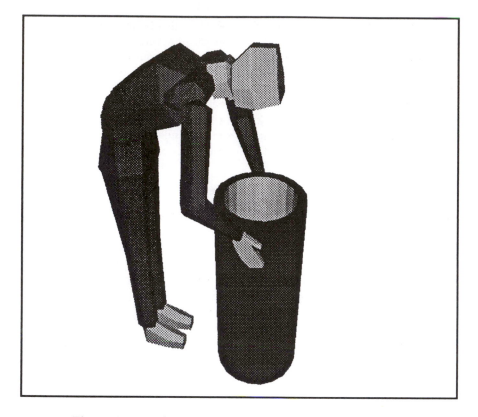

Figure 3.9: Looking Down Towards the End of the Tube.

3.4   Reachable Spaces

[2]The *workspace* is the volume or space encompassing all points that a reference point on the hand (or the end effector) traces as all the joints move through their respective ranges of motion [KW81]. An articulated chain is a series of links connected with either revolute or prismatic joints such as a robotic manipulator or a human limb. Visualizing the 3D workspace for articulated chains has applications in a variety of fields: in computer graphics and artificial intelligence systems that generate plans for approaching and grasping an object in complex environments, in CAD systems to design the interior layout of cars, vehicles, or space shuttles, in the evolving areas of telerobots and parallel manipulators, in the coordination of different manipulators to perform certain tasks, and, finally, in ergonomic studies to help understanding the effects of body size, joint limits, and limb length on the workspace volume.

Previous workspace algorithms [Kum80, Sug81, GR82, TS83, TS81, Tsa86, YL83, Vij85, Muj87] are only capable of displaying 2D workspace cross-

---

[2]Tarek Alameldin.

sections. This is not adequate for redundant (more than 6 DOFs) manipulators with joint limits. We describe how to compute the 3D workspace for redundant articulated chains with joint limits.

The first efforts to compute the manipulator workspace, based on its kinematic geometry, started in the mid 1970's [Rot75, Sug81]. The first result was that the extreme distance line between a chosen point on the first joint axis and the center point of the hand/end effector (extreme reach) intersects all intermediate joint axes of rotation. This is not valid, however, if any joint has limits, any intermediate joint axis is parallel to the extreme distance line, or two joint axes intersect.

Kumar and Waldron [KW81] presented another algorithm for the manipulator's workspace. In their analysis, an imaginary force is applied to the reference point at the end effector in order to achieve the maximum extension in the direction of the applied force. The manipulator reaches its maximum extension when the force's line of action intersects all joint axes of rotation (since the moment of the force about each axis of rotation must be zero). Every joint of the manipulator can settle in either of two possible positions under the force action. Hence, this algorithm results in 2^{n-1} different sets of joint variables for a manipulator of n joints in the direction of the applied force. Each set of joint variables results in a point on the workspace boundary. The concept of stable and unstable equilibrium is used to select the set of joint variables that result in the maximum extension in the force direction. This algorithm is used to generate a shell of points which lie on the workspace boundary by varying the direction of the applied force over a unit sphere. This algorithm has exponential time complexity and deals only with those manipulators that have ideal revolute joints.

Tsai and Soni [TS83] developed another algorithm to plot the contour of the workspace on an arbitrarily specified plane for a manipulator with n revolute joints. The robot hand is moved to the specified plane, then the tip of the hand is moved on the plane until it hits the workspace boundary, and finally the workspace boundary is traced by moving the hand from one position to its neighbor. Each of these three subproblems is formulated as a linear programming problem with some constraints and bounded variables (to account for the joint limits). Accordingly, this algorithm is just a 2D workspace cross-section computation and, moreover, has excessive computational cost.

Yang [YL83] and Lee [LY83] presented algorithms to detect the existence of holes and voids in the manipulator's workspace. A workspace is said to have a hole if there exist at least one straight line which is surrounded by the workspace yet without making contact with it. The hole in a donut is a simple example for the above definition. A workspace is said to have a void if there exist a closed region R, buried within the reachable workspace, such that all points inside the bounding surface of R are not reached by the manipulator. Gupta [Gup86, GR82] classified voids into two different types. The first one, called *central*, occurs around the first axis of rotation and is like the core of an apple. The second type, called *toroidal* or *noncentral*, occurs within the reachable workspace and is like a hollow ring. He [Gup86] also presented qualitative reasoning about the transformation of holes to voids and vice versa. Both the qualitative method developed by Gupta [Gup86] and the analytical one developed by Yang and Lee [YL83, LY83] are based on mapping the workspace from the distal link to the proximal one and studying the relationship between the generated workspace and the new axis of rotation.

Tsai [Tsa86] presented another algorithm, based on the theory of reciprocal screws. In contrast to the above algorithms that only compute workspace points, this algorithm traces the 2D workspace boundary for a given manipulator. The use of reciprocal screw theory has made computing piecewise continuous boundary that consists of straight line segments and circular arcs possible. The manipulator's workspace is computed by performing the union operation on all the workspaces of the manipulator's aspects. An aspect of a robot is interpreted as a set of joint variables such that the manipulator can reach points inside the workspace at one configuration without hitting a joint limit [Tsa86]. The computed workspace has interior surfaces which are the boundaries of aspects. This algorithm is limited to manipulators which do not have holes or voids in their workspaces.

Korein [Kor85] created conservative approximations to 3D reach volumes by taking polyhedral unions of reach polyhedra, working along an articulated chain from the distal joint inwards. The major drawbacks of his approach are the high computational cost and numerical sensitivity of the polyhedral unions which are very difficult to perform once they become many-sided.

3.4.1   Workspace Point Computation Module

The purpose of this module is to compute a suitably dense set of workspace points. The inputs to this module are a chain of linkages with a proximal and distal end, the joint limits associated with each DOF and the desired resolutions in the x, y and z directions (res_x, res_y, res_z) for the end effector position.

We classify the algorithms that can be used to implement this module as follows:

1. Algorithms based on forward kinematics. The basic idea is to generate end effector positions by cycling each DOF through some number of discrete angles (if revolute) or distances (if prismatic).

2. Algorithms based on nonlinear programming. Here a collection of points in space is provided as targets for the end effector and the linkage attempts to solve for a satisfying posture.

3. Algorithms based on force application at the end effector. A series of force directions is used to pull the chain to its maximum extension.

Each class is better than the others for some applications. Direct kinematics algorithms lend themselves easily to volume visualization applications since they require less time and space than the other algorithms. It is difficult, however, to determine the adequate density (the number of points to be generated) that would compute a workspace with the given resolution (res_x, res_y, and res_z) . Hence, direct kinematics based algorithms cannot be used alone to compute the workspace volume since they are not guaranteed to compute all the reachable points. The resolution values divide the space into cells of dimensions $res_x \times res_y \times res_z$. A cell is marked with one if it contains a workspace point. A cell marked with zero does not necessarily mean that it is unreachable since the direct kinematics based algorithm might not have computed enough workspace points. This limitation is serious especially if the application requires surface visualization which use edge detection algorithm as will be described in the next section. On the other hand, algorithms based on nonlinear programming are more appropriate for applications that only require computing the envelope of the reachable workspace since these algorithms compute only points that lie on the workspace envelope. However, the cost of computing each point by the nonlinear programming based algorithms is higher than the cost using forward kinematics based algorithms. Finally, nonlinear programming based algorithms are more appropriate for applications that require partial surface computation in predetermined directions. They can also be used in volume visualization applications by dividing the space into voxels (of dimension $res_x \times res_y \times res_z$) and using the inverse kinematics algorithm to determine whether the cell is occupied or not. However, this operation is very costly and does not guarantee the correct result since the nonlinear programming algorithms do not necessarily return the global maximum or minimum (they might stop at local ones). Algorithms that are based on force application are very costly since they require exponential time to compute each point. All these algorithms can be hybridized to compute better quality volumes or surfaces [Ala91, ABS90].

3.4.2 Workspace Visualization

We believe that either surface based techniques or voxel based techniques can be used in workspace visualization depending on the application type. If the application goal is to compute the workspace boundary in order to find the intersection with other psurf objects in the environment, surface based techniques can be used. On the other hand, binary voxel based techniques lend themselves easily to applications that require computing cut-away views, changing the view point, finding the union or the intersection with other objects that are represented by voxels, and trading off computation time against image quality.

This module constructs a surface that encompasses the workspace points that were computed by the workspace point generation module. We have developed an algorithm that accepts the workspace contours computed by the direct kinematics algorithm. The algorithm can be summarized in four steps:

1. Region Filling. This step involves determining the number of regions in a given workspace contour. The number of holes and voids in the

given workspace contour can be determined. Region filling algorithms
are a common graphics utility and are widely used in paint programs
[Sha80, FB85, Fis90]. A region is a collection of pixels. There are two
types of regions: 4-connected and 8-connected. A region is 4-connected
if adjacent pixels share a horizontal or vertical edge. A region is 8-
connected if adjacent pixels share an edge or a corner. Region filling
algorithms start with a given seed point (x, y) and set this pixel and all
of its neighbors with the same pixel value to a new pixel value. A good
region-filling algorithm is one that reads as few pixels as possible. The
algorithm computes the number of regions in a given workspace cross-
section (contour). We search the contour for a reachable workspace
cell (marked with 1) and use it as a seed point. The set of all cells
connected to the seed point comprise a reachable region. The region
filling algorithm sets those cells to a new value that greater than 2. The
region filling algorithm is called as many times as necessary in order to
set different regions with unique values.

2. Boundary Detection. The purpose of this step is to compute the boundary of different regions in a workspace cross-section. This is done by
   testing the neighbors of each cell in the workspace cross-section. An
   array element of the workspace cross-section is considered a boundary
   cell if it has a different value from its neighbor.

3. Contour Tracing. This step computes the edges that connect the boundary points for a given region.

4. Triangulation. This step constructs the 3D workspace by tiling adjacent
   contours with triangles. We have used the Fuchs' algorithm [FKU77]
   that interpolates the triangular faces between parallel slices in order to
   construct the 3D workspace surface from the different cross sections.

3.4.3   Criteria Selection

This module interacts with the user and selects the most suitable point computation and visualization algorithms based on the application requirements.
Those requirements (parameters) include:

- *Surface/volume.* This parameter allows the user to select to either compute the workspace boundary (envelope) or compute the workspace volume based on the application requirements.

- *Complete/partial.* This parameter allows the user to compute either the
  full 3D workspace or just the portion of interest. If the user selects a
  partial workspace, it then asks for either the bounding cube or sphere
  that limits the portion of interest. The criteria selection would call the
  nonlinear-programming based algorithms from the point computation
  module since they are most suitable for computing partial workspaces.

- *Holes and voids.* This parameter allows the user to select computing holes and voids based on the application requirements. Computing the workspace envelope without holes and voids is important for some applications. On the other hand, computing the holes and voids is often unnecessary and anyway requires more time and space.

- *Resolution.* This parameter allows the user to select between a simple plot and a complex image based on the application deadline. The criteria selection asks the user to enter values for the required resolution in x, y, and z directions. These parameters are denoted res_x, res_y, and res_z respectively. The criteria selection passes those values to the point computation algorithms so that they can compute the right number of workspace points. If the user is interested in a quick response regardless of the image quality, low resolution values for the res_x, res_y, and res_z parameters can be entered.

We can now compute 3D workspaces for articulated chains with redundant DOFs and joint limits. The criteria selection module interacts with the user and selects the most suitable workspace computation and visualization algorithms based on the application requirements. The second module of that system computes workspace points for the given chain. The third module fits a 3D surface around the volume that encompasses the workspace points computed by the second module. An example of a 3D workspace for the left arm of a seated figure is illustrated in Plates 4 and 5. In Plate 4 the global shape of the workspace is visible as a translucent surface surrounding the body, while in Plate 5 we see what the figure can simultaneously reach with his left hand and *see* within the cockpit.

Chapter 4

Behavioral Control

The behaviors constitute a powerful vocabulary for postural control. The manipulation commands provide the stimuli; the behaviors determine the response. The rationale for using behavioral animation is its economy of description: a simple input from the user can generate very complex and realistic motion. By defining a simple set of rules for how objects behave, the user can control the objects through a much more intuitive and efficient language because much of the motion is generated automatically.

Several systems have used the notion of behaviors to describe and generate motion [Zel91]. The most prominent of this work is by Craig Reynolds, who used the notion of behavior models to generate animations of flocks of birds and schools of fish [Rey87]. The individual birds and fish operate using a simple set of rules which tell them how to react to the movement of the neighboring animals and the features of the environment. Some global parameters also guide the movement of the entire flock. William Reeves used the same basic idea but applied it very small inanimate objects, and he dubbed the result *particle systems* [Ree83].

Behaviors have also been applied to articulated figures. McKenna and Zeltzer [MPZ90] describe a computational environment for simulating virtual actors, principally designed to simulate an insect (a cockroach in particular) for animation purposes. Most of the action of the roach is in walking, and a gait controller generates the walking motion. Reflexes can modify the basic gait patterns. The stepping reflex triggers a leg to step if its upper body rotates beyond a certain angle. The load bearing reflex inhibits stepping if the leg is supporting the body. The over-reach reflex triggers a leg to move if it becomes over-extended. The system uses inverse kinematics to position the legs. *Jack* controls bipedal locomotion in a similar fashion (Section 5), but for now we focus on simpler though dramatically important postural behaviors.

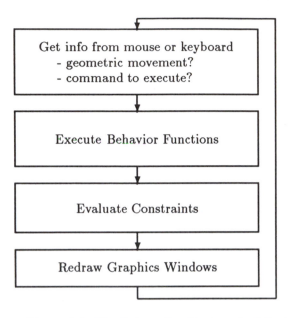

Figure 4.1: The Interactive System Architecture.

4.1   An Interactive System for Postural Control

The human figure in its natural state has constraints on its toes, heels, knees, pelvis, center of mass, hands, elbows, head and eyes. They correspond loosely to the columns of the staff in Labanotation, which designate the different parts of the body.

The heart of the interactive system is a control loop, shown in Figure 4.1. The system repeatedly evaluates the kinematic constraints and executes the *behavior functions* [PB91]. It also polls the user for information, which can be geometric movements through the direct manipulation operator described in Section 3.1, or commands to execute which can change the state of the system or the parameters of the constraints. The behavior functions can also modify the state of the environment or the parameters of the constraints, as described below. Each iteration of the control loop is a time step in a simulated movement process, although this is an imaginary sense of time.

There are four categories of controls for human figures, illustrated in Table 4.1. First, there are *behavioral parameters*. These are the parameters of the body constraints and govern things like whether the feet should remain planted on the floor or whether they should be allowed to twist as the body moves. Second, there are *passive behaviors*. These behaviors express relationships between different parts of the figure. These relationships are usually more complex than can be expressed through the behavioral parameters. An example of a passive behavior is the parametrization of the distribution of weight between the feet. Third, there are *active behaviors*. Active behaviors have a temporal component. They wait for events or conditions to occur and then fire off a response which lasts for a specified duration. An example of an active behavior is the automatic stepping action the figure takes just before it loses its balance. Finally, there are *manipulation primitives*. These are the commands which allow the user to interactively drag or twist parts of a figure. These are the principal sources of input, the stimuli for the postural adjustments, although much of the movement during a postural adjustment usually comes from the response generated by the behavioral controls. Table 4.1 provides a summary of *Jack*'s current vocabulary for postural control.

4.1.1 Behavioral Parameters

The behavioral parameters are the properties of the constraints which model the posture. Mostly, these parameters describe the objective functions of the constraints, as in whether the constraint specifies position, orientation, or both. The parameters can include the goal values of the constraints as well. These are simple relationships which require no computation on the part of the system.

The *Jack* behaviors provide control over the position and orientation of the feet, the elevation of the center of mass, the global orientation of the torso, the orientation of the pelvis, and the gaze direction of the head and eyes. There are additional non-spatial controls on the knees and elbows. These controls were originally designed for the human figure in a rather ad hoc fashion, although they correspond loosely to the columns of the staff in Labanotation.

Most of *Jack*'s current behavioral parameter commands, listed in Table 4.1, allow the user to instruct the figure to maintain the current posture of the part of the body that it controls, such as the position and orientation of feet or the elevation of the center of mass. This means that this property will be maintained whenever possible even as the other parts of the figure change posture. This works well in an interactive manipulation context: the user manipulates the body part into place, and it stays there. This is the "what you see is what you get" approach. This also obviates the need for a complex syntax for describing positions and orientations grammatically, since the method of describing the location is graphical and interactive, through direct manipulation.

The Position and Orientation of the Feet

The foot behaviors are shown in Table 4.2. These are options to the set foot behavior command. The standard human figure model in *Jack* has a foot with two segments connected by a single toe joint, and two natural constraints, one on the toes and another on the heel. The toe constraint keeps the toes on the floor; the heel constraint can keep the heel on the floor or allow it to rise if necessary. For a standing figure, the pair of behaviors *keep heel on floor* and *allow heel to rise* control the height of the heel. The *pivot* behavior instructs

behavioral parameters
set foot behavior
pivot
hold global location
hold local location
keep heel on floor
allow heel to rise
set torso behavior
keep vertical
hold global orientation
set head behavior
fixate head
fixate eyes
release head
release eyes
set hand behavior
hands on hips
hands on knees
hold global location
hold local location
release hands
hand on site
grab object

passive behaviors
balance point follows feet
foot orientation follows balance line
pelvis follows feet orientation
hands maintain consistent orientation
root through center of mass

active behaviors
take step when losing balance
take step when pelvis is twisted

manipulation primitives
move foot
move center of mass
bend torso
rotate pelvis
move hand
move head
move eyes

Table 4.1: Behavioral Controls.

set foot behavior
pivot
hold global location
hold local location
keep heel on floor
allow heel to rise

Table 4.2: Foot Behaviors.

the toes to maintain the same position, and to maintain an orientation flat on the floor while allowing them to rotate through a vertical axis. The *hold global location* behavior disables the *pivot* behavior and fixes the toe orientation in space. This is the appropriate behavior when the foot is not on the floor. The *hold local location* behavior attaches the foot to an object such as a pedal. If the object moves, the foot will follow it and maintain the same relative displacement from it. If the figure is seated, then the heel behaviors and the *pivot* behavior have no effect, and the *hold* behaviors control the position and orientation of the heel instead of the toes.

The behavior of the feet is usually activated by the manipulation of some other part of the figure, such as the center of mass or the pelvis. A good example of the *pivot* behavior is when the center of mass is dragged towards one foot: should the other foot pivot in order to extend the leg, or should it remain planted and inhibit the movement of the center of mass? The behaviors say which should occur.

The Elevation of the Center of Mass

The horizontal location of the center of mass is a passive behavior which determines balance, as described below. The elevation of the center of mass is more straightforward. This concept has a direct analog in Labanotation: the *level of support* [Hut70]. A middle level of support is a natural standing posture, a low level of support is a squat, and a high level of support is standing on the tip-toes. The *hold current elevation* behavior is an option of the set balance behavior command. It instructs the figure to maintain the current elevation of the center of mass. This behavior is off by default. This behavior is necessary because under normal circumstances, the center of mass of the figure is free to rise and fall as necessary to meet the requirements of the feet. After adjusting the center of mass to an appropriate level, if no control holds it there, it may rise or fall unintentionally.

The Global Orientation of the Torso

The torso behaviors are listed in Table 4.3. The default behavior is *keep vertical*, which causes the torso to maintain a vertical orientation. Biomechanics research tells us that one of the most constant elements in simple human

set torso behavior
keep vertical
hold global orientation

Table 4.3: Torso Behaviors.

locomotor tasks is the global orientation of the head. One theory explaining this suggests that the head is the principle sensor of stability [BP88]. The *keep vertical* behavior mimics this nicely through a directional constraint on the chest to remain vertical, while not affecting its vertical rotation. This means that as the pelvis of the figure rotates forward, backward, or side to side, the torso will automatically compensate to keep the head up. Since the constraint is on the upper torso, not the head, the neck is free to move in order for the figure to look at certain reference points, as described below with the head and eye behaviors.

The *hold global orientation* behavior involves all three DOFs of the torso. This allows other parts of the body to be adjusted while the head and chest stay relatively fixed. This is particularly important in making adjustments to the pelvis and legs after positioning the torso acceptably. This behavior does not involve position, because it is usually acceptable to have the position float with the rest of the body.

Movements of the spine are described in terms of total bending angles in the forward, lateral, and axial directions. The technique uses weighting factors that distribute the total bending angle to the individual vertebrae in such a way that respects the proper coupling between the joints. Different weight distributions generate bends of different flavors, such as neck curls or bends confined to the lower back. These parameters are options to the torso behavior controls through the set torso behavior command because they govern how the torso behaves as it bends to maintain the proper orientation. The user can select one of the standard *curl from neck* or *bend from waist* options, or alternatively input the range of motion of the spine by selecting a top and bottom joint, and *initiator* and *resistor* joints which control the weighting between the vertebrae.

The Fixation Point for the Head and Eyes

The head and eyes can be controlled by specifying a fixation point, modeled through aiming constraints which orient them in the proper direction. The constraint on the head operates on a reference point between the eyes, oriented forwards of the head. The head constraint positions only the head, using the neck. The constraint on the eyes rotates only the eyeballs. The eyeballs rotate side to side and up and down in their sockets. The behavioral parameters control the head and eyes independently during postural adjustments. The active behaviors described below simulate the coupling between head and eye movement.

set head behavior
fixate head
fixate eyes
release head
release eyes

Table 4.4: Head Behaviors.

set hand behavior
hands on hips
hands on knees
hold global location
hold local location
release hands
hand on site
grab object

Table 4.5: Hand Behaviors.

The *fixate head* behavior option of the set head behavior command allows the user to select a fixation point for the head. The *fixate eyes* behavior does the same for the eyes. When these behaviors are active, the head and eyes will automatically adjust to remain focused on the fixation point as the body moves.

The Position and Orientation of the Hands

The principal control for the hands involves holding them at particular points in space as the body moves. Postural control of the arms and hands is usually a two step process. First, get the hands into position using the active manipulation facilities, and second, set a control to keep them there as some other part of the body moves. The *hold global location* and *hold local location* behaviors serve much the same for the hands as their counterparts for the feet. The desired geometric positions and orientations are either global or local to some other object. The set hand behavior command provides several standard postures. For a standing figure, a pleasing reference point is the figure's hips. The hands rest on the hips with the elbows out to the side, the arms akimbo posture. For a seated position, a pleasing reference point is the figure's knees. The *site* behavior moves the hand to a particular site, in both position and orientation. This simulates a reaching movement, but its real purpose is to hold the hand there once it reaches the site.

The controls for the hands are invoked whenever the body moves or whenever an object to which the hand is constrained changes location. A good

analogy is holding onto an object such as a doorknob. If the door closes, the
arm goes with it. Likewise, if the body bends over, the door stays fixed and
the arm adjusts accordingly.

Jack also allows the converse relationship which is more suited to the way
a person holds a screwdriver. A screwdriver is controlled completely by the
hand and is not fixed in space in the same sense as the door. If the body
bends over, the screwdriver should move along with the arm, not remain in
place like the doorknob. This type of a relationship comes from the *grab object*
behavior. "Grab" in this context does not mean "grasp"; it doesn't mean the
fingers will wrap around the object. Such an action is available as a type of
motion (Section 4.2.7). It actually means that the object will subsequently
be attached to the figure's hand, as if the figure grabbed it. Once again, the
process has two-steps: first, position the hand and the object relative to each
other, then specify the *grab* behavior to hold it there.

The constraints on the hands are logically separate from the other constraints on the body. *Jack* evaluates the hand constraints *after* the other
constraints, not simultaneously. The reasons for structuring the arm behaviors this way are partly practical and partly philosophical.

In practice, the inverse kinematics algorithm does not perform well when
the hand constraint is considered collectively with the other body constraints.
With the human figure rooted through the toes, there are too many DOFs
between the toes and the hands to be controlled effectively. Even though the
constraints on the pelvis, center of mass, and opposite foot help to resolve
this redundancy, if the hand constraint is on equal par with the other parts of
the body, the hand constraint can frequently cause the other constraints to be
pulled away from their goals. Since the potential energy function describing
the equilibrium state for the figure is a weighted combination of all of the
constraints, the center of mass and pelvis constraints must have significantly
higher weight to avoid having the hand pull the body off balance. It has been
difficult to arrive at a set of weights which give the right behavior. It has been
much easier to simply localize the movements of the arms and isolate them
from the rest of the body.

Philosophically, it is acceptable to consider the arm movements independently as well. Normally, a reaching task does not initiate much movement of
the lower body, unless there are explicit instructions to do so. For example,
consider what happens when a human being reaches for a nearby object such
as a doorknob. If the door is near enough, this won't involve any bending
of the waist, but if the door is farther away, it may be necessary to bend
the waist. If the door is farther away still, it may be necessary to squat or
counter-balance by raising a leg backwards. This system of behaviors requires
an explicit control specifying which approach the figure takes. If the torso
must bend or the center of mass must shift in order to perform a reaching
task, then the user, or some higher level behavior function, must initiate it.
Automatic generation of these intermediate postures is non-trivial. We discuss
two rather different approaches in Sections 5.4 and 5.5.

The Knees and Elbows

The knees and elbows require special care to prevent them from becoming locked at full extension. The fully extended position not only appears awkward, but it tends to cause the inverse kinematics algorithm to get trapped in a local minimum. Because the algorithm uses a gradient descent approach, if an elbow or knee reaches its limit, it has a tendency to stay there[1]. To prevent this, *Jack* uses *limit spring* constraints to discourage the knees and elbows from reaching their limiting value. The springs give a high energy level to the fully extended angle. The springs can be tuned to any angle, but the default is 10°, and in practice, this tends to work well.

This gives the figure in its natural standing position a more pleasing posture, more like "at ease" than "attention". Biomechanics literature describes this in terms of the stresses on the muscles [Car72]. Labanotation uses this posture as the default: the elbows are "neither bent nor stretched" [Hut70] and, in the middle level of support, the knees are "straight but not taut" [Hut70].

The Pelvis

The pelvis and torso are intricately related. The torso includes all joints in the spine from the waist to the neck, and rotating these joints allows the figure to bend over. However, when human beings bend over, they generally bend their pelvis as well as their torso. This means manipulating the two hip joints as a unit, which can be a problem for a computer model because there is no single fixed point below the hips from which to rotate. However, this problem is easy to handle by controlling the orientation of the pelvis through a constraint.

4.1.2 Passive Behaviors

Passive behaviors can represent more complex relationships than the behavioral parameters. They are like little processes attached to each figure. The passive behavior functions are executed at each interactive iteration. A passive behavior can involve a global property of the figure such as the center of mass or the shape of the figure's support polygon. An example of this kind of behavior is the parametrization of the distribution of the weight between the figure's feet: when the feet move, the balance behavior function must compute the proper location for the balance point and register this with the constraint on the center of mass. Passive behaviors are *instantaneous* in that they explicitly define a relationship to be computed at each iteration.

Passive behaviors are easy to implement in this basic system architecture because their only job is to compute the necessary global information and supply it to the behavioral controls. Because of the general nature of the inverse

---

[1] Essentially the algorithm sees a zero gradient and hence finds no advantage to moving the locked joint as that does not decrease the overall distance to the goal: the required motion is in fact exactly perpendicular to the aligned segments.

kinematics constraints, the behaviors can overlap to a degree not possible with other systems, like Zeltzer's local motion processes [Zel82, Zel84].

Currently, *Jack* has implemented six basic passive behavior functions for human figures, and they illustrate a range of capabilities. They control the location of the balance point, the orientation of the feet, the orientation of the pelvis, and the orientation of the hands. The final two behaviors control the figure root.

Balance as a Passive Behavior

Probably the most important human postural behavior, and the one demanding the most coordination, is balance. The need to remain balanced dictates much of the subtle and elusive behavior of a human figure. The location of the balance point of a figure is significant in both cause and effect. The location of the balance point is dependent on other parts of the figure, namely, the feet. Also, the balance point sends information to the other parts of the body regarding the figure's state of balance. Requiring a process to handle balance in a global fashion was recognized long ago [BS79, BOK80], but significant progress in computer interactivity and posture behavior algorithms was needed to realize that design.

To parametrize the location of the balance point with respect to the feet we use the *balance line*, which is the line between a fixed reference point in the middle of each foot. Biomechanics literature [Car72] states that in the standing rest position, the body's vertical line passes 2-5cm in front of the ankle joint, midway through the arch of the foot. This line between the feet divides the support polygon down the middle.

Given the location of the center of mass, the balance point parameters, call them x and z, can be determined as shown in Figure 4.2. To do this, project the balance point on the $y = 0$ plane and call the point $\mathbf{b}$. Then find the point on the balance line closest to this point, and call it $\mathbf{p}$. z is the distance between $\mathbf{b}$ and $\mathbf{p}$, that is, the balance point's distance forward from the balance line. However, it is more convenient to normalize z between 0.0 and 1.0 according to the placement of $\mathbf{b}$ between the balance line and the front edge of the support polygon. Therefore, if $z > 1$ then the balance point lies outside the support polygon. If the balance point is behind the balance line, then let z be normalized between -1.0 and 0.0. Likewise, x is the interpolation factor which gives $\mathbf{p}$ in terms of the left and right foot reference points, normalized between 0.0 and 1.0, with $x = 0$ being the left foot. If x is outside of the $[0, 1]$, then the balance point is to the side of the support polygon.

Once the system has the ability to measure balance, these parameters are available for the behavior functions to use. The *balance point follows feet* behavior, described in Section 4.1.2, falls directly out of this parametrization. This behavior causes the distribution of weight between the feet to remain constant even as the feet move. The active stepping behavior *take step when losing balance*, described in Section 4.1.3, uses this parameter as its trigger.

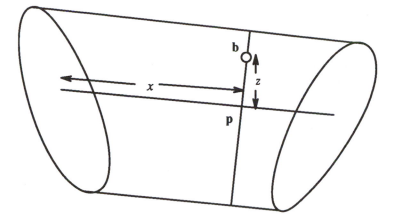

Figure 4.2: The Parametrization of the Balance Point.

Global Effects of Local Manipulations

Another capability of the passive behaviors in this system is to telegraph changes in the posture of a local part of the figure to the rest of the figure as a whole. This can provide coordination between the different parts of the figure. The behavioral parameters as described above generally hold the different parts of the figure in place, but sometimes it is better to have them move automatically. A good example of this is the *pelvis follows foot orientation* behavior, described in Section 4.1.2, in which the orientation of the pelvis automatically adjusts to the orientation of the feet. Whenever the feet change orientation, they radiate the change to the pelvis which mimics the rotational spring-like behavior of the legs.

Negotiating Position and Orientation

The passive behaviors offer a solution to the problem of negotiating the overlapping influence of position and orientation while interactively dragging part of the body. Because of the nature of the direct manipulation technique described in Section 3.1, it is not possible to rotate and translate during a single movement of the mouse. This has come up before, in Section 3.2.5: either the dragging procedure has *no* control over orientation, in which case the orientation is arbitrary and unpredictable, or the dragging procedure *does* have control over orientation, in which case the orientation remains globally fixed during spurts of translation. Fixing the orientation during translation can, for example, cause the hand to assume an awkward orientation as it is translated.

Passive behavior functions allow the direct manipulation operator to have control over the orientation and avoid awkward orientations. While the user is translating with the mouse, the behavior function can automatically determine a suitable orientation based on heuristic observations. While rotating, the user has complete control over the orientation. The heuristics can simply be embedded in the behavior functions (Section 2.4).

The pair of behaviors *foot orientation follows balance line* and *hands maintain consistent orientation*, use heuristics taken from Labanotation to predict suitable orientations for the hands and the feet during their manipulation. This allows the user to position them mostly by translating them, making changes to the orientation only as necessary.

The Figure Root

One passive behavior deserves special attention: the figure root. The principal disadvantage of modeling an articulated figure as a hierarchy is that one point on the figure must be designated as the figure root. Section 3.2.3 explains the effect of the figure root on the inverse kinematics algorithm: the positioning algorithm itself cannot move the figure root. It can only manipulate chains emanating from the root. Any movement of the figure root must be programmed explicitly. Therefore, a major element of **Peabody** is the ability to change the setting of the figure root when necessary.

The figure "root" is an unnatural concept. It has no natural analog for a mobile figure like a human being, so it has no place in the language for controlling human figures. Since it is a necessary internal concept, can it be controlled internally as well? For certain postures of a human figure, there are distinct reference points on the figure which serve as good figure roots: the feet, the lower torso, and the center of mass. It should be possible to have the system choose these automatically and thus make the root transparent to the user.

There are several possibilities for the figure root of a human figure. Many systems which don't have the ability to change the root choose to locate it at the lower torso [BKK+85]. However, this complicates the process of moving the lower torso during balance adjustments. Using this approach, it can be very difficult to get the figure to bend over convincingly because the hips need to shift backwards and downwards in ways that are difficult to predict. However, for a seated posture, the lower torso is a good choice for the root. When a figure is standing, the feet are natural choices for the root.

The choice of the figure root can be handled by designing a behavior function which monitors the figure's posture and automatically changes the figure root when necessary to provide the best behavior. This behavior function uses the following rules:

- It roots the figure through a foot whenever the weight of the body is more than 60% on that foot. This ensures that if the figure is standing with more weight on one leg than the other, the supporting leg serves as the root. It also ensures that if the figure is standing with weight equally between the two legs but possibly swaying from side to side that the root doesn't rapidly vacillate between the legs.

- If the height of the center of mass above the feet dips below 70% of the length of the leg, then the root changes to the lower torso. This predicts that the figure is sitting down. Heuristically, this proves to be a good choice even if the figure is only squatting, because the constraint on the non-support leg tends to behave badly when both knees are bent to their extremes.

Balance Point Follows Feet

Labanotation has a notion for the distribution of the weight between the feet and the shifting of the weight back and forth [Hut70]. This notion is well-defined regardless of the position of the feet: after specifying the distribution of weight between the feet, this proportion should remain fixed even if the placement of the feet need adjustment during a postural manipulation. This is the job of the *balance point follows feet* behavior.

Given these two parameters, a new balance point can be computed based on any new position of the feet. Holding these parameters fixed as the feet move ensures that the balance point maintains the same relationship to the feet, both laterally and in the forward/backward direction.

Foot Orientation Follows Balance Line

During the active manipulation of the feet with the move foot command, the user can intersperse translations and rotations of the feet, centered around the toes. Since it is not possible to rotate and translate during a single movement, either the dragging procedure has *no* control over orientation, in which case the orientation is arbitrary and unpredictable, or the dragging procedure *does* have control over orientation, in which case the orientation remains globally fixed during spurts of translation. The *foot orientation follows balance line* behavior offers a convenient alternative.

The solution which the behavior offers is to predict the proper orientation of the foot based on the balance line and adjust the orientation automatically as the foot is translated with the move foot command. The balance line, as described above, is an imaginary line between the middle of the feet. Actually, this rule fixes the orientation of the foot with respect to the balance line. As the foot translates, the balance line changes, and the orientation of the foot changes to keep the same relative orientation. This behavior is particularly appropriate when the figure is taking a step forward with the intention of turning to the side.

Pelvis Follows Feet Orientation

The muscles in the leg make the leg act like a rotational spring. The hip and ankle joints provide only a little more than 90° of rotation in the leg around the vertical axis. This means that the orientation of the feet and the orientation of the pelvis are linked together. If the orientation of the feet are fixed, the orientation of the pelvis is severely limited. What is more, the extreme limits of pelvis orientation place an uncomfortable twist on the legs. If the legs are rotational springs, then the "middle" orientation of the pelvis can be determined by simply averaging the orientation of the feet. This seems to be in fact what happens when a person stands naturally: the pelvis is oriented to relieve stress on the legs. The *pelvis follows feet orientation* behavior simulates this.

Hands Maintain Consistent Orientation

The same problem with the orientation of the feet during the move foot command occurs with the hands with the move hand command. In fact, the problem is more intricate because the hands have a much greater range of movement than the feet. How is the orientation of the hand related to its position? How can this be determined automatically in order to predict reasonable postures when moving the hands?

Labanotation suggests an answer. Labanotation has a detailed system for describing arm postures and gestures, but what is most interesting here is what the notation does *not* say. To simplify the syntax, Labanotation has a standard set of orientations for the palms when the arms are in specific positions. Notations need be made only when the orientations differ from these defaults. The rules are [Hut70]:

- When the arms hang by the side of the body, the palms face in.

- When the arms are raised forward or upward, the palms face towards each other.

- When the arms are raised outward to the side, the palms face forward.

- When the arms cross the body, the palms face backward.

These rules are useful as defaults, but of course they do not dictate absolute behavior. These rules govern the orientation of the hands when the user translates them from one area to another without specifying any orientational change. These rules only take effect when the hand moves from one region to another.

Root Through Center of Mass

Most of the behaviors described so far are only appropriate for standing figures, which of course means that they are also only appropriate for earth-bound figures. But what about figures in zero-gravity space? This is actually quite easy to simulate by rooting the figure through the center of mass and disabling all other behaviors. The one constant element of zero-gravity is the center of mass. When the figure is rooted through the center of mass, the global location of the center of mass remains fixed as the figure moves.

4.1.3   Active Behaviors

Active behaviors mimic reflexive responses to certain conditions in the body. They can have temporal elements, so they can initiate movements of parts of the body which last for a certain duration. These behaviors make use of the concept of a *motion primitive*. A motion primitive has a distinct duration in terms of interactive iterations, and it typically involves a constraint which changes over this time interval. An example of this is the stepping movement of the feet which is initiated when the figure's center of mass leaves its support area. The interactive system architecture maintains a list of currently triggered active behaviors, and it advances them at each iteration until they are complete. The behaviors terminate themselves, so the duration can be explicit in terms of a number of interactive iterations, or they can continue until a certain condition is met.

Active behaviors are like motor programs, or *schemas* [Kee82, Ros91, Sch82b, Sch82a]. Considerable physiological and psychological evidence suggests the existence of motor programs, which are preprogrammed motor response to certain conditions. The theory of schemas suggests that humans and animals have catalogs of preprogrammed motor responses that are fired off to produce coordinated movements in the body. Schemas are parametrized motor programs which can be instantiated with different settings. For some motor programs, there even seems to be very little feedback involved. Evidence of this comes from experiments which measure the excitation of the muscles of the arm during reaching exercises. The patterns of excitation remain constant even if the movement of the hand is impeded [Ros91].

The incorporation of active behaviors into the postural control process begins to blur the distinction between motion and manipulation. The purpose of the behaviors is predictive: if the user drags the center of mass of a figure away from the support polygon, this probably means that the desired posture has the feet in a different location. The job of the active behavior is to anticipate this and hopefully perform the positioning task automatically.

There are two active behaviors, both involving the placement of the feet. The *take step when losing balance* and *take step when pelvis is twisted* behaviors automatically reposition the feet just before the figure loses its balance. They use the balance point parameters described above as their triggers. The purpose of these behaviors is to predict a proper posture for the figure given that its center of mass is leaving the support polygon.

Active behaviors can be used to simulate movement even in the context of postural control. The entire process of interactive postural control can serve as a good approximation to motion anyway. The active behaviors provide a way in which motion primitives can be incorporated into the interactive system. To do this more effectively, the interactive system needs a more sophisticated notion of time and timed events (Section 4.3).

Take Step When Losing Balance

This behavior fires a stepping response to the loss of balance of a figure. When this behavior is active, it monitors the parametrization of the balance point of the figure as described with the *balance point follows feet* behavior. If the balance point leaves the support polygon to the front or back, the behavior

move foot
move center of mass
bend torso
rotate pelvis
move hand
move head
move eyes

Table 4.6: The Manipulation Primitives.

moves the non-support foot forward or backward to compensate. The non-support foot in this case is the one which bears less weight. The behavior computes the new foot location such that the current balance point will lie in the middle of the new support polygon once the foot arrives there. If the balance point leaves the support polygon to the side, the stepping motion moves the support foot instead. In this case, the support foot is the only one which can be repositioned in order to maintain balance.

Take Step When Pelvis Is Twisted

The discussion of the *pelvis follows feet orientation* behavior above described the relationship between the global orientations of the feet and pelvis, particularly in terms of determining an orientation for the pelvis from the orientation of the feet. The opposite relationship is possible as well. Consider standing with your feet slightly apart, and then begin to twist your body to the right. After about 45° of rotation, your legs will not be able to rotate any more. In order to continue rotating, you will be forced to take a step, a circular step with either your left or right foot.

The *take step when pelvis twisted* behavior mimics this. When it senses that the orientation of the pelvis is near its limit relative to the feet, it repositions the non-support foot in an arc in front of or behind the other foot, twisted 90°.

4.2   Interactive Manipulation With Behaviors

This section discusses the *Jack* manipulation primitives, but in the process it describes the entire manipulation process, including the effect of all of the implemented behaviors. The effect of the manipulation commands cannot be treated in isolation. In fact, the very nature of the system of behaviors implies that nothing happens in isolation. This discussion serves as a good summary of these techniques because these are the commands (Table 4.6) which the user uses the most. These are the verbs in the postural control language.

The interactive postural control vocabulary includes manipulation primitives which allow the user to push, poke, and twist parts of the body, and behavior controls which govern the body's response. The manipulation commands are sufficiently intuitive to provide good handles on the figure, and the behavioral controls make the responses reasonable.

The structure of the behaviors for human figures did not come out of a magic hat. The rationale behind the behaviors comes partially from biomechanics and physiology literature, and partially from the semantics of movement notations such as Labanotation. Labanotation provides a good set of default values for the behaviors because it incorporates so many assumptions about normal human movement.

4.2.1 The Feet

The feet can be moved with the active manipulation command move foot. This command allows the user to drag the foot interactively. This automatically transfers the support of the figure to the other foot, provided the figure is standing. The control over the position of the feet is straightforward. The manipulation operator also gives control over the orientation. However, while translating the foot, its orientation depends upon the foot orientation behavior. The default behavior maintains a constant global orientation. The *foot orientation follows balance line* behavior causes the orientation of the foot to remain fixed with respect to the balance line during translation. This means that if the foot goes forward, it automatically rotates as if the figure is turning toward the direction of the stationary foot.

The move foot command automatically causes a change in the balance point according to the *balance point follows feet* behavior, which is the default. This means that the distribution of weight between the feet will remain constant as the foot moves. The location of the balance point within the support polygon, both side to side and forwards/backwards, will remain fixed as the support polygon changes shape. This is evident in Figure 4.3. The balance point shifts along with the foot. If this behavior is disabled, the balance point will remain fixed in space.

Manipulating the feet also telegraphs a change to the pelvis according to the *pelvis follows foot orientation* behavior, which is the default. This means that as the foot rotates, the pelvis automatically rotates as well. This keeps the body turned in the direction of the feet.

4.2.2 The Center of Mass and Balance

The move center of mass command allows the user to interactively drag the balance point of the figure, shifting its weight back and forth or forward and backward. This command changes the parametrization of the balance point in terms of the feet. If the *balance point follows feet* behavior is active, then when the move center of mass command terminates, the balance point will remain at its new location relative to the support polygon.

Figure 4.3: Moving the Left Foot, with Balance Point Following Feet.

The location of the balance point has a great effect on the feet. If the foot behavior is *pivot*, then shifting the weight laterally back and forth will cause the feet to twist back and forth as well. On the other hand, if the feet do not pivot, then they remain planted, possibly inhibiting the movement of the balance point. In Figure 4.4, the feet are held in place, not pivoting.

The move center of mass command also gives control over the elevation of the center of mass. Normally, the elevation of the center of mass is not controlled explicitly, except through the *hold current elevation* behavior option to the *set balance behavior* command. The move center of mass command gives control over the elevation, so moving the center of mass up and down allows the figure to stand on its tip-toes or squat down. Figure 4.5 shows the center of mass being lowered into a squatting posture. The constraint on the pelvis ensures that the hips remain square and straight.

The movement of the center of mass also tends to trigger the rooting behavior. This is mostly transparent, but to the trained eye, it is apparent in the movement of the feet. The support foot (the rooted one) is always very stationary.

The manipulation of the center of mass is the main instigator of the active stepping behavior. While the stepping behavior is active, if the balance point reaches the perimeter of the support polygon, the feet are automatically repositioned by the stepping behavior. Figure 4.6 illustrates the stepping behavior as the center of mass is dragged forward. When this occurs, the visual impression is of the figure being pulled and taking a step just to prevent a fall; it does not look like the figure is deliberately trying to walk somewhere. (In Section 5.2 more purposeful stepping and walking behaviors are utilized.)

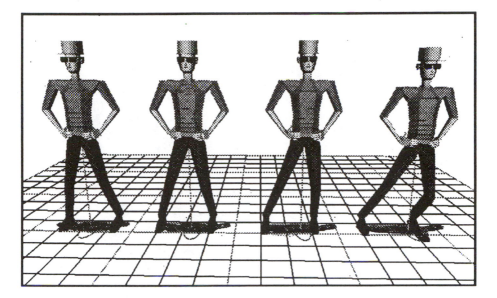

Figure 4.4: Shifting the Center of Mass.

Figure 4.5: Lowering the Center of Mass.

Figure 4.6: Taking a Step before Losing Balance.

4.2.3   The Torso

The *Jack* spine model provides a very important biomechanical feature for effective human behavioral control. Each vertebra has a current position defined by the three joint angles relative to its proximal vertebra. Also defined in the spinal database are joint rest positions and 6 joint limits for every joint. If each attribute is summed up for all joints, then 3D vectors are defined for current position, joint rest position, and two joint limits for the global spine. The target position – the 3D vector sum of final joint positions – is supplied as an input parameter. Movement towards the target position is either bending or unbending, meaning either towards the joint limits or towards the spine's rest position. Motion is defined as an interpolation between the current position and either the spine's position of maximum limit, or the spine's rest position.

Three rotations are calculated independently and then merged into one. For example, a 3D orientation vector (e.g. flex 45 degrees, rotate axially 20 degrees left, and lateral bend 15 degrees right) can be accomplished in one function with 3 loop iterations. It is assumed for the model that the maximum vertebral joint limit in one dimension will not affect the joint limits of another dimension.

The spine's rest position is included in the model, because it is a position of high comfort and stability. If the spine is unbending in one dimension of movement, it will move towards that position of highest comfort in that rotational dimension. The input parameters listed in Section 2.3 determine how much each vertebra bends as the spine moves. The three dimensions are done separately, then combined for the final posture.

A participation vector is derived from the spine's current position, target position, and maximum position. This global participation represents a 3D vector of the ratio of spine movement to the maximum range of movement. Participation is used to calculate the joint weights.

The following formulas are defined in each of three DOFs. Let

$Target$ = spine target position
$Current$ = spine current position
Max = spine sum of joint limits
$Rest$ = spine sum of joint rest positions.

If the spine is bending, then the participation P is

$$P = \frac{Target - Current}{Max - Current}.$$

Otherwise, the spine is unbending and

$$P = \frac{Target - Current}{Rest - Current}.$$

The joint positions of the entire spine must sum up to the target position. To determine how much the joint participates, a set of weights is calculated for each joint. The participation weight is a function of the joint number, the initiator joint, and the global participation derived above. Also, a resistance weight is based on the resistor joint, degree of resistance, and global participation. To calculate the weight for each joint i, let:

j_i = joint position
$limit_i$ = the joint limit
$rest_i$ = the rest position
p_i = participation weight
r_i = resistance weight.

If the spine is bending, then

$$w_i = p_i \cdot r_i \cdot (limit_i - j_i),$$

while if the spine is unbending,

$$w_i = p_i \cdot r_i \cdot (rest_i - j_i).$$

The weights range from 0 to 1. A weight of $k\%$ means that the movement will go $k\%$ of the differential between the current position and either the joint limit (for bending) or the joint rest position (for unbending).

To understand resistance, divide the spine into two regions split at the resistor joint. The region of higher activity contains the initiator. Label these regions *active* and *resistive*. The effect of resistance is that joints in the resistive region will resist participating in the movement specified by the parameter degree of resistance. Also, joints inbetween the initiator and resistor will have less activity depending on the degree of resistance.

Resistance does not freeze any of the joints. Even at 100% resistance, the active region will move until all joints reach their joint limits. Then, if there is no other way to satisfy the target position, the resistive region will begin to participate.

If the desired movement is from the current position to one of two maximally bent positions, then the weights calculated should be 1.0 for each joint participating. The algorithm interpolates correctly to either maximally bent position. It also interpolates correctly to the position of highest comfort. To calculate the position of each joint i after movement succeeds, let:

j_i = joint position
j_i^* = new joint position
$Target$ = spine target position
$Current$ = spine current position
$M = Target - Current$ = incremental movement of the spine.

Then

$$j_i^* = j_i + \frac{M w_i}{\sum w_i},$$

and it is easy to show that $\sum j_i^* = Target$:

$$\begin{aligned}
\sum j_i^* &= \sum (j_i + \frac{M w_i}{\sum w_i}) \\
&= \sum j_i + \sum \frac{M w_i}{\sum w_i} \\
&= Current + M \frac{\sum w_i}{\sum w_i} \\
&= Current + M \\
&= Target.
\end{aligned}$$

The bend torso command positions the torso using forward kinematics, without relying on a dragging mechanism. It consists of potentiometers which control the total bending angle along the three DOFs. The command also prompts for the flavor of bending. These controls are the same as for the set torso behavior command described above. They include options which specify the range of motion of the spine, defined through a top and bottom joint, along with *initiator* and *resistor* joints which control the weighting between the vertebrae.

Bending the torso tends to cause large movements of the center of mass, so this process has a great effect on the posture of the figure in general, particularly the legs. For example, if the figure bends forward, the hips automatically shift backwards so that the figure remains balanced. This is illustrated in Figure 4.7.

4.2.4   The Pelvis

The rotate pelvis command changes the global orientation of the hips. This can curl the hips forwards or backwards, tilt them laterally, or twist the entire body around the vertical axis. The manipulation of the pelvis also activates the torso behavior in a pleasing way. Because of its central location, manipulations of the pelvis provide a powerful control over the general posture of a figure, especially when combined with the balance and *keep vertical* torso constraints. If the torso is kept vertical while the pelvis curls underneath it, then the torso curls to compensate for the pelvis. This is shown in Figure 4.8.

The rotate pelvis command can also trigger the active stepping behavior if the orientation reaches an extreme angle relative to the feet.

4.2.5   The Head and Eyes

The move head and move eyes commands manipulate the head and eyes, respectively, by allowing the user to interactively move a fixation point. The head and eyes both automatically adjust to aim toward the reference point. The head and eyes rotate as described in Section 4.1.1.

4.2.6   The Arms

The active manipulation of the arm allows the user to drag the arm around in space using the mechanism described in Section 3.2.5. These movements utilize the shoulder complex as described in Section 2.4 so that the coupled joints have a total of three DOFs. Figure 4.10 shows the left hand being moved forwards.

Although it seems natural to drag this limb around from the palm or fingertips, in practice this tends to yield too much movement in the wrist and the wrist frequently gets kinked. The twisting scheme helps, but the movements to get the wrist straightened out can interfere with an acceptable position for the arm. It is much more effective to do the positioning in two steps, the first positioning the arm with the wrist fixed, and the second rotating the hand into place. Therefore, our active manipulation command for the arms can control the arm either from a reference point in the palm or from the lower

Figure 4.7: Bending the Torso while Maintaining Balance.

Figure 4.8: Rotating the Pelvis while Keeping the Torso Vertical.

Figure 4.9: Moving the Head.

Figure 4.10: Moving the Hand.

end of the lower arm, just above the wrist. This process may loosely simulate how humans reach for objects, for there is evidence that reaching involves two overlapping phases, the first a ballistic movement of the arm towards the required position, and the second a correcting stage in which the orientation of the hand is fine-tuned [Ros91]. If the target for the hand is an actual grasp, then a specialized *Jack* behavior for grasping may be invoked which effectively combines these two steps.

4.2.7   The Hands and Grasping

Jack contains a fully articulated hand. A hand grasp capability makes some reaching tasks easier [RG91]. The grasp action requires a target object and a grasp type. The *Jack* grasp is purely kinematic. It is a considerable convenience for the user, however, since it virtually obviates the need to individually control the 20 DOFs in each hand.

For a grasp, the user specifies the target object and a grip type. The user chooses between a predefined grasp site on the target or a calculated transform to determine the grasp location. A distance offset is added to the site to correctly position the palm center for the selected grip type. The hand is preshaped to the correct starting pose for the grip type selected, then the palm moves to the target site.

The five grip types implemented are the power, precision, disc, small disc, and tripod [Ibe87]. The grips differ in how the hand is readied and where it is placed on or near the object. Once these actions are performed, the fingers and thumb are just closed around the object, using collision detection on the bounding box volume of each digit segment to determine when to cease motion.

4.3   The Animation Interface

[2]The *Jack* animation system is built around the concept of a *motion*, which is a change in a part of a figure over a specific interval of time. A motion is a rather primitive notion. Typically, a complex animation consists of many distinct motions, and several will overlap at each point in time. Motions are created interactively through the commands on the *motion menu* and the *human motion menu*. There are commands for creating motions which control the placement of the feet, center of mass, hands, torso, arms, and head.

Jack displays motions in an animation window. This window shows time on a horizontal axis, with a description of the parts of each figure which are moving arranged vertically. The time interval over which each motion is active is shown as a segment of the time line. Each part of the body gets a different track. The description shows both the name of the figure and the name of the body part which is moving. The time line itself displays motion attributes graphically, such as velocity control and relative motion weights.

---

[2]Paul Diefenbach.

The numbers along the bottom of the animation grid are the time line. By default, the units of time are in seconds. When the animation window first appears, it has a width of 3 seconds. This can be changed with the arrows below the time line. The horizontal arrows scroll through time keeping the width of the window constant. The vertical arrows expand or shrink the width of the window, in time units. The current animation time can be set either by pressing the middle mouse button in the animation window at the desired time and scrolling the time by moving the mouse or by entering the current time directly through the **goto time**.

Motions actually consist of three distinct phases, although this is hidden from the user. The first stage of a motion is the pre-action step. This step occurs at the starting time of the motion and prepares the figure for the impending motion. The next stage is the actual motion function itself, which occurs at every time interval after the initial time up to the ending time, inclusive. At the ending time after the last incremental motion step, the post-action is activated disassociating the figure from the motion. Because of the concurrent nature of the motions and the possibility of several motions affecting the behavior of one moving part, these three stages must occur at each time interval in the following order: motion, post-action, pre-action. This allows all ending motions to finish before initializing any new motions affecting the same moving part.

While the above description implies that body part motions are controlled directly, this is not the true behavior of the system. The animation system describes postures through constraints, and the motions actually control the existence and parameters of the constraints and behaviors which define the postures. Each motion has a set of parameters associated with it which control the behavior of the motion. These parameters are set upon creation of the motion and can be modified by pressing the right mouse button in the animation window while being positioned over the desired motion. This changes or deletes the motion, or turns the motion on or off.

Each motion is active over a specific interval in time, delimited by a *starting time* and an *ending time*. Each motion creation command prompts for values for each of these parameters. They may be entered numerically from the keyboard or by direct selection in the animation window. Existing time intervals can be changed analogously. Delimiting times appear as vertical "ticks" in the animation window connected by a velocity line. Selecting the duration line enables time shifting of the entire motion.

The yellow line drawn with each motion in the animation window illustrates the motion's *weight function*. Each motion describes movement of a part of the body through a kinematic constraint. The constraint is only active when the current time is between the motion's starting time and ending time. It is entirely possible to have two motions which affect the same part of the body be active at the same time. The posture which the figure assumes is a weighted average of the postures described by the individual motions. The weights of each constraint are described through the weight functions, which can be of several types:

constant The weight does not change over the life of the constraint.

increase The weight starts out at 0 and increases to is maximum at the end time.

decrease The weight starts out at its maximum and decreases to 0 at the end time.

ease in/ease out The weight starts at 0, increases to its maximum halfway through the life of the motion, and then decreases to 0 again at the end time.

The shape of the yellow line in the animation window illustrates the weight function. The units of the weight are not important. The line may be thought of as an icon describing the weight function.

The green line drawn with each motion in the animation window represents the velocity of the movement. The starting point for the motion comes from the current posture of the figure when the motion begins. The ending position of the motion is defined as a parameter of the motion and is specified when the motion is created. The speed of the end effector along the path between the starting and ending positions is controlled through the velocity function:

constant Constant velocity over the life of the motion.

increase The velocity starts out slow and increases over the life of the motion.

decrease The velocity starts out fast and decreases over the life of the motion.

ease in/ease out The velocity starts slow, increases to its maximum halfway through the life of the motion, and then decreases to 0 again at the end time.

The shape of the green line in the animation window illustrates the velocity function. The scale of the velocity is not important. This line can be thought of as an icon describing the velocity.

4.4   Human Figure Motions

The commands on the *human motion menu* create timed body motions. These motions may be combined to generate complex animation sequences. Taken individually, each motion is rather uninteresting. The interplay between the motions must be considered when describing a complex movement. These motions are also mostly subject to the behavioral constraints previously described.

Each one of these commands operates on a human figure. If there is only one human figure present, these commands automatically know to use that figure. If there is more than one human figure, each command will begin by requiring the selection of the figure. Each of these commands needs the starting and ending time of the motion. Default or explicitly entered values may be used. The motion may be repositioned in the animation window using the mouse.

A motion is a movement of a part of the body from one place to another. The movement is specified in terms of the final position and the parameters of how to get there. The *initial* position of the motion, however, is defined implicitly in terms of where the part of the body is when the motion starts. For example, a sequence of movements for the feet are defined with one motion for each foot fall. Each motion serves to move the foot from its current position, wherever that may be, when the motion starts, to the final position for that motion.

4.4.1 Controlling Behaviors Over Time

We have already seen how the posture behavior commands control the effect of the human movement commands. Their effect is permanent, in the sense that behavior commands and constraints hold continuously over the course of an animation. The "timed" behavior commands on the *human behavior menu* allow specifying controls over specific intervals of time. These commands, create timed figure support, create timed balance control, create timed torso control, create time hand control, and create time head control each allow a specific interval of time as described in Section 4.3 just like the other motion commands. The behavior takes effect at the starting time and ends with the ending time. At the ending time, the behavior parameter reverts to the value it had before the motion started.

4.4.2 The Center of Mass

A movement of the center of mass can be created with the create center of mass motion command. This controls the balance point of the figure. There are two ways to position the center of mass. The first option positions the balance point relative to the feet by requiring a floating point number between 0.0 and 1.0 which describes the balance point as an interpolation between the left (0.0) and right (1.0) foot; thus 0.3 means a point $\frac{3}{10}$ of the way from the left foot to the right. Alternatively, one can specify that the figure is standing with 30% of its weight on the right foot and 70% on the left.

The global location option causes the center of mass to move to a specific point in space. Here *Jack* will allow the user to move the center of mass to its desired location using the same technique as with the move center of mass command on the *human manipulation menu*.

After choosing the positioning type and entering the appropriate parameters, several other parameters may be provided, including the weight function and velocity. The weight of the motion is the maximum weight of the constraint which controls the motion, subject to the weight function.

The behavior of the create center of mass motion command depends on the setting of the figure support. It is best to support the figure through the foot which is closest to the center of mass, which is the foot bearing most of the weight. This ensures that the supporting foot moves very little while the weight is on it.

The effect of the center of mass motion depends upon both the setting of the figure support at the time the motion occurs and when the motion is created. For predictable behavior, the two should be the same. For example, if a motion of the center of mass is to take place with the figure seated, then the figure should be seated when the motion is created.

The support of the figure can be changed at a specific moment with the create timed figure support command. This command requires starting and ending times and the figure support, just like the set figure support command. When the motion's ending time is reached, the support reverts to its previous value.

4.4.3   The Pelvis

The lower torso region of the body is controlled in two ways: through the center of mass and through the pelvis. The center of mass describes the location of the body. The pelvis constraint describes the orientation of the hips. The hips can rotate over time with the command create pelvis motion.

The create pelvis motion command allows the user to rotate the pelvis into the final position, using the same technique as the rotate pelvis command. It also requires the velocity, and weight functions, and the overall weight.

4.4.4   The Torso

The movement of the torso of a figure may be specified with the create torso motion. This command permits bending the torso into the desired posture, using the same technique as the move torso command. Like the move torso command, it also prompts for the torso parameters.

The create torso motion command requires a velocity function, but not a weight or a weight function because this command does not use a constraint to do the positioning. Because of this, it is not allowable to have overlapping torso motions.

After the termination of a torso motion, the vertical torso behavior is turned off. The behavior of the torso can be changed at a specific moment with the create timed torso control command. This command requires starting time and ending times and the type of control, just like the set torso control command. When the motion's ending time is reached, the behavior reverts to its previous value.

4.4.5   The Feet

The figure's feet are controlled through the pair of commands create foot motion and create heel motion. These two commands can be used in conjunction to cause the figure to take steps. The feet are controlled through constraints on the heels and on the toes. The toe constraints control the position and orientation of the toes. The heel constraint controls only the height of the heel from the floor. The position of the heel, and the entire foot, comes from the toes. The commands allow the selection of the right or left foot.

The create foot motion command gets the ending position for the foot by the technique of the move foot command. In addition, a height may be specified. The motion causes the foot to move from its initial position to its final position through an arc of a certain elevation. A height of 0 implies that the foot moves in straight-line path. If both the initial and final positions are on the floor, then this means the foot will slide along the floor. A height of 10cm means the toes will reach a maximum height from the floor of 10cm halfway through the motion.

The effect of the create foot motion command depends upon how the figure is supported. Interactively, the move foot command automatically sets the support of the figure to the moving foot, and the create foot motion command does the same. However, this does *not* happen during the generation of the movement sequence. The behavior of the feet depends very much on the support of the figure, although the effect is quite subtle and difficult to define. A foot motion can move either the supported or non-supported foot, but it is much better at moving the non-supported one.

The general rule of thumb for figure support during a movement sequence is the opposite of that for interactive manipulation: during a movement sequence, it is best to have the support through the foot on which the figure has most of its weight. This will ensure that this foot remains firmly planted.

The behavior of the feet can be changed at a specific moment with the create timed foot control command. This command needs starting and ending times and the type of control, just like the set foot control command. When the motion's ending time is reached, the behavior reverts to its previous value.

4.4.6 Moving the Heels

The movement of the foot originates through the toes, but usually a stepping motion begins with the heel coming off the floor. This may be specified with the create heel motion command. This command does not ask for a location; it only asks for a height. A height of 0 means on the floor.

Usually a stepping sequence involves several overlapping motions. It begins with a heel motion to bring the heel off the floor, and at the same time a center of mass motion to shift the weight to the other foot. Then a foot motion causes the foot to move to a new location. When the foot is close to its new location, a second heel motion causes the heel to be planted on the floor and a second center of mass motion shifts some of the weight back to this foot.

4.4.7   The Arms

The arms may be controlled through the command create arm motion. This command moves the arms to a point in space or to a reference point such as a site. The arm motion may involve only the joints of the arm or it may involve bending from the waist as well. The command requires the selection of the right or left arm and whether the arm movement is to be confined to the arm or include a bending of the torso. Arm movements involving the torso should *not* be combined with a torso movement generated with the create torso motion command. Both of these control the torso in conflicting ways.

The hand is then moved to the new position in space, using the same technique as the move arm command. The user can specify if this position is relative to a segment; that is, to a global coordinate location or to a location relative to another object. If the location is relative, the hand will move to that object even if the object is moving as the hand moves during the movement generation.

4.4.8   The Hands

Hand behavior may also be specified over time with the create timed hand control command. The hand can be temporarily attached to certain objects over certain intervals of time. This command requires starting and ending times and the type of control, just like the set torso control command.

Objects can be attached *to the hands* over an interval of time with the create timed attachment command. The timing of the grasp action can be set accordingly. During animation, one can specify the hand grasp site, the approach direction, the starting hand pose, and the sequencing of finger motions culminating in the proper grasp. If one is willing to wait a bit, the hand pose will even be compliant, via collision detection, to changes in the geometry of the grasped object as it or the hand is moved.

4.5   Virtual Human Control

[3]We can track, in real-time, the position and posture of a human body, using a minimal number of 6 DOF sensors to capture full body standing postures. We use four sensors to create a good approximation of a human operator's position and posture, and map it on to the articulated figure model. Such real motion inputs can be used for a variety of purposes.

- If motion data can be input fast enough, live performances can be animated. Several other virtual human figures in an environment can react and move in real-time to the motions of the operator-controlled human figure.

---

[3]Michael Hollick, John Granieri

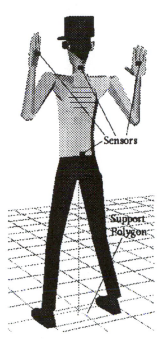

Figure 4.11: Sensor Placement and Support Polygon.

- Motion can be recorded and played back for analysis in different environments. The spatial locations and motions of various body parts can be mapped onto different-sized human figures; for example, a 5th percentile operator's motion can be mapped onto a 95th percentile figure.

- Virtual inputs can be used for direct manipulation in an environment, using the human figure's own body segments; for example, the hands can grasp and push objects.

We use constraints and behavior functions to map operator body locations from external sensor values into human postures.

We are using the **Flock of Birds** from Ascension Technology, Inc. to track four points of interest on the operator. Sensors are affixed to the operator's palms, waist, and base of neck by elastic straps fastened with velcro (Fig. 4.11). Each sensor outputs its 3D location and orientation in space. With an Extended Range Transmitter the operator can move about in an 8-10 foot hemisphere. Each bird sensor is connected to a Silicon Graphics 310VGX via a direct RS232 connection running at 38,400 baud.

One of the initial problems with this system was slowdown of the simulation due to the sensors. The Silicon Graphics operating system introduces a substantial delay between when data arrives at a port and when it can be accessed. This problem was solved by delegating control of the Flock to a separate server process. This server will configure the Flock to suit a client's

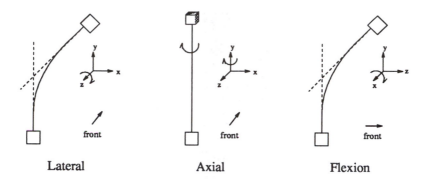

Figure 4.12: Extracting the Spine Target Vector

needs, then provide the client with updates when requested. The server takes updates from the Birds at the maximum possible rate, and responds to client requests by sending the most recent update from the appropriate Bird. This implementation allows access to the Flock from any machine on the local network and allows the client to run with minimal performance degradation due to the overhead of managing the sensors. The sensors produce about 50 updates per second, of which only about 8 to 10 are currently used due to the effective frame rate with a shaded environment of about 2000 polygons. The bulk of the computation lies in the inverse kinematics routines.

The system must first be calibrated to account for the operator's size. This can be done in two ways – the sensor data can be offset to match the model's size, or the model can be scaled to match the operator. Either approach may be taken, depending on the requirements of the particular situation being simulated.

Each frame of the simulation requires the following steps:

1. The pelvis segment is moved as the first step of the simulation. The absolute position/orientation of this segment is given by the waist sensor after adding the appropriate offsets. The figure is rooted through the pelvis, so this sensor determines the overall location of the figure.

2. The spine is now adjusted, using the location of the waist sensor and pelvis as its base. The spine initiator joint, resistor joint, and resistance parameters are fixed, and the spine target position is extracted from the relationship between the waist and neck sensors. The waist sensor gives the absolute position of the pelvis and base of the spine, while the rest of the upper torso is placed algorithmically by the model.

   The spine target position is a 3 vector that can be thought of as the sum of the three types of bending the spine undergoes – flexion, axial, and lateral. Since the sensors approximate the position/orientation of the base and top of the spine, we can extract this information directly. Lateral bending is found from the difference in orientation along the z axis, axial twisting is found from the difference in y orientation, and flexion is determined from the difference in x orientation (Fig. 4.12). Note that the "front" vectors in this figure indicate the front of the human. This information is composed into the spine target vector and sent directly to the model to simulate the approximate bending of the operator's spine.

3. Now that the torso has been positioned, the arms can be set. Each arm of the figure is controlled by a sensor placed on the operator's palm. This sensor is used directly as the goal of a position and orientation constraint. The end effector of this constraint is a site on the palm that matches the placement of the sensor, and the joint chain involved is the wrist, elbow, and shoulder joint.

4. The figure's upper body is now completely postured (except for the head), so the center of mass can be computed. The active stepping behaviors are used to compute new foot locations that will balance the figure. Leg motions are then executed to place the feet in these new locations.

One unique aspect of this system is the absolute measurement of 3D cartesian space coordinates and orientations of body points of interest, rather than joint angles. Thus, while the model's posture may not precisely match the operator's, the end effectors of the constraints are always correct. This is very important in situations where the operator is controlling a human model of different size in a simulated environment.

With a fifth sensor placed on the forehead, gaze direction can be approximated. Hand gestures could be sensed with readily available hand pose sensing gloves. These inputs would directly control nearly the full range of *Jack* behaviors. The result is a virtual human controlled by a minimally encumbered operator.

Chapter 5

Simulation with Societies of Behaviors

[1]Recent research in autonomous robot construction and in computer graphics animation has found that a control architecture with networks of functional behaviors is far more successful for accomplishing real-world tasks than traditional methods. The high-level control and often the behaviors themselves are motivated by the animal sciences, where the individual behaviors have the following properties:

- they are grounded in perception.

- they normally participate in directing an agent's effectors.

- they may attempt to activate or deactivate one-another.

- each behavior by itself performs some task useful to the agent.

In both robotics and animation there is a desire to control agents in environments, though in graphics both are simulated, and in both cases the move to the animal sciences is out of discontent with traditional methods. Computer animation researchers are discontent with direct kinematic control and are increasingly willing to sacrifice complete control for realism. Robotics researchers are reacting against the traditional symbolic reasoning approaches to control such as automatic planning or expert systems. Symbolic reasoning approaches are brittle and incapable of adapting to unexpected situations (both advantageous and disastrous). The approach taken is, more or less, to tightly couple sensors and effectors and to rely on what Brooks [Bro90] calls *emergent behavior*, where independent behaviors interact to achieve a more complicated behavior. From autonomous robot research this approach has been proposed under a variety of names including: *subsumption architecture* by [Bro86], *reactive planning* by [GL90, Kae90], *situated activity* by [AC87],

---

[1] Welton Becket.

and others. Of particular interest to us, however, are those motivated explicitly by animal behavior: *new AI* by Brooks [Bro90], *emergent reflexive behavior* by Anderson and Donath [AD90], and *computational neuro-ethology* by Beer, Chiel, and Sterling [BCS90]. The motivating observation behind all of these is that even very simple animals with far less computational power than a calculator can solve real world problems in path planning, motion control, and survivalist goal attainment, whereas a mobile robot equipped with sonar sensors, laser-range finders, and a radio-Ethernet connection to a Prolog-based hierarchical planner on a supercomputer is helpless when faced with the unexpected. The excitement surrounding the success of incorporating animal-based control systems is almost revolutionary in tone and has led some proponents such as Brooks [Bro90] to claim that symbolic methods are fundamentally flawed and should be dismantled.

Our feeling, supported by Maes [Mae90], is that neural-level coupling of sensors to effectors partitioned into functional groupings is essential for the lowest *levels of competence* (to use Brooks' term), though by itself this purely reflexive behavior will not be able to capture the long-term planning and prediction behavior exhibited by humans and mammals in general. Association learning through classical conditioning can be implemented, perhaps through a connectionist approach [BW90], though this leads only to passive statistics gathering and no explicit prediction of future events.

Our feeling is that symbolic reasoning is not flawed, it is just not efficient for controlling real-valued, imprecise tasks directly. The problem with traditional planning is its insistence on constructing complete, detailed plans before executing. Recent research in this area has focused directly on relaxing this constraint by interleaving planning and executing, reusing pieces of plans, delaying planning until absolutely necessary, and dealing directly with uncertainty. The distinction between the symbol manipulation paradigm and the emergent computation paradigm is even blurring—Maes has shown how a traditional means-ends-analysis planner can be embedded in an emergent computation framework, and Shastri [Sha88] has shown how simple symbol representation and manipulation can be accomplished in neural networks (which can be seen as the most fine-grained form of neuro-physiologically consistent emergent computation).

Our strategy for agent construction will be to recognize that some form of symbolic reasoning is at the top motivational level and biologically-based feedback mechanisms are at the bottom effector level. By putting them in the same programming environment we hope to gain insight into how these extremes connect. Hopefully, the result will be more robust than the harsh, rigid, feedback-devoid distinction between the planner and its directly implemented plan primitives. As will be discussed in Section 5.1.7, however, an important technique for understanding what is missing will be to make premature leaps from high-level plans to low-level behaviors appropriate for simple creatures. This approach is bidirectional and opportunistic. Blind top-down development may never reach the real world and pure bottom-up development faces the horror of an infinite search space with no search heuristic and no clear goals.

In this Chapter we first pursue this notion of societies of behaviors that create a forward (reactive) simulation of human activity. The remaining Sections present some of the particular behaviors that appear to be crucial for natural tasks, including locomotion along arbitrary planar paths, strength guided motion, collision-free path planning, and qualitative posture planning.

5.1 Forward Simulation with Behaviors

Figure 5.1 is a diagram of the control flow of a possible agent architecture. The cognitive model that will manage high-level reasoning is shown only as a closed box. It will not be discussed in this section other than its input/output relation — it is the topic of Chapter 6. The importance of encapsulating the cognitive model is that it does not matter for the purposes of this section how it is implemented. Inevitably, there are direct links between the subcomponents of the cognitive model and the rest of the system. However, we believe the level of detail of the current system allows ignoring these links without harm. The components of an agent are:

1. **Simulated Perception**: this will be discussed in Section 5.1.1, but note that raw perceptual data from the perception module is much higher level than raw data in a machine perception sense — our raw data includes relative positions of objects and their abstract physical properties such as object type and color. In a simulation we have perfect environmental information, so it is the job of the sensors to also simulate realistically limited values.

2. **Perceptual (Afferent) Behavior Network**: perceptual behaviors that attempt to to find high-level information from raw sensory data. Typically they respond to *focusing* signals which change field of view, thresholds, distance sensitivity, restrictions on type of object sensed, and the like.

3. **Cognitive Model**: the source of long-range planning and internal motivation (activity not triggered directly by perception).

4. **Efferent Behavior Network**: behaviors that derive activation or deactivation signals. (Note that the afferent and efferent behavior networks are separated only for organizational convenience — they could actually be one network.)

5. **Simulated Effectors**: attempt to modify objects embedded in the kinematics or dynamics simulation.

Although there may be a general feed-forward nature through the above components in order, the connectivity must be a completely connected graph with the following exceptions:

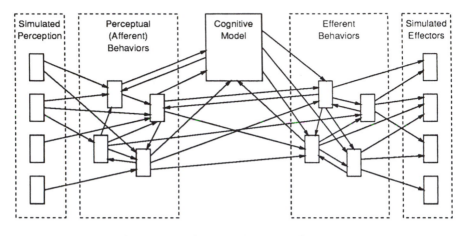

Figure 5.1: Abstract Agent Architecture.

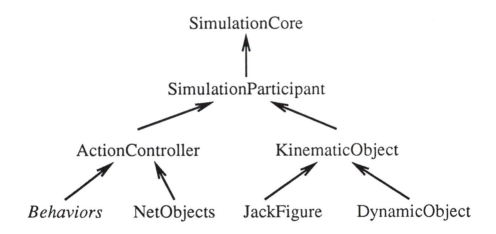

Figure 5.2: Outline of System Class Hierarchy.

1. The cognitive model cannot activate effectors directly.

2. There is no feedback directly from effectors — effector feedback is considered perception (usually proprioception, though pain from muscle fatigue is also possible) and is thus fed-back through the environment.

Raw perceptual information may go directly to the cognitive model or to efferent behaviors, but it is typically routed through perceptual behaviors which derive higher level information and are sensitive to various focusing control signals from the cognitive model, efferent behaviors, or perhaps even other perceptual behaviors. The cognitive model may attempt to re-focus perceptual information through signals to the perceptual behaviors or it may activate or deactivate efferent behaviors in order to accomplish some type of motion or physical change. Efferent behaviors may send signals to effectors, send feedback signals to the cognitive model, or attempt to focus perceptual behaviors.

One typical pattern of activity associated with high-level motivation may be that the cognitive model, for whatever reason, wants to accomplish a complex motion task such as going to the other side of a cluttered room containing several moving obstacles. The cognitive model activates a set of efferent behaviors to various degrees, perhaps an object attraction behavior (to get to the goal) and a variety of obstacle avoidance behaviors. The efferent behaviors then continually activate effectors based on activation levels from the cognitive model and from information directly from perceptual behaviors. Note that this final control flow from perception directly to efferent behavior is what is traditionally called *feedback control*. In another typical pattern of activity, *reflex behavior*, efferent behavior is initiated directly by perceptual behaviors. Note, however, that especially in high-level creatures such as humans, the cognitive model may be able to stop the reflex arc through a variety of inhibitory signals.

5.1.1 The Simulation Model

Rather than implementing models on real robots we will implement and test in detailed simulations that by analogy to the world have a physically-based, reactive environment where some objects in the environment are under the control of agent models that attempt to move their host objects.

For the agent modeler, the main advantage to testing in simulations is the ability to abstract over perception. Because agents are embedded in a simulation, they can be supplied with the high-level results of perception directly, abstracting over the fact that general machine perception is not available. At one extreme agents can be omniscient, having exact information about positions, locations, and properties of all objects in the environment, and at the other extreme they can be supplied with a color bitmap image of what would appear on the agent's visual plane. A good compromise that avoids excessive processing but that also provides for realistically limited perception, is suggested by [Rey88] and also by [RMTT90]. They use the Z-buffering hardware on graphics workstations (or a software emulation) to render a bitmap projection of what the agent can see, except that the color of an object in the environment is unique and serves to identify the object in the image. The combination of the resulting image and the Z-buffer values indicate all visible objects and their distances, and this can be used for object location or determination of uncluttered areas.

Many models of reactive agents are accompanied by a simulation with 2D graphical output such as [AC87, PR90, HC90, VB90], however, these simulation environments are extreme abstractions over a real environment and assume discrete, two-dimensional, purely kinematic space. Such abstractions are, of course, necessary in initial phases of understanding how to model an intelligent reactive agent, but extended use of a system without real-valued input parameters and immense environmental complexity is dangerous. As will be discussed Section 5.1.3, Simon [Sim81] argues that complex behavior is often due to a complex environment, where the agent responds to environmental complexity through simple feedback mechanisms grounded in sensation. When environmental complexity is not present, the agent modeler, noticing the lack of complexity, may commit *agent bloating*, also discussed in Section 5.1.3, where environmental complexity is accounted for artificially in the agent model.

5.1.2   The Physical Execution Environment

In our model, kinematic and dynamic behavior has been factored out of the agent models and is handled by a separate, common mechanism. The networks of efferent behaviors controlling a conceptual agent in the environment will *request* motion by activating various effectors. The requested movement may not happen due to the agent's physical limitations, collision or contact with the environment, or competition with other behavioral nets.

Simulations of agents interacting with environments must execute on reasonably fine-grained physically-based simulations of the world in order to result in realistic, useful animations without incurring what we call the *agent-bloating* phenomenon, where motion qualities arising from execution in physical environment are stuffed into the agent model. One of Simon's central issues [Sim81] is that complex behavior is often not the result of a complex control mechanism, but of a simple feedback system interacting with a complex environment. Currently, for simplicity, our animations are done in a *kinematic* environment (one considering only velocity and position) and not a *dynamic* one (also considering mass and force). Using only kinematics has been out of necessity since general dynamics models have not been available until recently, and even then are so slow as to preclude even near real time execution for all but the simplest of environments. Kinematic environments are often preferred by some since kinematic motion is substantially easier to control with respect to position of objects since there is no mass to cause momentum, unexpected frictional forces to inhibit motion, and so on. But as we demand more of our agent models we will want them to exhibit properties that result from interaction with a complex physical world with endless, unexpected intricacies and deviations from desired motion. Unless we execute on a physically reactive environment we will experience one form of agent-bloating where we build the physical environment into the agents. If we build an actual simulation model into agents we have wasted space and introduced organizational complexities by not beginning with a common physical environment. If we build the environmental complexity into the agents abstractly, perhaps through statistical models, we will have initial success in abstract situations, but never be able to drive a meaningful, correct, time-stepped simulation with multiple agents interacting with an environment and each other. We do not mean that statistical and other abstract characterizations of behavior are not necessary – just that abstract description is essential to understanding how the underlying process works and judging when a model is adequate.

The much cited loss of control in dynamic simulations needs to be overcome, and the message of emergent behavior research is that perhaps the most straightforward approach to this is by looking at the plethora of working existence proofs: real animals. Even the simplest of single-celled creatures executes in an infinitely complex physical simulation, and creatures we normally ascribe little or no intelligence to exhibit extremely effective control and goal-orientedness. Animals do this primarily through societies of feedback mechanisms where the lowest levels are direct sensation and muscle contraction (or hormone production or whatever).

In our system dynamic simulations should enjoy the following properties:

- Effectors request movement by applying a force at a certain position to an object.

- Collisions are detected by the system, which will communicate response forces to those participating in the crash or contact situation.

- Viscous fluid damping is simulated by applying a resistance force opposite and proportionate to instantaneous velocity.

For simplicity, and especially when the motion is intended to be abstract, a simulation may still be run on a purely kinematic environment which has the following properties:

1. Effectors request changes in position and orientation, rather than application of force.

2. Every object has some maximum velocity.

3. No motion takes place unless requested explicitly by effectors.

4. Collisions are resolved by stopping motion along the system's estimated axis of penetration.

5. The system adapts the time increment based on instantaneous velocity and size of object along that object's velocity vector so that no object could pass entirely through another object in one time step.

The particular physical simulation approach is to use a simple finite-difference approximation to the equations for elastic solids. Objects are modeled as meshes of point masses connected by springs (including cross connections to maintain shape), where tighter spring constants yield more rigid looking bodies. This approach is discussed by Terzopoulos [TPBF87] and Miller [Mil91] and has the advantage of extreme simplicity and generality. Because it is a discrete approximation to the "integral-level" analytical physics equations it can solve many problems for free, though in general the cost is limited accuracy and much slower execution times than the corresponding direct analytical methods (the results, however, are not only "good enough for animation" but are good enough considering our abstraction level). The model can easily account for phenomena such as collision response, elastic deformation, permanent deformation, breakage, and melting. Finite element analysis yields a better dynamic behavior to the point-mass mesh (for accuracy and execution time), but is not as general as the mass/spring approach and cannot model breakage and melting.

5.1.3   Networks of Behaviors and Events

The insulation of the cognitive model with networks of behaviors relies on emergent computation. It is important to understand, then, why emergent computation works where a strict hierarchy would not, and what problems an emergent computation approach poses for the agent designer and how these problems can be overcome.

For simplicity, existing high-level task-simulation environments tend to model activity in strict tree-structured hierarchies, with competition occurring only for end effectors in simulation models as in [Zel82], or for position of a body component in purely kinematic models. However, for some time behavior scientists and those influenced by them have argued that although there is observable hierarchy, behavior – especially within hierarchical levels – is not tree structured but may have an arbitrary graph of influence [Gal80, Alb81]. In particular a theory of behavior organization must anticipate behaviors having more than one parent and cycles in the graph of influence.

The central observation is that in many situations small components communicating in the correct way can gracefully solve a problem where a direct algorithm may be awkward and clumsy. Of course this approach of solving problems by having a massive number of components communicating in the right way is nothing new: cellular automata, fractals, approximation methods, neural networks (both real and artificial), finite-difference models of elastic solids [TPBF87], simulated annealing, and so on use exactly this approach.

The drawback to such massively parallel systems without central control is typically the inability to see beyond local minima. Certainly a high-level planner may periodically exert influence on various system components in order to pull the system state from a local minimum. The appropriate introduction of randomness into component behavior, however, can help a system settle in a more globally optimal situation. This randomness can be from explicit environmental complexity, introduction of stochastic components, limited or incorrect information, or mutation.

This general approach is not limited to low-level interaction with the environment. Minsky proposes a model of high-level cognition in [Min86] where a "society of agents" interacts (organized as a graph) to accomplish high-level behavior. Pattie Maes [Mae90] has proposed an approach to high-level planning through distributed interaction of plan-transformation rules. Ron Sun proposed a distributed, connectionist approach to non-monotonic reasoning [Sun91].

All of these approaches rest on emergent computation — behavior resulting from communication of independent components. Common objections to such an approach are:

1. it is doomed to limited situations through its tendency to get stuck in local minima.

2. in order to implement, it requires an unreasonable amount of weight fiddling.

The first objection has already been addressed. The second is a serious concern. Our proposed solution will be to transfer the weight assignment process to some combination of the behavioral system and its environment. An evolution model is one way to do this, as Braitenberg [Bra84] does with his vehicles, or as the Artificial Life field would do. Another is to combine simple behavioral psychology principles and a connectionist learning model in a creature that wants to maximize expected utility [Bec92], then provide a reinforcement model that punishes the creature whenever it does something wrong (like hits something).

Making it easy for a human designer to engage in an iterative design and test process is another approach. Wilhelms and Skinner's [WS90] system does exactly this by providing a sophisticated user interface and stressing real-time or at least pseudo-real-time simulation of creatures interacting with the environment. However, we will not pursue this approach for the following reasons:

- Self-supervised weight assignment as agents interact with their environment is clearly more desirable from a simulation point of view, though it sacrifices direct control for realism and ease of use.

- For reasons discussed in Section 5.1.2, we encourage execution in complex physically-based environments — an emphasis precluding real-time playback on standard displays.

5.1.4 Interaction with Other Models

Our approach then, is to control physical simulation with the abstract findings of the animal sciences, beginning by using the tricks that low-level animals use. Low-level animal behavior tends, through its extensive use of environmental feedback, to be incremental — it makes a new decision at every moment considering the current state of the environment. For this reason it is considered *reactive* because it will incorporate unexpected events in constant time as though they had been planned for in advance. Certainly human behavior exhibits short and long term planning that cannot be explained by purely reactive processes. We hope to discover and elaborate abstraction layers with long-term symbolic planning at the top and feedback mechanisms at the bottom.

However, there are countless areas in the neuro-physiological level study of humans that are not well enough understood to allow direct or even abstract implementation. Behavior such as human walking, to our knowledge, cannot be described accurately in terms of feedback from proprioceptive sensors and perhaps the vision system. Many such components of human behavior can, however, be modeled directly by abstract methods and we ought to be able to incorporate these as we progress. These direct methods will often be considerably faster than the corresponding neuro-physiological models which typically rely an massive parallel computation and will not run efficiently on sequential machines. So even if there were a neural-level walking algorithm for humans, in cases where the robustness and correctness of locomotion are unlikely to contribute to the usefulness of the overall simulation, say because the are very few obstacles and the terrain is simple, it would be useful to use the direct method to save time.

Algorithms that are designed to manipulate human body parts directly can be incorporated into the described system as long as an approach to conflict resolution is also implemented should there be more than one behavior attempting to control a given body segment (this can be weighted averaging, or strict prioritization, or whatever). Since the rest of the system is totally reactive and considers the current state of the environment at every instant, it does not matter whether the physical model, kinematic model, or some other process modified a given object.

As will be discussed later, if a collision is detected, all behaviors controlling the offenders will be sent messages indicating the points of collision and the impulse forces. For objects that do not have explicit velocity information a velocity is simply computed by looking at the system's current δt and how far the object was moved over the previous time step. The receiving behaviors can do whatever they wish with the information — replan, respond to it, ignore it, or anything appropriate. The only difficulty is when two objects both controlled by unyielding direct control methods collide — they both will fail to move any further. This can be avoided by keeping the number of objects under direct control limited, or by always implementing some sort of failure recovery method. Since communication is based on contact positions and forces, different control approaches can always communicate through their effects on the environment.

Even other physically-based object controllers such as finite element analysis, or direct rigid body dynamics can be incorporated. Direct control messages across computer networks or through operating system pipes to dynamics simulation packages can also be used. Direct manipulation is also possible though there must be a way to compensate for speed differences if the simulation is running much slower than real time. One way to do this is to have the user move an object while the simulation is frozen, ask the user how long in simulation time that action should take, then use a direct kinematic controller to do a spline-smoothed approximation of the user's motion as the simulation continues.

5.1.5 The Simulator

The simulation of intelligent agents interacting with a reactive environment is advanced incrementally in small adaptive time steps. The Δt for a time slice will be no greater than $\frac{1}{30}$th of a second (the typical video frame rate) and can be as small as floating point precision will allow. Typically, kinematically controlled objects will update on $\frac{1}{30}$ths of a second but dynamically controlled objects when experiencing high-impact collisions will want very small time steps. The distinction made in earlier sections between agents and the environment is only conceptual at the simulator level— both components of agent models and components of physical models are considered first-class participants in a single simulation. Every time step is broken down into a number of synchronizing phases. The synchronizing phases are motivated by Haumann and Parent's behavioral simulation system [HP88], but augmented with features for adaptive time steps. The following messages are broadcast in the given order to every participant on every time step:

start   This tells participants a time step is beginning. Typically buffers for collecting messages in the affect stage are cleared here, and state information is saved in case there is a backup.

affect   Participants that attempt to modify the state of other participants may do so here by looking at the state of the environment and sending messages calling for change. However, no participant is allowed to change the appearance of an internal state – all calls for change must be buffered and dealt with in the respond stage.

respond   Objects are allowed to change their externally accessible state variables, such as position and color for environmental objects or activation level for behavioral network components.

data inject Rigid rules, such as static non-interpenetration, are enforced here after objects have had a chance to update themselves. Pure kinematic scripting may be done here also.

In addition, at any phase any object may request that the time step be restarted with a smaller time step if it feels the simulation is running too fast. A participant need only suggest a new Δt, perhaps half the previous Δt, then call for a global backup. All participants are required to store persistent state information in the start phase, and restore this state if a backup is called. Participants may also request new Δt values without requesting a backup and if no requests are made, the system will try to double the Δt on every step until it reaches $\frac{1}{30}$th of a second.

The Class Hierarchy

An object-oriented approach is natural for implementing such a system, and in order to allow fast execution for interactive development, we chose to use C++. The cognitive model is based on Lisp and Prolog and will communicate through C-callout functions to C++.

The class hierarchy is outlined in Figure 5.2. The `SimulationCore` class manages the clock, the current Δt, and a list of participants to which it broadcasts synchronizing messages on each time step. `SimulationParticipant` encapsulates all participants in the simulation. A distinction is made between participants that have spatial qualities (the `KinematicObj` class, which tends to operate in the respond stage) and participants that try to modify the state of other participants (the `ActionController` class which operates in both the affect and respond stages).

Objects, actions, and networks

The `KinematicObj` class is broken into a `JackFigure` class which allows use of the *Jack* figures. The `DynamicObj` class is for objects controlled by dynamic simulation and is a subset of kinematic objects because any dynamic object ought to be able to respond to any message intended for a purely kinematic object.

`ActionControllers` are broken down into *Behaviors* which include perceptual and efferent behaviors discussed above and `NetObjects` which connect them. Our network package allows general neural network-type constructions, though it is important to note that the system is not a neural network because:

- the 'neurons' (nodes) may be of arbitrary complexity.

- the messages passed along network links may be very complicated, in particular, they can be pointers to objects.

Neural networks can be used within behaviors, however, and we have begun experimenting with backpropagation learning [FS91, HKP91] and recurrent networks [Bec92, Sch90] as ways of learning how to behave.

All `ActionController` instances must respond to messages requesting the start and end time of activation or an indication that the action has not started or ended. This allows general implementation of conditional action sequencing through meta-behaviors that on each time step check to see of a particular action has started or ended or if an action of a particular type has begun or ended.

5.1.6 Implemented Behaviors

Presently, reactive agents resemble Reynolds' birds [Rey87] in that on each time step the agent moves along its local z-axis. Efferent behaviors attempt to modify the global orientation of the local z-axis and also determine by how much it will move forward.

Our primary perceptual behavior is the `Closest-k` sensor. Its arguments are the number and type of objects to which it is sensitive. In addition the sensor needs to know what its relative position is to its host environmental object (the z-axis of this transformation will be the forward direction). The sensor produces k groups of outputs which will contain information on the closest k objects of the defined type. Each group will have three floating-point output nodes: the distance from the sensor's current global origin, the angle between the sensor's z-axis and a vector to the detected object's centroid, and the radius of the detected object (we currently use bounding cylinders and bounding spheres around objects to simplify calculations). We have found no pressing need yet to construct a corresponding `furthest-k` sensor.

Another perceptual behavior that is not behaviorally motivated, but useful for abstract control is the `ObjectSensor` that is sensitive only to a particular object in the environment and has outputs similar to a `closest-k` sensor.

The efferent behaviors we have implemented are loosely motivated by neuro-ethological findings about real creatures and are discussed by Wilhelms and Skinner [WS90] in their implementation and abstraction of Braitenberg's *Vehicles* [Bra84] and in Anderson and Donath's emergent reflexive behavior system [AD90]. What is novel about our behaviors is their dynamically adjustable tuning parameters:

1. threshold distance

2. field of view (angular threshold)

3. sensitivity of activation level to distance of object and angular distance of object. Distance from threshold and angle from center scaled by an exponent and a constant (both focusing parameters).

these can be adjusted directly by the cognitive component or by other behaviors. We have found the following behaviors particularly useful:

Attract go toward either closest-k of a certain type of object or a specific object. Loosely corresponds to *teleotaxis* in animals [Gal80].

Avoid go away from a particular object or from a certain type of object. Also a form of teleotaxis.

GoAround uses the incremental obstacle avoidance approach outlined by Reynolds [Rey88], which is based on how birds avoid obstacles while flying.

Achieve   go to a particular place or a particular place relative to another object.

AttractLine go directly towards a line in space – used to follow walls.

AvoidLine go directly away from a line in space – used to avoid walls.

5.1.7   Simple human motion control

An important approach to developing human behaviors is to attempt to apply the behaviors appropriate for low level animals directly to humans and see where they appear awkward in order to understand what is missing. Our initial attempt allows the above efferent and perceptual behaviors to be used directly in a human model except that instead of simply moving along the z-axis the human agent attempts to reduce its current and desired headings by taking steps. The stepping is accomplished by using a locomotion algorithm (Section 5.2). Our walking algorithm is incremental in that it only needs to know where the next footstep should go and how it should be oriented. Our approach to supplying footsteps clips the difference between the current and desired headings to 45 degrees and places the next foot to be moved alongside the new heading. Heading is determined by the orientation of the lower torso (which is oriented by the walking algorithm). The size of the step is currently based on the curvature of the turn (smaller steps for larger turns), though certainly step length should have other influences.

Simulations involving this simple human agent model show very clearly that humans anticipate the effects of placing the next step (perhaps through behavioral gradient estimation) rather than blindly following influences of the current situation. In all complicated situations under the described model the agent tends to oscillate around the behavior gradient.

There are other agent behaviors that are in the process of migrating into this behavioral framework. In the next sections we look at locomotion, strength-guided lifting, collision avoidance, and posture planning.

5.2   Locomotion

[2]Locomotion provides a tremendous extension of the workspace by moving the body to places where other activities may be accomplished. A locomotion system should provide a reasonable configuration of the figure at any time as it moves along a specified input path. There have been many efforts to make this process more realistic and automatic, which can roughly be summarized into two major approaches: kinematic and dynamic controls. Rotoscopy data and biomechanics knowledge can be utilized to control locomotion kinematically, but empirical data must be generalized to get walking under parametric control. A dynamics computation can be done to get the locomotion path and some of the body motion characteristics, but biomechanics knowledge is

---

[2]Hyeongseok Ko.

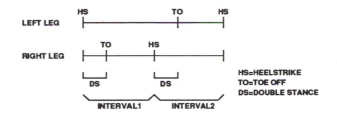

Figure 5.3: The Phase Diagram of a Human Walk.

useful in determining the details and reducing the complexity of the whole body dynamic system.

These two approaches can be applied to get straight path walking. The natural clutter and constraints of a workplace or other environment tend to restrict the usefulness of a straight path so we must generalize walking to curved paths. We have already seen the stepping behavior and the collision avoidance path planning in *Jack*, so a locomotion capability rounds out the ability of an agent to go anywhere accessible. First we give some necessary definitions for the locomotion problem, then look at feasible ways of implementing curved path walking.

At a certain moment, if a leg is between its own heelstrike (beginning) and the other leg's heelstrike (ending), it is called the *stance leg*. If a leg is between the other leg's heelstrike (beginning) and its own heelstrike (ending), it is called the *swing leg*. For example, in Figure 5.3, the left leg is the stance leg during interval 1, and the right leg is the stance leg during interval 2. Thus at any moment we can refer to a specific leg as either the stance or swing leg with no ambiguity. The joints and segments in a leg will be referenced with prefixes *swing* or *stance*: for example, swing ankle is the ankle in the swing leg.

Let $\Theta = [\theta_1, \ldots, \theta_J]$ be the joint angles and $\Lambda = [l_1, \ldots, l_S]$ be the links of the human body model. Each θ_i can be a scalar or a vector depending on the DOFs of the joint. Let Σ be the sequence of $(\vec{h_i}, \vec{d_i}, sf_i, lorr_i), i = 0, 1, \ldots, n$, where h_i is the heel position of the ith foot, d_i is the direction of the ith foot, sf_i is the step frequency of the ith step, and $lorr_i$ ("left" or "right") is 0 when the ith foot is left foot and 1 otherwise. The locomotion problem is to find the function f that relates Λ and Σ with Θ at each time t:

$$\Theta = f(\Lambda, \Sigma, t). \tag{5.1}$$

Usually the function f is not simple, so the trick is to try to devise a set of algorithms that computes the value of Θ for the given value of (Λ, Σ, t), depending on the situation.

5.2.1   Kinematic Control

The value of Θ can be given based on rotoscopy data. Two significant problems in this approach are the various error sources in the measurements and the discrepancy between the subject's body and the computer model. When applying kinematic (empirical) data to the model, obvious constraints imposed on the walking motion may be violated. The most fundamental ones are that the supporting foot should not go through nor off the ground in the obvious ways depending on the situation, and that the global motion should be continuous (especially at the heel strike point). The violation of these constraints is visually too serious to be neglected. During motion generalization the error is likely to increase. Therefore in the kinematic control of locomotion, one prominent problem is how to resolve errors and enforce constraints without throwing away useful information that has already been obtained.

So how can we generalize empirical data? The walk function Θ depends on many parameters, and simple interpolation cannot solve the problem. Boulic, Magnenat-Thalmann and Thalmann's solution for this problem [BMTT90] is based on the relative velocity (RV), which is simply the velocity expressed in terms of the height of the hip joint H_t (e.g. $2H_t/sec$). For example the height of the waist O_s during the walk is given by

$$-0.015RV + 0.015RV \sin 2\pi(2t - 0.35)$$

where t is the elapsed time normalized by the cycle time. Because this formulation is based on both body size and velocity, the approach can be applied under various body conditions and velocities.

5.2.2   Dynamic Control

Bruderlin and Calvert built a non-interpolating system to simulate human locomotion [Bru88, BC89]. They generated every frame based on a hybrid dynamics and kinematics computation. They could generate a wide gamut of walking styles by changing the three primary parameters step length, step frequency, and speed. The example we use here is based on their work.

Their model is divided into two submodels. The one (stance model) consists of the upperbody and the stance leg. The other (swing model) represents the swing leg. In the stance model, the whole upperbody is represented by one link and the stance leg is represented with two collinear links joined by a prismatic joint. So the stance leg is regarded as one link with variable length ω. In the swing model, the two links represent the thigh and calf of the swing leg. In both models, links below the ankle are not included in the dynamic analysis and are handled instead by kinematics.

Two sets of Lagrangian equations are formulated, one set for each leg phase model. To do that, the five generalized coordinates, ω, θ_1, θ_2, θ_3, θ_4 are introduced: ω is the length of stance leg; θ_1, θ_2, θ_3 is measured from the vertical line at the hip to the stance leg, upperbody, and the thigh of the swing leg, respectively; and θ_4 is the flexion angle of the knee of the swing leg. During the stance phase the stance foot remains at (x, y), so x and y are regarded as constants. Once those five values of general coordinates are given, the configuration of the whole body can be determined by kinematics.

So the goal of the dynamics computation is to obtain the general coordinate values.

We will focus only on the stance model here. By formulating the Lagrangian equation on the stance model, we get the three generalized forces F_ω, F_{θ_1}, and F_{θ_2}.

$$
\begin{aligned}
F_\omega =\ & m_2\ddot{\omega} - m_2 r_2 \ddot{\theta}_2 \sin(\theta_2 - \theta_1) - m_2 r_2 \dot{\theta}_2(\dot{\theta}_2 - \dot{\theta}_1)\cos(\theta_2 - \theta_1) \\
& -m_2\omega\dot{\theta}_1^{\,2} - m_2 r_2 \dot{\theta}_2 \dot{\theta}_1 \cos(\theta_2 - \theta_1) \\
& +m_2 g \cos\theta_1
\end{aligned}
\tag{5.2}
$$

$$
\begin{aligned}
F_{\theta_1} =\ & (I_1 + m_1 r_1^2 + m_2\omega^2)\ddot{\theta}_1 + 2m_2\omega\dot{\omega}\dot{\theta}_1 \\
& -(m_1 r_1 + m_2\omega)g\sin\theta_1 + m_2 r_2 \ddot{\theta}_2 \omega \cos(\theta_2 - \theta_1) \\
& -m_2 r_2 \dot{\theta}_2^{\,2}\omega \sin(\theta_2 - \theta_1)
\end{aligned}
\tag{5.3}
$$

$$
\begin{aligned}
F_{\theta_2} =\ & -m_2 r_2 \ddot{\omega}\sin(\theta_2 - \theta_1) + m_2 r_2 \omega\dot{\theta}_1 \cos(\theta_2 - \theta_1) \\
& +(I_2 + m_2 r_2^2)\ddot{\theta}_2 - m_2 g r_2 \sin\theta_2 \\
& +2m_2 r_2 \dot{\omega}\dot{\theta}_1 \cos(\theta_2 - \theta_1) + m_2 r_2 \omega\dot{\theta}_1^{\,2}\sin(\theta_2 - \theta_1)
\end{aligned}
\tag{5.4}
$$

which can be written in a matrix form as

$$
\begin{bmatrix} a_{11} & a_{12} & a_{13} \\ a_{21} & a_{22} & a_{23} \\ a_{31} & a_{32} & a_{33} \end{bmatrix}
\begin{bmatrix} \ddot{\omega} \\ \ddot{\theta}_1 \\ \ddot{\theta}_2 \end{bmatrix}
=
\begin{bmatrix} F_\omega + b_1 \\ F_{\theta_1} + b_2 \\ F_{\theta_2} + b_3 \end{bmatrix}
\tag{5.5}
$$

Let $x(t)$ be the value of x at time t; x can be a scalar, a vector, or a matrix. In equation 5.5 at time t, everything is known except $\ddot{\omega}, \ddot{\theta}_1, \ddot{\theta}_2, F_\omega, F_{\theta_1}, F_{\theta_2}$. If we give the generalized force values at time t, the above linear equation can be solved for accelerations. The position at the next time step is

$$
\begin{aligned}
\vec{q}_r(t + \Delta t) &= \vec{q}_r(t) + \Delta t \dot{\vec{q}}_r(t) \\
\vec{q}(t + \Delta t) &= \vec{q}(t) + \Delta t \dot{\vec{q}}_r(t).
\end{aligned}
\tag{5.6}
\tag{5.7}
$$

The internal joint torques $F(t) = [F_\omega, F_{\theta_1}, F_{\theta_2}]^T$ are not fully known. Bruderlin adopted some heuristics from biomechanics to handle this problem. For example, to get F_{θ_1}, he noted

> A significant torque at the hip of the stance leg occurs only just after heel strike and lasts for about 20% of the cycle time. Also, the torque during this time interval is such that it rapidly reaches a maximum value and decays quickly towards the end [IRT81, Win90].

and approximated it by a constant function

$$
F_{\theta_1} = \begin{cases} c & \text{for the first 20\% of cycle time} \\ 0 & \text{for the remaining cycle time.} \end{cases}
\tag{5.8}
$$

Similarly, in modeling the hip joint and waist joint as springs, the internal torques were given by the following formulas:

$$F_\omega = k_\omega(\omega_{des} + pa_3 - \omega) - v_\omega \dot{\omega} \tag{5.9}$$

$$F_{\theta_2} = -k_2(\theta_2 - \theta_{2\_des}) - v_2 \dot{\theta}_2. \tag{5.10}$$

To handle the errors coming from these approximations, several checkpoints were set. For example, the posture at the heel strike after the current step can be derived based on the step symmetry. Integrating $F(t)$ until the checkpoint, we can compare the result with the desired one. The constants in the equations above (e.g. c, a_3) are adjusted according to the difference. This process is repeated until the integration brings it close enough to the desired posture.

5.2.3   Curved Path Walking

Research on biped locomotion has focused on sagittal plane walking in which the stepping path is a straight line. Unfortunately, simply treating a complex walking path as a sequence of straight-line path segments does not work. The problems of turning and coordinating the limb motions at the turns is frequently neglected and the rigid appearance of the resulting abrupt mid-air turns is clearly unacceptable animation.

In building a general planar locomotion behavior, we utilized pre-existing straight path ideas. We will call a linear path locomotion algorithm a 1D system; we will use it as a process within our 2D behavior. For every 2D step, we will consider its *underlying 1D step*, and the 1D system will provide some needed information. Our generalization algorithm from 1D to 2D is based on the intuition that there should be a smooth transition between linear and curved locomotion. If the curvature is not large, the 2D walk generated should be close to the 1D walk given by the underlying 1D system. In particular, the degenerate 2D case of a straight line should be exactly the same as that produced by the underlying 1D system. Since no assumptions are made about the underlying 1D system, any 1D locomotion algorithm can be generalized into our 2D one. Moreover, the underlying 1D system will determine the stylistics (or faults) of the curved path walk.

When requested to create a step, the 1D step generation algorithm provides information to the 2D system. The 2D system first computes the center [of mass] site trajectory and the locations of both hip joints. The locations of the feet are computed based on the 1D step information. Because we have the hip and foot locations of both legs, the configurations of both stance and swing legs can be determined. The banking angle is computed, and the upper body is adjusted to move the center of mass to achieve the required banking. The parameters Θ that determine the configuration of the whole body is now available for *Jack* display. This entire process is incremental at the step level, so that it fits neatly into the behavioral simulation paradigm.

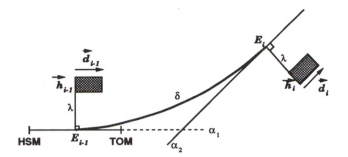

Figure 5.4: The Step Length of the Underlying 1D Step.

Specifying the Walk

The direct input to the locomotion behavior is a *step sequence* Σ of 4-tuples,

$$\sigma_i = (\vec{h_i}, \vec{d_i}, sf_i, lorr_i), i = 0, \ldots, n. \tag{5.11}$$

Each tuple σ_i is called the *i*th *foot description*. The pair of adjacent two foot descriptions (σ_{i-1}, σ_i) is called the *i*th *step description* or simply the *i*th *step*.

Even though we have maximum control of locomotion by using the step sequence, generating such a sequence directly is a tedious job. The behavioral simulation can generate a path incrementally, or an interactive user could specify a curved path. In either case, the specification is automatically transformed to a step sequence.

The specification of a walk in 1D can be done by giving a sequence of $(sl_i, sf_i), i = 1, \ldots, n$. Each (sl_i, sf_i) affects the type of current step, starting from the current heelstrike to the next one. For every step description (σ_{i-1}, σ_i) in 2D, we consider its *underlying 1D step*. The step frequency sf_{1D} of this 1D step is given by sf_i of σ_i. We can draw 2 lines α_1, α_2 on the horizontal plane as shown in the Figure 5.4: α_1 is in the direction of $\vec{d_{i-1}}$ displaced by λ from $\vec{h_{i-1}}$; α_2 is in the direction of $\vec{d_i}$ displaced by λ from $\vec{h_i}$. Let δ be the arc length of the spline curve from E_{i-1} to E_i, where E_{i-1} and E_i are the projections of the heel positions to the lines α_1, and α_2, respectively. (The derivatives at the end points of this spline curve are given by $\vec{d_{i-1}}$ and $\vec{d_i}$.) The step length sl_{1D} of the underlying 1D step is given by this δ.

Path of the Center Site

For this discussion we will keep the model simple by assuming that the center of mass moves along a straight line from the heelstrike moment of the stance leg (HS) to the toe off moment of the swing leg (TO) (Figure 5.5). The trajectory of the center site during this double stance phase (DS) is given by the current stance foot direction $\vec{d_{i-1}}$. From the TO to the next HS, the center site moves along a spline interpolation (Figure 5.5). At both ends of the spline, the derivative of the must match that of the adjacent line segments for

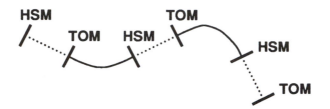

Figure 5.5: The Trajectory of the Center Site (Top View).

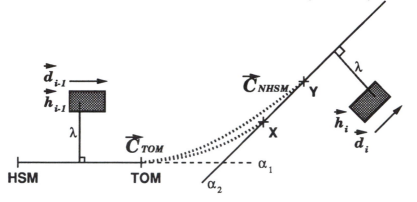

Figure 5.6: The Position of Center Site at Heelstrike Moment.

first order continuity. Through the whole locomotion, the pelvis is assumed to face the derivative direction of the center site path, and be vertical to the ground. The torso can be bent in any direction, a part of which is given by the underlying 1D algorithm, and another part is given from a banking adjustment.

To derive the spline curve, we need the position $\vec{C}_{NHS}$ and derivative $\dot{\vec{C}}_{NHS}$ of the center site at the *next* HS, as well as $\vec{C}_{TO}$ and $\dot{\vec{C}}_{TO}$ at TO which are provided by the underlying 1D system (Figure 5.6). The assumptions above imply that $\dot{\vec{C}}_{NHS} = \vec{d}_i$, and $\vec{C}_{NHS}$ should be put at point X somewhere on the line α_2. Let η_{1D} and τ_{1D} be the length of the center site trajectory from HS to TO, and from TO to the next HS, respectively, during the underlying 1D step. Let η_{2D} of corresponding 2D step be similarly defined. Let $\tau_{2D}(X)$ be the arc length (top view) of the spline from $\vec{C}_{TO}$ to X in Figure 5.6. Now the position of the center site $\vec{C}_{NHS}$ at the next HS is set to the point X on the line α_2 such that

$$\frac{\eta_{1D}}{\tau_{1D}} = \frac{\eta_{2D}}{\tau_{2D}(X)}. \tag{5.12}$$

This definition of $\vec{C}_{NHS}$ is based on the smooth transition assumption from 1D locomotion to 2D. By a mapping which preserves arc length ratio [Gir87, SB85, Far88], we can find the correspondence between the 2D trajectory of the center site and underlying 1D one. Note that this definition also makes

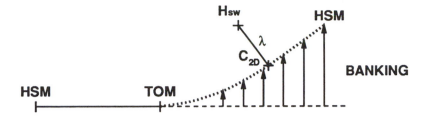

Figure 5.7: Banking of the Center Site.

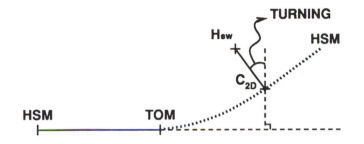

Figure 5.8: Turning of the Center Site.

the degenerate case of 2D walk exactly same with the corresponding 1D walk.

The displacement of the curved path from the underlying linear path is produced by banking as shown in Figure 5.7. The position of the displaced center site in 2D step is C_{2D}, and H_{sw} is the position of the swing hip. Banking mostly results from ankle joint adjustment. Even though the center site is put on the spline curve by the ankle angle, the upper body has not bent yet to generate the overall correct banking of the whole body. The banking should be considered in terms of the center of mass of the body. The overall banking is given by

$$\phi = \arctan(\frac{\kappa v^2}{g}) \tag{5.13}$$

where v is the velocity, g is the gravity, and κ is the curvature of the path [Gir87]. Here we use the spline curve of the center site as an approximation to get the curvature. The upper body should be bent so that the center of mass (which is in the upper body) may make the angle ϕ around the stance ankle with respect to the ground. Iteration can be used to compute the current center of mass and reduce the difference from the current one and the desired one.

We assume that the length of the dynamic leg ω in 2D locomotion at a moment t, is the same as ω at the corresponding moment in the underlying 1D step. So the displaced center site C_{2D} will be lower than the corresponding 1D center site C_{1D}. The position (x_1, y_1, z_1) of the hypothetical ankle is available from the old foot location. Let (x_2, y_2, z_2) be the position of the swing hip H_{sw} in Figure 5.7. The horizontal components x_2 and z_2 can be computed from the derivative at C_{2D} and λ. In Figure 5.7, λ is the distance between H_{sw} and C_{2D}, and this distance is along the perpendicular direction of the derivative.

Because we assumed that ω is the same in 1D and 2D locomotion, we have

$$\mid (x_1, y_1, z_1) - (x_2, y_2, z_2) \mid = \omega \qquad (5.14)$$

where ω is given by the underlying 1D system. The value of y_2 that satisfies the above equation is the height of both H_{sw} and C_{2D}. Because the pelvis is assumed to be upright through the steps, the height of the stance hip H is also y_2.

The Stance Leg

The center site movement of 2D locomotion during DS is the same as that of the 1D one, including the height component, so the stance leg configurations are given by the underlying 1D system. During the single stance phase, we still use 1D system to get the joint angle at the ball of foot. But because the center site begins to deviate, the other joint angles should be computed.

In the stance leg, after the foot is put flat on the ground, the toetip is regarded as the root because that point is not moved until the next toe off. Because the joint angle at the ball of the foot is provided by the 1D algorithm, we have the location A of the ankle. Since the location of the hip is also available the configuration of the stance leg can be determined.

The Swing Leg at the Double Stance Phase

Because a revolute joint is assumed at the ball of foot, if we exclude the possibility of sliding, the toe group of the swing foot should stay fixed on the ground during the DS. Because there are 3 links between the swing hip and the ball of foot, we should resolve the redundancy in a reasonable way. If we use the ball of the foot joint angle in the 1D algorithm this redundancy goes away. This approximation works well in most of the cases. But when both the direction change and the step length (the distance between the adjacent steps) are extremely large, the distance $\mid \vec{\rho}_{sw} \mid$ from H_{sw} to A_{sw} becomes too long to be connected by the lengths of thigh and calf. This problem is solved by increasing the angle at the ball of foot until $\mid \vec{\rho}_{sw} \mid$ becomes less than the sum of thigh and calf. Then $\vec{\rho}_{sw}$ is used to get the joint angles at ankle, knee, and hip.

The Swing Leg at the Single Stance Phase

The trajectory (top view) followed by the swing ankle is approximated by a second degree Casteljau curve [Far88]. The 3 control points are given by the position D_1 of the current swing ankle at TO, D_2 which is the symmetric point of the stance ankle with respect to the line α, and the ankle position D_3 at the next heel strike point (Figure 5.9).

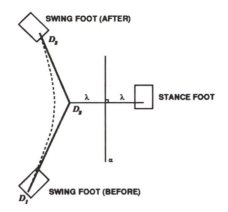

Figure 5.9: The Path of the Swing Foot.

The height component of the ankle is determined by the underlying 1D algorithm. So now we have the locations A_{sw} and H_{sw}, and can determine the swing leg configuration except for the two indeterminacies. At the moment of heelstrike, the swing leg should have been prepared for the next step. Because linear walking is assumed from HS and TO, the hip and ankle angles in swing leg should become 0 except for the bending direction. So we should somehow adjust the swing leg and foot from the *chaos configuration* (at TO) to the *ordered configuration* (at the next HS).

At toe off, the displaced (rotated around the forward axis) foot gets to the normal position very quickly and it is approximated by an exponential function that decreases rapidly to 0: for some positive constant G, we let θ_3^x at time t be

$$\bar{\theta}(t) = \bar{\theta}(0) \cdot \exp^{\frac{-Gt}{t_{sw}}} \tag{5.15}$$

where t is the elapsed time after TO, and t_{sw} is the duration between the TO and the next HS. The rotation of the swing leg around the the axis from the swing hip to the swing ankle is approximated by a parabola given by

$$\tilde{\theta}(t) = \tilde{\theta}(0) \cdot (\frac{t_{sw} - t}{t_{sw}})^2 \tag{5.16}$$

If the 2D locomotion path is actually a straight line, the walk generated is exactly the same as the walk given by the underlying 1D system. For example, in the consideration of swing leg motion during the single stance phase, D_1, D_2, and D_3 will be collinear and parallel to the walking path. Also in the equations 5.15 and 5.16, both $\theta_3^x(0)$ and $\theta_7^z(0)$ will be 0 and the trajectory of the swing leg will be exactly the same as that of 1D walking.

5.2.4 Examples

Figure 5.10 shows foot steps generated by the interactive *step editor*. Figure 5.11 shows the walking path generated by the interactive *path editor*. Fig-

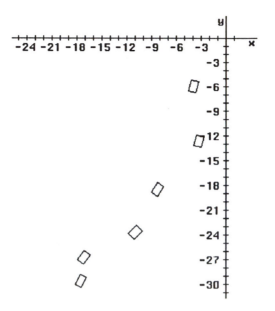

Figure 5.10: Steps Generated by the Step Editor.

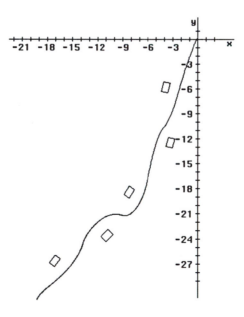

Figure 5.11: Steps Generated by the Path Editor.

ure 5.12 shows snapshots during a turning step. Finally, Figure 5.13 shows a path generated incrementally by the approach and avoidance behaviors.

5.3 Strength Guided Motion

[3]Human motion is likely to be hybrids of many motion and path generation techniques. The task is to find effective combinations that provide realistic motion behaviors while simultaneously offering the user reasonable and intuitive control mechanisms. We have already seen several methods using constraints and other simple control methods that implement various *basic* human activities such as reaching, looking, grasping, and balancing. Now we will look closer at a task-level control algorithm for object manipulation by an end-effector, such as lifting a load to a specified position in space. The resulting motion is certainly dictated by the geometric limits and link structure of the body; but more importantly the motion is strongly influenced by the *strength* and *comfort* of the agent.

5.3.1 Motion from Dynamics Simulation

Torques may be used to physically simulate motions of a figure. Typically the joint responses are conditioned by springs and dampers so that responses to external forces can be computed. Such force- and torque-based methods are called dynamic simulations [Gir87, Gir91, AGL87, IC87, WB85, Wil87, FW88, Wil91, Hah88, HH87, Bar89]. Solving the dynamic equations, an initial value problem, is computationally expensive, especially if the joints are stiff [AGL87]. Natural external forces such as gravity and collision reactions easily yield motions which are free-swinging or passive (purely reactive), but which give the unfortunate impression of driving a hapless mannequin or puppet. As might be expected, the best examples of dynamic simulation come from crash studies [Pra84] where rapid deceleration produces forces that typically overwhelm any agent-initiated torques. In less violent motions, the torques may be derived from a spring or vibration model. Such have been used to create convincing motions of worms, snakes, and other flexible objects [Mil88, PW89], but this cannot be the same mechanism used for human figure motion. Dynamic simulations are annoyingly difficult to control by an animator since force space specifications are highly non-intuitive.

Kinematic and inverse kinematic approaches are easier to manipulate and may create the right "look," but suffer from potentially unrealistic (or unspecified) velocities or torques in the body joints. These problems have been addressed as boundary value problems with objective functions. The trajectories are then solved by global optimization approaches [WK88, Bre89] or control theory [BN88], but their methods presume complete knowledge of the driving conditions and overall constraints.

---

[3]Philip Lee.

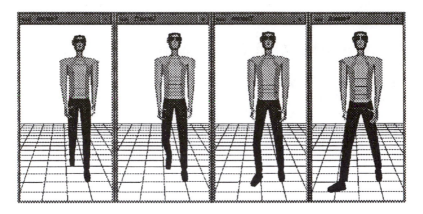

Figure 5.12: Snapshots during a Turning Step.

Figure 5.13: Incremental Walk Behavior.

Robotics emphasizes accomplishing a motion within constraints and optimizing it with respect to some criteria such as time, torque, energy, or obstacles [Bob88, HS85b, KN87, Kha87, MK85, SL87]. Bioengineers try to determine if human motion conforms to some optimality criterion, such as time or energy [BC68, CJ71, YN87, Yeo76]. Given its range and diversity, human motion is not optimal with respect to a single criteria.

Despite these various approaches to the human motion problem, none has been successful at specifying a task by describing a load and a placement goal, and then completing the task in a realistic (though possibly suboptimal) manner. There have been efforts to generate a path between two endpoints [AAW74, Ayo91, SH86, KR79, SSSN85], but the usual solution incorporates constraints and a single objective function that is optimized.

5.3.2 Incorporating Strength and Comfort into Motion

We offer a solution which blends kinematic, dynamic and biomechanical information when planning and executing a path. The task is described by the starting position, the load (weight) that needs to be transported, and a goal position for the load. Some simple additional parameters help select from the wide range of possible paths by invoking biomechanical and performance constraints in a natural fashion. Thus a path is determined from a general model rather than provided by default or by an animator. In addition, the algorithm is incremental: it has the ability to adapt to changing forces that are required to complete a task. The basic premise of the method is that a person tends to operate within a *comfort* region which is defined by *available strength*. This is even more probable when the person has to move a heavy object.

We assume that a person tends to operate within a comfort region dictated by muscular strength, especially when moving a heavy object. When a person has to accomplish a given task, say lifting a box or cup, he starts from some initial posture and then plans the direction for his hand to move. This planning is based on the person's perception of his strength, comfort range, and the importance of staying along a particular path. After a direction is determined, he tries to move in that direction for a short distance with joint rates that maintain the body's discomfort level below a particular threshold. Once the position is reached another direction is selected by balancing the need to finish the task as directly as possible with restrictions derived from the body's limitations. Again, joint rates can be determined once a new direction is established.

The objective is to find the trajectories, both joint and end-effector, that a human-like linkage would traverse to complete a lifting task The task can be specified as a force that has to be overcome or imparted to reach a goal position over an entire path. The task specification can be generalized to describe a complicated task by letting the force be a function of body position, hand position, time, or other factors. In general, task specification can be represented by a *force trajectory*. In addition to task specification by a force trajectory, we have seen other behaviors in which human motion is guided by constraints limiting joint and end-effector trajectories. Constraints that guide the end effector motion are *discomfort level, perceived exertion*, and *strength*.

Discomfort level is defined in a mechanical sense. It is found by calculating, over the entire body, the maximum torque ratio: current torque divided by the maximum torque at each individual joint for the current joint position and velocity. The *Comfort level* is just $1 - discomfort$. In general, when humans move they try to maintain their effort below a particular discomfort level. Therefore, it is desirable to dictate a motion that minimizes the maximum torque ratio of a body in order to maximize the comfort level.

Perceived exertion is a variable used to indicate the expected level of difficulty in completing a task. It depends on the perception of the amount of strength required (an implicit function of the force trajectory) and the amount of strength available. If perceived exertion is low then the discomfort level is not expected to be exceeded for the paths "likely" to be taken to satisfy a task, especially for a path that travels a straight line between the initial body position and the goal. However, if the perceived exertion is high, then the end-effector path needs to deviate from a straight path in order to abide by the comfort constraint. Perceived exertion is represented by a cone which is defined by the maximum deviation angle of a path from its current position.

Strength – the maximum achievable joint torque – also dictates end effector motion and path. For testing the strength-guided motion behavior any suitable strength formulation would suffice; we used empirical data collected by Abhilash Pandya of NASA Johnson Space Center [PMA+91]. There are two strength curves to represent the two muscle group strengths (flexor and extensor) at each DOF.

5.3.3   Motion Control

The motion controller consists of three components (Figure 5.14):

1. Condition Monitor which monitors the state of a body and suggests motion strategies.

2. Path Planning Scheme (PPS) which plans the direction that an end-effector will move.

3. Rate Control Process (RCP) which determines the joint rates for motion.

The *condition monitor* reports on the current state of a body: current position, maximum strength for a current position, current joint torques, etc. It then suggests motion strategies to the *path planning scheme* which determines an end-effector's direction of travel. The amount of motion of the end-effector in the suggested direction of travel can be arbitrarily set. The rate of travel, constrained by torque, for a path interval can then be computed by the *rate control process*. After the joint rates are resolved and new joint positions are found, these procedures are repeated until the entire joint path is mapped

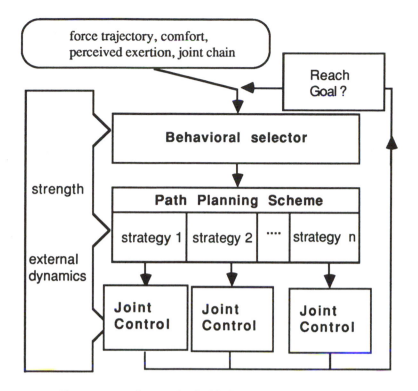

Figure 5.14: Strength Guided Motion Architecture.

out in a manner that satisfies the specified task. This system architecture is an iterative process which allows changes to the parameters at any time through other external processes. Possible situations to alter any of the parameters are dropping or changing the mass of a load, redirecting the goal, or encountering an obstacle. This is different from the global nature of optimal control-based algorithms. We handle similar global considerations through an external process [LWZB90].

Condition Monitor

The condition monitor gathers information about the current state of a body, assembles the information, and suggests a motion strategy for the next procedure to process. The motion strategies are a function of the constraint parameters: comfort, perceived exertion, and strength. Each motion strategy, based on the constraints, concentrates on a separate fundamental aspect of motion. The strategies can be divided into those that represent indirect joint control and those that represent direct joint control. For indirect joint control strategies, the end-effector's need to reach a goal is more important than joint considerations; and for direct joint control, joint considerations are more important than reaching a goal. We can also interpret the strategies as particular optimization problems. The condition monitor is the highest level of the three procedures in predicting a path.

Path Planning Scheme

The path planning scheme, guided by the condition monitor, determines the direction to move. In general, the output of any system is bounded by its headroom: the available range of a variable within a constraint. In the case when there is much strength in a system (a situation where indirect joint control applies) the headroom can be used to suggest incremental joint displacements, $d\theta$. A larger headroom allows a larger displacement. The mapping between the cartesian displacement and the joint displacement is

$$d\mathbf{x} = \mathbf{J}d\theta \tag{5.17}$$

where $\mathbf{J}$ is the $3 \times n$ Jacobian matrix and n is the number of joint displacements. If the headroom for each joint is represented by a weighting vector $\mathbf{w}$ proportional to $d\theta$, then

$$d\hat{\mathbf{x}} = \mathbf{J}\mathbf{w} \tag{5.18}$$

where $d\hat{\mathbf{x}}$ is a normalized direction of reach. The direction $d\hat{\mathbf{x}}$ is then compared against a cone representing the feasible directions of travel derived from perceived exertion. If $d\hat{\mathbf{x}}$ is within the cone then the direction of motion should be $d\hat{\mathbf{x}}$, otherwise the direction can be $d\hat{\mathbf{x}}$ projected onto the cone.

When the system is relatively weak, the suggested direction of motion must not violate the strength constraints. The decision process should shift importance from one strategy where the desirability to reach a goal is a major component of determining a suggested motion to an alternative strategy of avoiding positions where the joints are greatly strained. This leads to schemes where direct joint control is imperative to avoid positions where joints are strained [Lee92].

Rate Control Process

The rate control process, the most basic of the three procedures, resolves the speed with which a body moves along a prescribed end-effector path. This requires the use of dynamics, especially when the motion is fast. However, the incorporation of dynamics is difficult. When torques are specified to drive a motion (direct dynamics), control is a problem; when the driving forces are derived by kinematic specification (inverse dynamics), the forces are useful for only a short time interval and they may violate the body's torque capacity; and finally, when the forces optimize a particular function between two sets of positional constraints (boundary value problem), the method presumes that the optimization criteria is valid for the body's entire range of motion.

Dynamics equations can be interpreted as constraint equations solving for joint trajectories if they satisfy the conditions imposed by specific end-effector path and torque limits. The dynamics equations can be reformulated so that they provide a mapping between an end-effector path and a binding torque constraint. A binding torque constraint is the maximum torque allowed to drive a body with maximum end-effector acceleration without the end-effector deviating from the prescribed path. A greater torque would cause excessive inertial force and therefore, undesirable path deviation. From the derivation of the reformulated dynamics equations originally derived to solve for path completion in minimum time [Bob88], joint trajectories can be found from the acceleration of an end-effector. In addition to finding the trajectories, the reformulated dynamic equations implicitly determine the force functions (joint torques) to guide an end-effector along a specified path.

Torque limits are established by the current discomfort constraint. The discomfort level variable dcl determines the torque limit at each joint by a simple relation:

$$dcl = \frac{\tau_{c,i}}{\tau(\theta)_{max,i}} \qquad (5.19)$$

where $\tau_{c,i}$ is the torque load for a particular joint i. The value $\tau(\theta)_{max,i}$ is the maximum torque for the joint's current position obtained by querying the strength curves. When the value of dcl becomes greater than one, there is no more strength to accomplish a task and therefore the attempt to complete a task should cease. The discomfort level can be adjusted to achieve a desired motion. It influences both the rate of task completion and the direction of travel.

5.3.4 Motion Strategies

This is a catalogue of human motion strategies that are evaluated in the condition monitor and are executed in the path planner. The strategies are given in the order of increasing discomfort.

Available Torque

When a person moves, the tendency is to move the stronger joint. This is similar to the forces due to a spring or other types of potential forces. A stronger spring, based on the spring's stiffness coefficient, would yield a larger displacement per unit time than a weaker spring. Similarly, for a human, the amount of displacement for a joint depends not only on the strength that a joint is capable of, but mainly on the amount of strength that is currently available. The amount of strength available, which is based on the difference between the current required torque to support a particular position and the *effective maximum strength* (the maximum strength factored by comfort), is called *torque availability*. If torque availability is low, motion should not be encouraged. Conversely, if the torque availability is high, the joint should do more of the work. Torque availability is the driving factor for a joint to move and to thereby redistribute the joint torques so that the comfort level is more uniform.

Reducing Moment

As a joint approaches its effective maximum strength, the joint should move in a manner that avoids further stress (discomfort) while still trying to reach the goal. A path towards the goal is still possible as long as the maximum strength is not surpassed for any of the joints. As the body gets more stressed it should attempt to reduce the moment caused by a force trajectory by reducing the distance normal to the force trajectory's point of application. In addition, a reduction in moment increases the torque availability of (at least) the joint that is rapidly approaching its maximum strength. The reduction in the total moment involves examining the moments on a joint by joint basis. At each joint a virtual displacement is given to determine if that displacement provides sufficient moment reduction to continue moving in that direction. This strategy assumes that the body has enough effective strength to allow its joints to move to positions where the overall stress level of the body is smaller than if the joints were only guided by kinematic demands.

Pull Back

The two previous strategies depend on the current torque being less than the maximum strength. In these cases, maneuverability in torque space is high and therefore an end-effector can still consider moving toward a goal without exceeding any joint's maximum strength.

When a particular joint reaches its maximum strength, however, then that joint can no longer advance toward a goal from the current configuration. The Pull Back strategy proposes that the end-effector approach the goal from another configuration. In an effort to determine another approach to the goal, the constraint of moving toward a goal within a restricted path deviation can be relaxed. The emphasis of the strategy is one where the joints dictate an improved path in terms of torques. This can be accomplished by increasing the *ultimate available torque* – the difference of maximum strength to current torque – for a set of *weak joints* – joints that are between the joint which has no ultimate available strength and an end-effector.

In general, the joint with the least amount of ultimate available torque will reverse direction and cause the end-effector to pull back (move away from its goal). The idea is to increase the overall comfort level. When the joints form a configuration that has a greater level of comfort, there might be enough strength to complete the task. Then the governing strategy could return to Reducing Moment, which allows the end-effector to proceed toward the goal.

The Pull Back strategy leads to a *stable configuration*. This is a posture that a set of joints should form so that it can withstand large forces, such as those caused when changing from a near-static situation to one that is dynamic.

Added Joint, Recoil, and Jerk

When the three strategies, Available Torque, Reducing Moment, and Pull Back have been exhausted and an agent still cannot complete a task, it is obvious that the *active joints* – the joints that were initially assigned to the task – cannot supply sufficient strength. When this occurs it should be determined if the task should be aborted or if there are other means of acquiring additional strength. One mode of acquiring more strength is to add a joint to the chain of active joints. This assumes that the added joint is much stronger than any of the active joints.

Another mode to consider is to use the added joint to jerk – apply with maximum force – the set of active joints. Jerk reduces the forces necessary to complete a task for the set of active joints. Before jerking is initiated, a stable configuration should be formed by the active joints. After a stable configuration has been formed and the added joint has jerked, the active joints can then proceed to reach their goal since the required torques have decreased. A third possibility is to recoil another set of joints and then jerk with the recoiled set of joints in order to reduce the forces needed by the set of active joints to complete a task. For example, a weight lifter sometimes recoils his legs and then pushs off to reduce the force required in his arms.

5.3.5 Selecting the Active Constraints

The path determination process has been uncoupled into two active constraints: comfort and perceived exertion. In the rate control process involving dynamics, the two constraining parameters must be active to determine the joint rates.

At higher levels of control (such as in the path planner), both need not be active simultaneously. In fact, as the torque levels change the applicability of a particular constraint to predict motion also changes. We use a model that relates the comfort level to the constraints. The strategies bound various comfort levels.

High Comfort. The perceived exertion constraint is not active but the comfort constraint is, because any changes in acceleration (not necessarily large) may cause a joint to exceed the allowable discomfort level. In general, the force trajectory associated with a motion of high comfort is negligible, but dynamics is important because of the relatively large inertial effects of the body. This group is bounded by motions that are categorized by *zero jerk* condition [Gir91] and Available Torque.

Regular Comfort. The end-effector can advance toward the goal. Perceived exertion and comfort are loosely constraining and dynamics should be evaluated. Available Torque and Reducing Moment bounds this comfort level.

Discomfort. At this point the discomfort level for one or more joints are surpassed. The perceived exertion constraint needs to be changed so that a larger path deviation is allowed. Motion should have slowed down considerably, therefore dynamics is not important and, most likely, is not meaningful. This group is formed by Reducing Moment and Pull Back.

Intolerable Discomfort Many of the joints' comfort levels have been exceeded and there may be other joints which could be approaching their maximum available torque. In such a situation, strategies can be combined. The pool of strategies are Added Joint, Pull Back, Recoil, and Jerk. Perceived exertion is relaxed and depending on the combination of the strategies, dynamics might be important.

5.3.6   Strength Guided Motion Examples

The strategies for Available Torque, Reducing Moment, Pull Back, and Added Joint are implemented in *Jack*. Figures 5.15, 5.16, 5.17, and 5.18 show the paths that were produced from these conditions. The task is to place an increasingly heavy load from various initial positions at a goal which is located above the body's head.

In Figure 5.15, there are two curves which outline the path of the hand. The right curve is for a task that involves lifting a 10 pound object; the left curve is for a 20 pound object. For the right curve, because the object is relatively light, a fast motion is predicted and the solution resembles a minimum time path. For the left curve, the heavier weight draws the hand closer to the body. This path is rough because it is at the boundary of a solution determined by Available Torque and Reducing Moment. In Figure 5.16, the right curve is for the 20 pound lift, and the left curve is for a lift of 30 pounds. Once again the algorithm predicts that a heavier object would bring the hand closer to the body.

Figure 5.17 shows the body with a heavier load (35 pounds). The body immediately executes Pull Back. In this case, the body pulls back to a region of high comfort and therefore the approach to the goal is smooth, without the rough path evident in the previous figures. In Figure 5.18, the joint chain, initially composed of the joints between the hand and the shoulder, is allowed to extend to the waist. The algorithm decides that it is better to distribute the weight with more joints. Figure 5.18 shows the advantage of including the waist in the set of active joints.

These algorithms can be applied to any type of task, as long as it is force-based: even rising from a chair. A force trajectory is used to represent the body weight and the shoulder's normal position when standing is used as the force goal. The body leans forward to balance its weight (a consequence of Reducing Moment) to reach the shoulder goal.

The average time of a path generation is under 10 seconds. Since our examples mainly involved heavy loads, static torque computations were used. The internal joint chain positions are determined by *Jack* inverse kinematics.

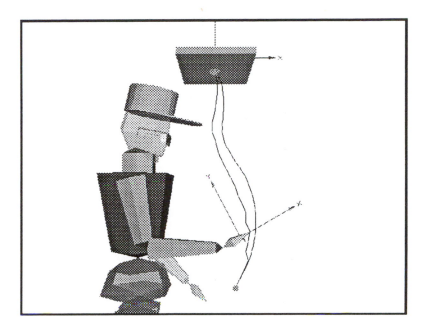

Figure 5.15: Lifting a 20 pound and 10 pound Object.

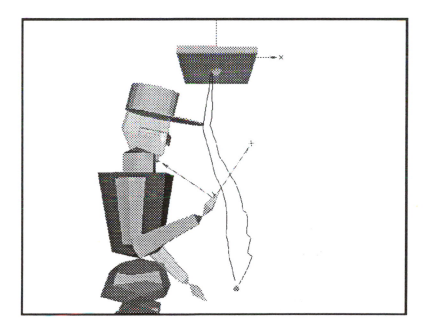

Figure 5.16: Lifting a 30 pound and 20 pound Object.

Figure 5.17: Pull Back.

Figure 5.18: Added Joint.

5.3.7 Evaluation of this Approach

We have tried to generate a realistic motion path for a slow, weight-lifting task represented by a time- and position-dependent force trajectory. The method maps out an entire path automatically and incrementally for a force trajectory over a set of constraints based on comfort level, perceived exertion, and strength. Because the body state is constantly updated, these constraints can also be a function of an external model, such as fatigue.

Motion is generated by integrating a condition monitor which suggests basic motion strategies, a path planning scheme which locally plans the end-effector's path and a rate control process which controls the joint rates. The condition monitor offers strategies to pursue by balancing the goal of the task against the resources that are currently available. The path planning scheme proposes a direction of travel by executing the basic strategies. The elusive force function that previous investigators have sought can be found by changing the role of the dynamic equations to a constraint equation which is established with a dynamics model. By selecting the most restrictive constraint from the constraint equations, the maximum joint rates can be computed.

Altering the constraints used in this problem still gives a goal-directed motion that conforms to physical laws. We see this capability as an inherently model-driven, flexible, and crucial component for generating more natural human behaviors. We will see shortly in Section 5.4 how this approach can be extended to include collision avoidance during more complex actions.

5.3.8 Performance Graphs

Three types of graphs are developed for the user to analyze some pertinent mechanical relations of the agent's movements. The properties that are tracked and graphed are comfort levels, work, and energy (Figure 5.19, 5.20, and 5.21).

The histogram of comfort shows the current discomfort value as well as the user-specified desired maximum. The effective comfort level is the actual comfort level that controls the movements. It includes factors that may affect the desired comfort level. Currently, an exponential function representing fatigue is one of the factors that can alter the effective comfort level.

The graph of work the agent performs at each iteration is computed as

$$\Delta W_j = \sum_{i=n}^{n} \tau_i \, \Delta \theta_i \qquad (5.20)$$

where n is the number of DOFs, τ_i is the current torque of the ith joint, and $\Delta\theta_i$ is the change in joint position ($\theta_j - \theta_{j-1}$).

The energy graph represents the sum of all the work performed by the joints since the beginning of the task. Because the amount of energy that is expended grows very fast, the curve that represents energy is automatically rescaled to fit within the designated plot area when necessary.

Figures 5.22, 5.23, and 5.24 show the comparative trajectories of the hand as load, comfort level, and perceived exertion are varied.

5.3.9   Coordinated Motion

Coordinated motion is when the execution of a task requires more than one set of linkages either from the same agent or from two separate agents. Our implementation of coordinated motion follows the same parameter control philosophy. As in the task specification of a single linkage, a coordinated task is made a function of comfort and path deviation.

The coordination between the two joint chains is based on a master and slave relation: the weaker chain is the master and the stronger chain is the slave. The algorithm first determines which is the weaker linkage (master), then its path is generated according to the strategy that is appropriate for its comfort level. The other joint chain (slave) must comply with the master's new position. Simple geometry from the master's new position, the dimension of the object, and the magnitude of the slave's incremental displacement is used to determine the slave's new position (see Figure 5.25). The magnitude of the master and slave's incremental path is a nominal distance factored by their respective comfort level; the master will travel less than the slave. The master-slave assignment switches whenever the relative comfort – the difference between the two linkages' comfort level – reverses.

The specification of a coordinated task begins by instantiating each of the joint chains as a separate task. Then the goal and the weight of the object to be moved is stated. Next, the kinematic relation between the two linkages is specified; this involves identifying the attachment points on the object (handle) with the corresponding end-effector. This is done for each of the chains that participates in the coordinated task. The end-effectors are automatically attached to the handle.

Finally, two control parameters which control the characteristics of the path need to be specified. The first control parameter, *allowable comfort difference*, specifies a tolerance in the relative comfort level before a master-slave switch is made. A graph can be called to display the difference in comfort between the two joint chains. The other parameter controls the amount of *allowable path deviation*. The user can control the amount of path deviation by entering a ratio that determines the relative propensity between the path of moving to the goal directly and the path that is sensitive to the agent's stress level. Unlike a task involving a single chain, the motion of each chain cannot deviate or switch strategy without considering the other chain. This means that the strategies of the two linkages should coincide; both linkages performing Pull-Back would not be permitted. Because of this limitation, the strategies available in this current implementation are only Available-Torque and Reduce-Moment.

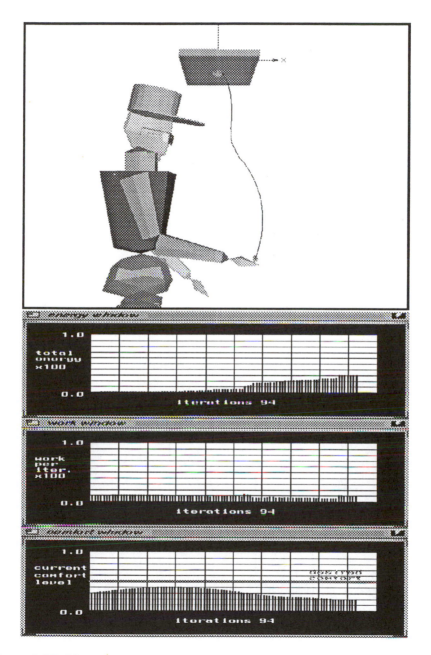

Figure 5.19: Plots of Comfort Level, Work, and Energy (10 lb., pe = 0.30, cl = 0.50)

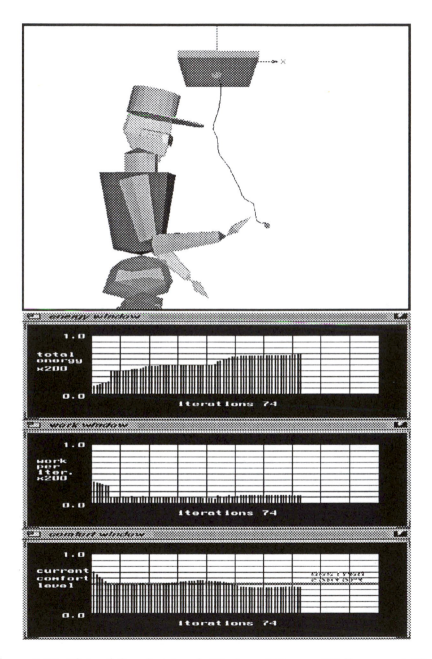

Figure 5.20: Plots of Comfort Level, Work, and Energy (20 lb., pe = 0.30, cl = 0.50)

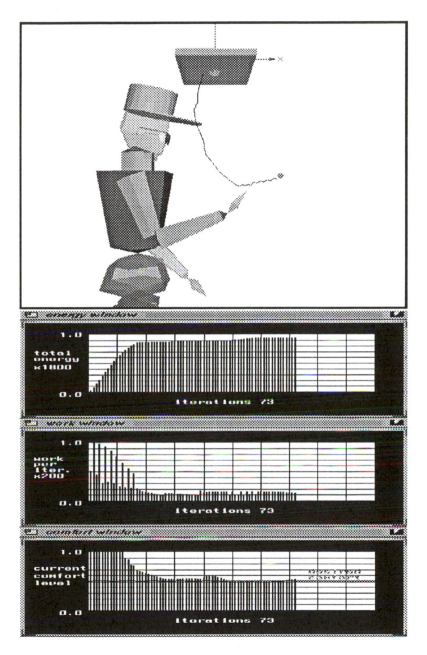

Figure 5.21: Plots of Comfort Level, Work, and Energy (30 lb., pe = 0.30, cl = 0.50)

Figure 5.22: 30 lb., pe = 0.30, cl = (0.40, 0.50, 0.85)

Figure 5.23: 30 lb., pe = 0.30, cl = (0.40, 0.50, 0.75, 0.85)

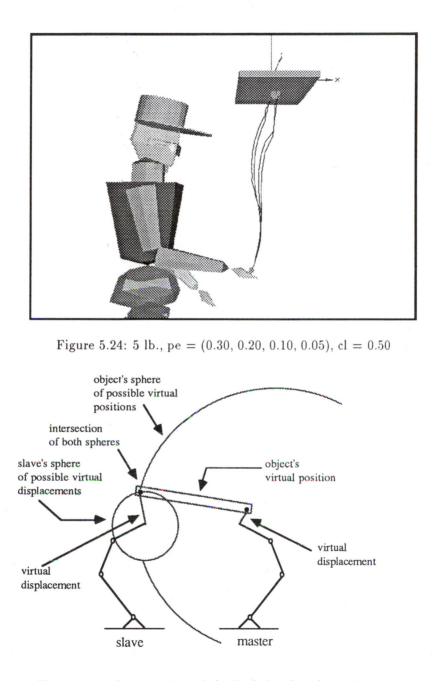

Figure 5.24: 5 lb., pe $= (0.30, 0.20, 0.10, 0.05)$, cl $= 0.50$

Figure 5.25: Construction of the Path for Coordinated Motion.

5.4   Collision-Free Path and Motion Planning

[4]Collision-free path planning has applications in a variety of fields such as robotics task planning, computer aided manufacturing, human figure motion studies and computer graphics simulations. A collision-free path for an articulated figure is the path along which the articulated figure moves from an initial configuration to a final configuration without hitting any obstacles residing in the same environment as the articulated figure.

A great deal of research has been devoted to the motion planning problem in the area of robotics within the last 10 years, e.g. [LPW79, LP87, LP83, Bro83b, BLP83, Bro83a, Don84, DX89, KZ86, Gou84]. However, despite the applicability of motion planning techniques to computer graphics simulations, the problem has not been addressed much in the computer graphics community [Bre89, DLRG91].

Articulated human figures are characterized by a branching tree structure with many DOFs. Existing algorithms in robotics fall short in handling some of the issues encountered when dealing with these types of figures. We present novel algorithms that can address all these issues. The basic idea is that instead of treating all the DOFs in the figure together, we divide them up into groups and treat these groups one by one and playback the path in a coordinated manner when all the groups are considered. Our motion planning system can also take into consideration the strength data of human figures so that the planned motion will obey strength availability criteria (Section 5.3).

5.4.1   Robotics Background

The major challenge of our problem is to handle a redundant branching articulated figure with many DOFs. Many of the robotics algorithms deal with manipulators with relatively few DOFs, e.g. mobile robots which typically have 3 DOFs or arm-like robots which have 6. Many of these algorithms are based on the use of the configuration space (C space) which is the space encompassing the DOFs of the robot [LPW79, LP83]. The inherent difficulty with this approach is due to the high dimensionality of the C space. It is well known that the worst case time bound for motion planning for a robot arm is exponential in the dimensionality of its C space [SS83a, SS83b]. It is only during the last few years that motion planning algorithms that can handle manipulators with many DOFs have been presented [BLL89b, BLL89a, BL89, Gup90, Fav84, Bre89].

Very few studies consider articulated figures with branches. Barraquand *et al* gave an example involving a manipulator with 2 branches [BLL89b, BLL89a, BL89]. In their work, they create an artificial potential field in the 3D workspace and the free path is found by tracking the valleys. A gain in efficiency is obtained as a result of the clever selection of potential functions and heuristics. However, it is not clear how these can be selected in general.

---

[4] Wallace Ching.

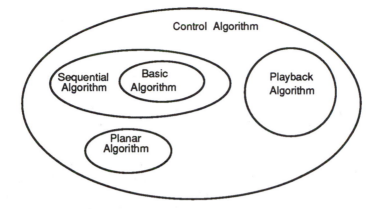

Figure 5.26: Different Modules and their Associated Algorithms in the Path Planning System.

Faverjon *et al* [Fav84] partition the free space into oct-trees and uses some probability measures to cut down the search tree during the A* search. Gupta [Gup90] handles sequential linkages with many DOFs using a sequential search technique which basically treats the individual DOFs one by one instead of considering all of them together. The initial stage of our path planner is based on his work.

5.4.2 Using Cspace Groups

The main idea of our path planner is to handle the DOFs of the articulated figure not all at once but a certain number at a time. The general principle of our path planner is first to divide the DOFs into a number of groups which we call *Cspace groups*. We then compute the collision-free motion for the DOFs in each group successively, starting from the first group. After the motion of the DOFs in group i has been planned, we parameterize the resulting motion with a parameter t. The motion for the DOFs in group $i + 1$ will then be planned along this path by controlling the DOFs associated with it. The problem is then posed in a $t \times \theta^k$ space if there are k DOFs in this group. We proceed in this manner along the whole figure structure and solve for the motion for all the groups. Finally a playback routine is invoked to playback the final collision-free path for the figure.

Our system adopts a modular design in that it is made up of a number of modules each of which is based on an algorithm (Figure 5.26). Each module carries out a particular function and contributes to the whole path finding process.

On a more global perspective, the path finding procedure can be viewed as consisting of two phases: the *computation* phase and the *playback* phase. All of the steps involved in these phases are performed by the algorithms described in later sections.

The overall path planning procedure is outlined as follows:

- **Computation** Phase:

  1. Partition the articulated figure's DOFs into *Cspace groups* according to a grouping scheme.

  2. Impose an order of traversal among the Cgroups. For a human figure, we use a depth-first traversal. This means we plan the motion for one arm and then another.

  3. Invoke the *control algorithm* that handles traversal of the tree and finds the final collision-free path. This algorithm will actually call upon a subsidiary algorithm, *sequential algorithm*, to compute the free path along a branch of the tree structure. The *sequential algorithm* will in turn call another subsidiary algorithm, the *basic algorithm*, to compute the path for the DOFs within each Cgroup.

- **Playback** Phase:

  After all the Cspace groups have been considered, a special *playback algorithm* will be called upon to traverse the tree structure in a reverse order, collect and coordinate all the computed information and finally playback the overall collision-free path in discrete time frames. These time frames can be further interpolated to produce smooth motion. Ideally the behavioral simulation loop controls the frame timing and hence the production of the output postures.

The translational movement of the articulated figure as a whole on a plane can also be generated with this planner. In this case, the figure resembles a mobile robot with two degrees of translational freedom and one degree of rotational freedom. The module that handles this case is named the *Planar Algorithm*.

Figure 5.27 shows the general redundant branching articulated structure and symbols that we will use for reference. We will mainly focus on the upper body of the human figure. The system can be easily applied to the legs to provide stepping or foothold movements as we will show later.

5.4.3 The Basic Algorithm

The particular algorithm we have chosen is the one presented by Lozano-Pérez in [LP87] due to its simplicity and intuitiveness. It first constructs the C space for the articulated figure. For the sake of completeness, the process is described below.

If the manipulator has n links, its configuration space can be constructed as follows:

1. $i = 1$.

2. While $(i < n)$ do

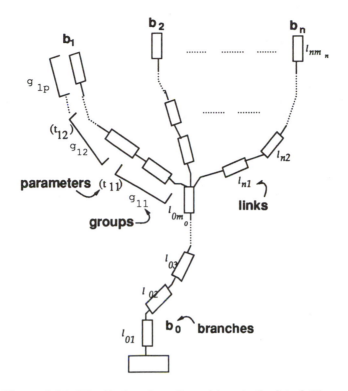

Figure 5.27: The Redundant Branching Articulated Figure.

(a) Ignore links beyond link i, and find the ranges of legal values of q_i by rotating link i around the position of joint i determined by the current value ranges of $q_1, ..., q_{i-1}$ and check for collision with the surrounding obstacles. Self collision can be avoided by checking collision with linkages from the same figure as well. Mark those joint values at which link i will have a collision as forbidden.

(b) Sample the legal range of q_i at the specified resolution.

(c) Increment i and repeat step (a) for each of these value ranges.

The free space is then represented by a *regions* data structure to explore the connectivity between the cells. A graph is then built on these region nodes and an A* search is conducted to search for a free path from the start node to the goal node.

5.4.4   The Sequential Algorithm

The *Sequential Algorithm* handles the motion planning problem for the Cspace groups along a sequential branch. This algorithm is based on but differs from Gupta's work.

Referring to Figure 5.28, let n be the total number of *Cspace groups* on this branch. Let the joint DOFs associated with the groups be represented by q_{ij} where i is the group number and j is from 1 to m_i where m_i is the maximum number of DOFs group i has. Let r_i be the reference vertex for group i. It is basically the distal vertex of the link associated with the DOFs in the group i. Let $r_i(t)$ denote the trajectory of the reference vertex r_i. The initial and goal configurations of the arm are given as q_{ij}^s and q_{ij}^g, $i=1..n$; $j = 1..m_i$.

The algorithm is as follows:

1. Compute a collision-free trajectory for the links associated with group 1. The trajectory of the reference vertex on its link will be $r_1(t)$.

2. $i = 2$.

3. While ($i < n$)

   (a) along $r_{i-1}(t)$, discretize the path according to a pre-specified resolution. Compute a collision-free trajectory for the DOFs in the ith group from q_{ij}^s to q_{ij}^g for $j = 1..m_i$ using the *basic* algorithm.

   (b) given $q_{1j}(t), q_{2j}(t), ..., q_{ij}(t)$, compute $r_i(t)$ using forward kinematics.

   (c) Increment i.

The parameter used in parameterizing the path already computed can be either interpreted as temporal or non-temporal. For a temporal interpretation of the parameter, the path computed has to be monotonic with respect to the parameter t simply because we cannot travel backward in time. Hence backtracking within the Cspace group is not allowed and the chance of finding a path is greatly restricted. In the example shown in Figure 5.29, we will not be able to come up with a path without backtracking. We have adopted a non-temporal interpretation of the parameter in most cases as this will increase the chance of finding a path.

Each C group deals with one parameter and a certain number of DOFs. The number of DOFs can vary between C groups so as to fit into the structure of the figure. For example, the shoulder joint can be handled by one C group with 3 DOFs.

The number of DOFs handled at a time also affects the degree of optimality of the resulting path (with respect to some criteria). Theoretically, the optimal path can only be obtained by searching through the n-dimensional C space built from considering all n DOFs together. However, such an algorithm has been proven to be exponential in the dimensionality of its C space [SS83a]. There is a customary trade off between speed and optimality.

Our choice of using the region graph instead of the visibility graph allows for the path to be positioned farther away from the obstacles, hence leaving more room for the next linkage (Figure 5.30).

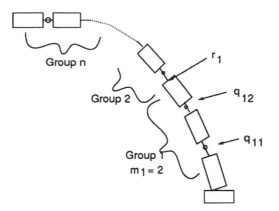

Figure 5.28: A Sequential Linkage.

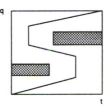

Figure 5.29: An Example Showing the Case that a Path can only be Found with Backtracking which Means the Parameter Takes on a Non-Temporal Interpretation.

5.4.5 The Control Algorithm

The control algorithm performs the entire path planning process:

1. Apply the Planar Algorithm to the whole figure to obtain the planar collision-free translational movement of the figure taken as a whole.

2. Parameterize the resulting motion.

3. Repeat the following to every branch, starting from the first.

   (a) Apply the *Sequential* algorithm to the branch using the last parameter in the first group.

   (b) Parameterize the resulting path computed for this branch according to some prespecified resolution.

   (c) Invoke the PlayBack Algorithm to the branch to obtain the sequence of joint angle values of the branch when moving along the computed path.

   (d) Record this sequence of joint angles in the array *FREEANGLES*.

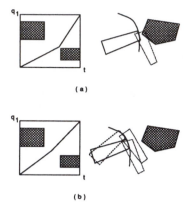

Figure 5.30: (a) A Path that is Too Close to an Obstacle. This Leaves Little Room for the Next Linkage to Maneuver. (b) A Better Path that is Farther Away from the Obstacle.

4. Apply the PlayBack Algorithm to the whole figure, starting from the last group of the very last branch.

5. The angle values obtained can then written into frames for continuous playback.

5.4.6   The Planar Algorithm

The articulated figure can translate and rotate on a plane, navigating around obstacles. The whole figure behaves just like a mobile robot. The path planning algorithm in this case deals with a three dimensional (2 translational, 1 rotational) Cspace. We can handle this case simply with our *basic* algorithm or other existing mobile robot path planning techniques.

5.4.7   Resolving Conflicts between Different Branches

Although the different branches are attached to the same rear link of branch b_0, we do not use the same parameter t that parameterizes the motion of branch b_0 in all these branches. The reason is that the parameters t_{ij} are interpreted as non-temporal in general. Hence, backtracking within the Cspace group is allowed and the values of t_{ij} along the computed path can be non-monotonic. If we use the same parameter in computing the motion for the first groups in all other branches, some of the joint angle values cannot be obtained uniquely during the final playback phase. This reasoning may become clear after looking at the playback algorithm.

Our solution to this problem is to further *parameterize* the already *parameterized path* of the previous branch and then use the new parameterization variable in the next branch.

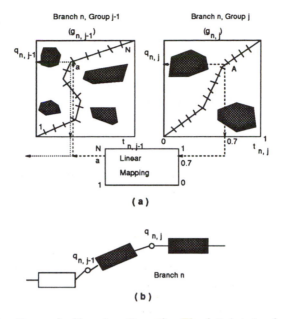

Figure 5.31: An Example Showing How the Final Joint Angle Values of the Whole Figure are Obtained from the Cspace Associated with the Cspace Groups.

5.4.8 Playing Back the Free Path

During the playback phase, we start from the *last group* of branch b_n and then traverse the branches in a backward manner along branch b_{n-1}, b_{n-2} and so on and finally to branch b_0. For example, let Figure 5.31 (a) represent the configuration space for the *last group* of the last branch, i.e. group g_{n,p_n} of branch b_n. We then discretize the free path according to a pre-specified playback resolution. The number of discretization intervals for this last group will be equal to the number of *time frames* for the final simulation.

At every discretized point, say A, there is a corresponding (q, t) pair: the q value is what we should set the last joint DOF to, and the *parameter t* is used to deduce the motion of the preceding group. We first set the last DOF to the q value. Then we use the parameter t in the pair to trace back to the *preceding* (proximal) group. Note that within this preceding group, the parameter t is *monotonic* by definition. Hence we can uniquely determine the corresponding (q, t) pair within this preceding group. By the same token, we can continue tracing back to the groups further preceding this one (Figure 5.31 (a)). We carry on in this fashion recursively until we come to the first group within this branch.

Note that at this point, all joint DOFs along this branch will have been set to their correct value for this simulation time frame. The sequence of joint values along the free path for all the other branches should have also been recorded in the array $FREEANGLES_i$. The parameter value left unused will then be used as an index into the recorded joint angle array and to uniquely determine the set of angles corresponding to the movement of the preceding branch. The rest of the branches are processed similarly.

We will examine the *playback* algorithm by looking into its two components separately: the *Final Playback* algorithm and the *Single Branch Single Frame Playback* algorithm.

The Final Playback Algorithm

The Final Playback algorithm is driven by the behavior simulation cycle and generates the intermediate body postures culminating in the final goal achievement.

- Discretize the path computed for the last group in the last branch into N discrete points according to some pre-specified resolution. This number also determines the total number of key postures or time frames we will generate for the final simulation.

- For each time frame, do the following steps to get back the computed angles.

  1. Apply the **Single Branch Single Frame Playback Algorithm** to branch b_n, the last branch in the figure.

  2. A parameter value will be obtained at the termination of this algorithm. Use this parameter as an array index into $FREEANGLES$ for the next branch. The joint angles recorded for the next branch will be read from the array element pointed to by this parameter value.

  3. Set the joint angles in the next branch to the values read from the array.

  4. The last parameter value read from the array is used to index into the $FREEANGLES$ array for the next branch in a similar manner.

  5. Repeat the same process for the rest of the branches.

  6. Now all the joint angles in the articulated figure have been set to their appropriate values in this time frame. What is left is the *position* of the whole figure. The last parameter value obtained from the last step is used to index into the path computed from the Planar Algorithm. Then we set the whole figure location to that indexed position.

The Single Branch Single Frame Playback Algorithm

Let the branch index we are considering be i. Here branch i has a total of p_i groups. This playback algorithm is called only after the motion for the last group in the branch is computed. This algorithm only deals with one discretized point, and hence only one time frame.

We start from the last group in the branch and go *down* the branch by doing the following on each group.

1. From the discretized point on the computed path, read the values of the $q_{i,j}$s associated with this Cspace group from the axes of the Cspace. This is illustrated in Figure 5.31 (a) with a 2D Cspace as an example.

2. Set the joints in the articulated chain corresponding to these q variables to the values just found.

3. Then read the normalized parameter value $t_{i,j}$ from the t axis.

4. Through a linear mapping, obtain the corresponding discretized point on the path computed for the next group down the branch from this parameter value.

Note that after this algorithm terminates, all the joint angles on this branch will be set to the appropriate values for this simulation time step.

5.4.9   Incorporating Strength Factors into the Planned Motion

In (Section 5.3) we demonstrated that realistic animation of lifting motions can be generated by considering the strength of the human figure. The basic premise of the method is that a person tends to operate within a *comfort* region which is defined by the amount of available torque. The static torque values at all the joints required to sustain a load is a function of figure configuration. The path planner incrementally updates the next joint angle values according to the *available torque* at the current configuration based on a number of motion strategies.

The planning methodology we have described so far divides the DOFs into groups and plans the motion for each group sequentially. Therefore, only after the control algorithm terminates do we have the complete path for each DOF. However, we need to make use of the strength information *during* the planning process. This requires values of all joint angles at a certain configuration. The solution is to use the value of the current parameter and project it over to the rest of the angles that have not yet been computed. The projection function $PROJ$ is arbitrary (since this is only an approximation of reality), so we use just a simple linear interpolation:

$$PROJ(t) = \theta_{initial} + t(\theta_{final} - \theta_{initial}) \ .$$

Since our searching process uses the A* algorithm, a heuristic function is evaluated at every step to find the node that has the smallest value. So far we have been using only a spatial distance measure in this heuristic function. The path found will be optimal up to the size of the *regions* used. Now, however, we have a means to compute the required torque value of a particular configuration, so this heuristic function can include terms representing strength information. The weights attached to these terms represent the relative importance of the quantities they represent. Possible terms to include are:

- **Work Done**. The total work done or energy expended can be measured by the term $\int T(\vec{\theta}) \cdot d\vec{\theta}$. The integration is done over the path taken.

- **Comfort**. The *comfort level* of the resulting motion can be measured by the *available torque* which is the quantity obtained by subtracting the required torque from the strength limit at that particular joint configuration. We can sum up all the contributions along the path as $\int AvailTorque(\vec{\theta}) \cdot d\vec{\theta}$ where the available torque is defined in terms of its elements:

$$AvailTorque(\vec{\theta})_i = \begin{cases} Str(\vec{\theta})_i - T(\vec{\theta})_i & \text{if } Str(\vec{\theta})_i > T(\vec{\theta})_i \\ 0 & \text{otherwise} \end{cases}$$

  The subscript i stands for the i-th element in the vector. Str is the strength limit vector. This integral value will then represent the overall comfort level.

  This term will properly be useful only in the g function as it only affects future actions.

- **Fatigue**. Humans are not like robots: our strength will decrease with time as a result of fatigue. We may include a term such as $\int \|T(\vec{\theta})\| dt$ to avoid taking a path that has a high torque value maintained over a prolonged period of time.

The path found by the collision-free path planner is the best up to the size of the *regions* (the basic entities). Paths within regions are chosen by the strength guided motion heuristics. For example, in Figure 5.32 (a), the left path may be chosen by search to be better than the one on the right. This path can then be further refined by examining local comfort levels and invoking one of the motion heuristics such as *Available Torque*, *Reducing Moment* and *Pull Back*.

5.4.10   Examples

We have experimented with a variety of reaches involving shelves and apertures. Figure 5.33 shows a human figure reaching through two apertures with both arms. The path computed is collision-free and involves more than 20 DOFs. These and similar examples take about 12 to 20 minutes elapsed time to compute, depending on the complexity of the environment.

Simulating the wide range of human motions requires a number of different behavioral skills such as walking, grasping, and lifting. The path planner

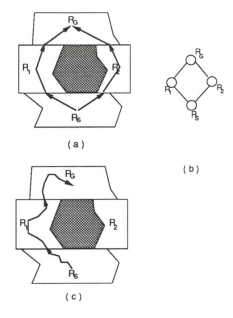

Figure 5.32: (a) Part of a Sample Cspace Showing Two Possible Paths Leading from the Start to the Goal Node. (b) The Corresponding Regions Graph. (c) Path Refinement after Considering Comfortable Motion Heuristics.

interfaces with other existing techniques in simulating more complex human behaviors. Figure 5.34 shows a human figure climbing up a rocky surface. The climbing movement of each limb and the torso translation are produced by the path planner. Each limb is considered in turn by the planner; the other three limbs are fixed by a point (reach) constraint. The spatial locations for each hand grasp and foothold must be pre-specified by the user. Even though our path planner cannot handle closed loop systems directly, such motions can be simulated with the help of other behaviors.

5.4.11 Completeness and Complexity

This planner is an approximate algorithm when backtracking among groups is not employed: it may fail to discover a path even though one exists. When backtracking is employed between groups, the algorithm is turned into a complete algorithm. Alternatively, the DOFs can be re-grouped differently if a path cannot be found for the previous grouping scheme.

The *basic* algorithm within a Cspace group has complexity $O(r^{k-1}(mn)^2)$ where k is the number of DOFs, r is the discretization interval, m is the number of faces and edges for the figure and n for the environment [LP87]. Since the number of DOFs in a Cspace group is bounded, the run time for the *basic* algorithm can be treated as a constant. Consequently the whole algorithm runs in $O(p)$ time where p is the total number of groups in the tree structure without backtracking between groups. With backtracking, the worst case run time for the algorithm is exponential with respect to the number of DOFs. This is the same as a conventional exhaustive search algorithm. We believe that the average run time of the algorithm is fast enough for practical though not interactive use.

5.5 Posture Planning

[5]Motion generation algorithms for geometric figures typically start with initial, final, and sometimes intermediate configurations or postures. From these input postures, "natural" motion sequences are generated which satisfy given optimization criteria, e.g., time or energy. The assumption that the final joint angle configuration of a highly redundant articulated figure such as the human body is known – in advance – is rather unrealistic. Typically, only the task-level goals of the end effectors are known. In order for an agent to move in accordance with such task-level goals, we need to provide the agent with an ability to plan both intermediate and final postures. *Posture planning* uses explicit reasoning along with numerical procedures to find a relatively natural and collision-free sequence of postures that terminates at the desired goal.

The inputs to the posture planner are positional or orientational goals for end effectors. The posture planner finds the appropriate movements of relevant body parts needed to achieve the goals. It discovers a final global posture satisfying the given goals by finding intermediate motions that avoid collision. Typical motions used in the plan include stepping towards the workspace, spreading the legs, bending the upper body at the waist while the whole body remains balanced, and moving the upper arm with respect to the shoulder. Only the geometric aspects of body motion are considered at this time. The agent is assumed to be initially located in the vicinity of the target object so that an end effector goal can be achieved by taking only one or two steps. It is assumed that a given goal is not changed during the posture planning process. Collision-avoidance will be alluded to as necessary but the details are not addressed here [Jun92].

The fundamental problem in achieving postural goals is controlling the massively redundant skeletal DOFs. There are 88 DOFs in the *Jack* model (not counting fingers). Figure 5.35 shows a simplified tree containing only 36 DOFs that are necessary for gross motion. This excludes the vertebrae which account for most of the remaining freedom. To solve the redundancy problem, we should reduce the relevant DOFs to a manageable set at any given moment during motion planning. We use constraints to supplement the traditional methods of robot motion planning in joint space done solely using numeric computations [LPW79, LP81, LP83, BHJ+83, LP87, Bro83b, Bro83a, Don87, Kha86, MK85, BLL89a, Bre89, CB92]. We reduce the complexity of the numeric computations by applying cues from qualitative knowledge and reasoning.

---

[5]Moon Jung.

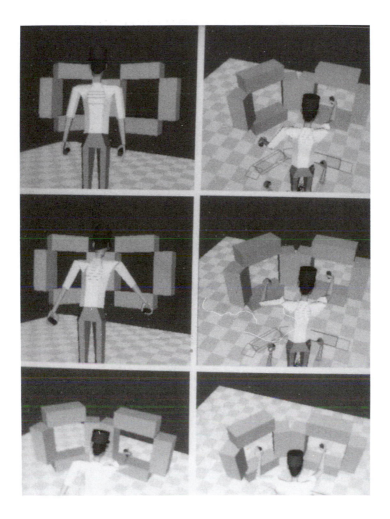

Figure 5.33: A Human Figure Reaching Through Two Apertures with Both Arms.

Figure 5.34: A Human Figure Climbing up a Rocky Surface. This Animation is Created with a Hybrid of Simulation Techniques.

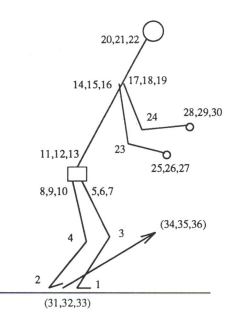

Figure 5.35: The Reduced Degrees of Freedom of the Human Body.

Here are the basic steps needed to determine postures needed to achieve a given end effector goal.

1. Postulate primitive motions for the end effector goal considering motion dependencies and a *minimum disturbance constraint.* For example, a motion dependency causes the palm to move forward and downward when the upper body is bent forward about the waist. While deciding on movement of body parts, the body is subjected to a constraint which requires minimal movements. For example, the agent does not bend if a relevant object can be grasped just by extending the hand. Primitive motions are defined in terms of salient parameters defined in the 3D Cartesian *task space.* These parameters are called *control points* and *control vectors.* They are points and vectors defined on parts of the body that allow the conversion from task-level goals into an intuitive subset of body DOFs.

2. Use *mental simulation* to bind parameters of primitive motions and to detect collisions. The body is subject to inherent constraints such as one that requires that the body remain balanced when a task is performed.

3. If the mental simulation indicates that a body part would collide with an obstacle, identify collision-avoiding spatial constraints or suggest intermediate collision-avoiding goals by reasoning about the qualitative geometric relations among the body part, the goal placement, and the obstacle.

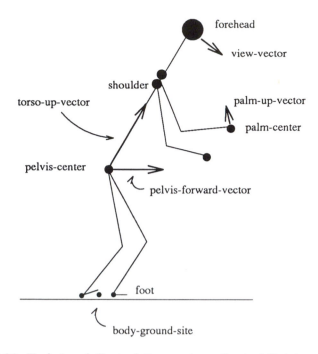

Figure 5.36: Task-Level Control Parameters: Control Points and Vectors.

4. If the postulated motions violate already achieved goals or collision-avoiding constraints, use the amount of violation to replan and compensate for the violation.

5.5.1 Functionally Relevant High-level Control Parameters

To control body postures effectively, we represent spatial configurations of the body in terms of "lumped" control parameters: control points and control vectors (Figure 5.36). Control points are points defined on important body parts such as feet, pelvis, head, and hands) to control their positions. Control vectors are vectors defined to control orientations. The task-space control points or vectors are considered to be the reduced set of DOFs of the body with respect to the task-space. The number of task-space DOFs that we consider is 14.

A control point or vector moves relative to a *base site* of the control point or vector. For example, the palm-center may be moved with respect to a base site at the shoulder, the pelvis-center, or the body-ground-site. Or it may be moved as the whole body moves with respect to the base site outside of the body, that is, the origin of the world coordinate frame. The pelvis-forward-vector controls the horizontal orientation of the body and so is confined to rotate along the horizontal circle centered at the pelvis-center. The torso-up-vector controls the forward/backward orientation of the upper body. Note that the rough configuration of the body is defined by the four *primary* control parameters: body-ground-site, pelvis-center, pelvis-forward-vector, and torso-up-vector.

5.5.2 Motions and Primitive Motions

Motions are defined by specifying control parameters and the directions and the distances to move them. We use the three standard directions along which to move or rotate: sagittal (forward/backward), vertical (upward/downward), and sideward (leftward/rightward). These relative directions are considered unit vectors defined with respect to the body-centered coordinate frame. When we say that a control point moves *forward*, it means that the movement of the control point has the *forward* component. It may have other motion components. For example, we use the motion goal *move-by(forehead, downward, Dist)* to refer to a goal of moving the forehead downward by distance *Dist* and *orient-by(torso-up-vector, forward, Angle)* to refer to a goal of rotating the torso-up-vector forward by angle *Angle*. A motion along a given direction is decomposed into the three components along the standard directions. This is convenient for two reasons. First, the component motions can be independently planned, although interference among them must be taken into account. Second, it is easy to find cooperative motions that contribute to a given standard motion component.

Note that motion *move-by(forehead, downward, Dist)* does not specify the base site relative to which the forehead is to move. The forehead may move relative to the pelvis-center (by bending the torso-up-vector forward), or relative to the body-ground-site (by lowering the pelvis-center down), or do both in sequence or parallel. A motion which specifies the base site of a control point or vector is called a *primitive motion*. Examples of primitive motions are given in Table 5.1. Primitive *move-by(left.palm-center, downward, Dist, pelvis-center)* means that the agent moves the left palm center downward by distance *Dist* with respect to base site *pelvis-center*. When the body-ground-site is moved, its base site is the world origin *world*. For example, *move-by(body-ground-site, forward, Dist, world)* means that the body-ground-site is moved forward by distance *Dist* with respect to the world origin.

The consequences of a primitive motion are not specified in terms of precondition-action-effect rules. Rather they are computed by incremental motion simulation by taking advantage of the underlying geometric properties of the body and the body balance constraint. Enumerating effects of primitive motions under different conditions is simply not feasible in the continuous domain of motion planning with massively redundant bodies.

5.5.3 Motion Dependencies

A positional goal is translated into a conjunction of simultaneous goals. For example, given a positional goal *positioned-at(right.palm.center, GoalPos)*,

Table 5.1: Primitive Motions for Manipulating Control Parameters.

move-by(left.palm-center, downward, Dist)
move-by(left.palm-center, downward, Dist, shoulder)
move-by(left.palm-center, downward, Dist, pelvis-center)
move-by(body-ground-site, forward, Dist, world)
orient-by(pelvis-forward-vector, leftward, Ang)
orient-by(pelvis-forward-vector, leftward, Ang, pelvis-center)
orient-by(pelvis-forward-vector, leftward, Ang, body-ground-site)

the difference vector from the current position of the palm center to the goal position *GoalPos* is decomposed into the forward, downward, and rightward component vectors, with their distances being F, D, and R respectively . That is, positional goal *positioned-at(right.palm-center, GoalPos)* is translated to the conjunction of the three component motion goals: *move-by(right.palm-center, forward, F)*, *move-by(right.palm-center, downward, D)*, and *move-by(right.palm-center, rightward, R)*.

There are several ways to achieve each component motion goal. They are determined based on the motion dependencies among different body parts. More precisely, they are relationships among control parameters described as follows:

1. move-by(right.palm-center, forward, Dist) has four contributors:

    (a) move-by(right.shoulder, right.palm-center, forward, D1),

    (b) rotate-by(pelvis-forward-vector, leftward, Ang2),

    (c) rotate-by(torso-up-vector, forward, Ang3, pelvis-center),

    (d) move-by(body-ground-site, forward, D4, world),

    such that Dist = D1 + D2(Ang2) + D3(Ang3) + D4, where D2(Ang2) is the distance that the right-palm-center travels due to the rotation of the pelvis-forward-vector leftward by angle Ang2 and D3(Ang3) is the distance that the right-palm-center travels due to the rotation of the torso-up-vector forward by angle Ang3. In general, these distances are dependent on the body context, the situation in which the body is placed. Hence it would be extremely hard to compute them analytically in advance without incremental simulation.

2. move-by(palm-center, downward, Dist) has two contributors:

    (a) move-by(palm-center, downward, D1, shoulder),

    (b) move-by(shoulder, downward, D2)

    such that Dist = D1 + D2.

3. move-by(shoulder, downward, Dist) has two contributors:

   (a) rotate-by(torso-up-vector, forward, Ang1, pelvis-center),

   (b) move-by(pelvis-center, downward, D2, body-ground-site)

   such that Dist = D1(Ang1) + D2, where D1(Ang1) is the distance
   that the shoulder travels due to the rotation of the torso-up-vector with
   respect to the pelvis-center by angle Ang1.

4. move-by(palm-center, leftward, Dist) has four contributors:

   (a) move-by(right.shoulder, right.palm-center, leftward, D1),

   (b) rotate-by(pelvis-forward-vector, leftward, Ang2),

   (c) rotate-by(torso-up-vector, leftward, Ang3, pelvis-center),

   (d) move-by(body-ground-site, leftward, D4, world),

   such that Dist = D1 + D2(Ang2) + D3(Ang3) + D4, where D2 is the
   distance that the right-palm-center travels due to the rotation of the
   pelvis-forward-vector leftward by angle Ang2 and D3 is the distance
   that the right-palm-center travels due to the rotation of the torso-up-
   vector leftward by angle Ang3.

How much to move or rotate the contributing control parameters to achieve
a given goal is not part of what we call *motion dependencies*. They are
determined by mental simulation.

5.5.4   The Control Structure of Posture Planning

The control structure of posture planning (Figure 5.37) is described. The
planner maintains the partial plan (the plan under construction that has un-
ordered goals and motions) and the list of constraints on goals or motions.
The partial plan is initialized to the input goals: [*positioned-at(palm-center,
GoalPos), aligned-with(palm-up-vector, GoalVector)*], which are subject to the
proximity constraints. The **motion postulator** is invoked to suggest a sequence of primitive motions needed to achieve the current goal. The motions
are first postulated without considering collisions, while respecting the previously identified constraints. When the motions are postulated, the **motion
simulator** selects motions to achieve the positional goal. To do so, the motion dependencies among body parts are used. They permit many alternative
ways of achieving a given goal. They are partly constrained by the *minimum
disturbance* constraint which prescribes that body parts farther away from the
end effector or the upper body are to move only when movements of body
parts nearer the end effector or the upper body are not sufficient to achieve
a given postural goal. The minimum disturbance constraint is procedurally
incorporated into the motion postulator. To determine the values of distance
parameters, selected motions are simulated by incrementally changing the

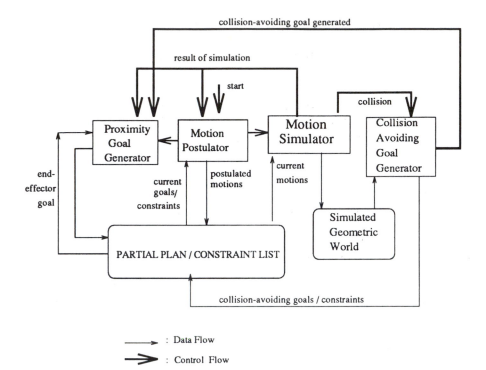

Figure 5.37: The Overall Control of Planning.

control parameters until the goal values are reached. The incremental step size for each control parameter is assumed to be fixed.

When the motions are determined, the **motion simulator** is again invoked to detect potential collisions of important body parts, hand(s), the upper body (including the head), and the lower body. Collision detection of important body parts seems sufficient for the purpose of finding a gross motion plan. If collisions are detected, the **motion simulator** marks the faces of the obstacles with which body parts collided for the first time and continues the simulation, even with object penetration, until the selected motions are fully achieved. This reveals all potential body part collisions and provides more lookahead without significant extra cost. If collision has occurred during the motion simulation the planner calls the **collision-avoiding goal generator** to generate intermediate goals. The achievement of the collision-avoiding goals is then planned by the **motion postulator**.

5.5.5   An Example of Posture Planning

The process of posture planning is best described using an example. Consider a positional goal *positioned-at(right.palm-center, GoalPos)*. Assume that the proximity constraints which the positional goal is subject to are already achieved and are maintained. For simplicity of exposition, the end effector goal is assumed to have only the *forward* and *downward* components, ignoring the *sideward* component. Consider the situation in Figure 5.38.

1. Translate the input goal *positioned-at(right.palm-center, GoalPos)* to its contributor motions: *move-by(right.palm-center, forward, F)* and *move-by(right.palm-center, downward, D)*, where the goal vector from the palm center to goal position *GoalPos* is decomposed to vectors F and D.

2. According to the minimum disturbance constraint, the shoulder is tried first as the base joint of the palm-center motions. This will be done if the distance between the shoulder and the goal position is less than the arm length. Otherwise, the shoulder should be first moved so that the distance between the new shoulder position and the goal position will be less than the arm length. A plausible goal position of the shoulder can be simply found as shown in Figure 5.39. To find it, first get the vector *ArmLine* between the shoulder and the goal position of the end effector. Get the vector *Arm* whose length is equal to the arm length and which is parallel to vector *ArmLine*. Then the difference vector $Diff = ArmLine - Arm$ becomes the motion vector of the base site, the shoulder. Suggest parallel primitive motions *move-to(right.palm-center, forward, F0, right.shoulder)* and *move-to(right.palm-center, downward, D0, right.shoulder)* and add them to the goal tree. Then, extract the downward and forward motion components from the difference vector *Diff*. Let the downward component be *DDist* and the forward component *FDist* (Figure 5.39). Add two goals *move-by(right.shoulder, downward, DDist)* and *move-by(right.shoulder, forward, FDist)* to the goal tree. They are parallel goals to be achieved at the same time. They are added to the goal tree to be achieved *before* the end effector motions previously added.

3. Get the top two goals from the goal tree. Nonlinear planning is used to plan for the goals, that is, each goal is planned for independently starting from the current situation. If the goals interfere, they are resolved by finding and removing the causes of the conflict. According to the motion dependencies, goal *move-by(right.shoulder, forward, FDist)* can be achieved by (i) *orient-by(torso-up-vector, forward, Ang2, pelvis-center)* and (ii) *move-by(body-ground-site, forward, F1, world)* where $FDist = F1 + F2(Ang2)$. Goal *move-by(right.shoulder, downward, DDist)* is achieved by (a) *orient-by(torso-up-vector, forward, Ang1, pelvis-center)* and (b) *move-by(pelvis-center, downward, D2, body-ground-site)*, where $DDist = D1(Ang1) + D2$. Here $D1(Ang1)$ is the movement of the shoulder caused by bending the torso-up-vector by angle *Ang1* and $D2$ is the movement of the shoulder caused by lowering the pelvis-center.

4. Consider subplan (i) *orient-by(torso-up-vector, forward, Ang1, pelvis-center)* and (ii) *move-to(body-ground-site, forward, FDist, world)* for

the forward component goal of the shoulder. Based on the minimum disturbance constraint, motion (i) alone is first tried, because its base site *pelvis-center* is more proximal to the control point, the shoulder, than is the base site (*world*) of motion (ii). Motion (i) *orient-by(torso-up-vector, forward, Ang2, pelvis-center)* helps achieve the first goal as long as the precondition holds that the shoulder is above the horizontal plane passing through the pelvis-center (Figure 5.40). Incrementally simulate motion (i) to determine angle parameter *Ang2* (Figure 5.39). This angle value is difficult to predict without incremental simulation, because this value is affected by the body balance constraint. Simulate the motion until the forward component goal of the shoulder is achieved or the precondition is violated. Because the precondition is violated before the forward component goal is achieved, it is concluded that motion (i) alone is not sufficient. Motion (ii) is used to fill the remaining gap. The distance *F1* that motion (ii) should achieve is easily predicted by simple arithmetic (Figure 5.41). The temporal relation between motions (i) and (ii) is determined, because the motion whose base site is the world origin *world* is to be achieved first.

Consider subplan (a) *orient-by(torso-up-vector, forward, Ang1, pelvis-center)* and (b) *move-by(pelvis-center, downward, D2, body-ground-site)*, where *DDist = D1(Ang1) + D2*, for the downward component goal of the shoulder. According the minimum disturbance constraint, motion (a) alone is chosen first, because its base site *pelvis-center* is more proximal to the hand than is the base site of motion (b), *body-ground-site*. This is compatible with the observation that lowering the pelvis-center requires bending the knees and is considered more difficult than bending the torso-up-vector. (This may not be possible if bending the torso causes collision. But in this example, collisions are not considered.) Incrementally simulate motion (b) to determine angle parameter *Ang2*. Simulate until the downward component goal of the shoulder is achieved, that is, *DDist = D1(Ang1)*. Because motion (a) for the downward component is the same (bending the torso) as motion (ii) for the forward component, the simulation of motion (a) will be done by augmenting or subtracting the simulation of motion (ii).

5. The above reasoning suggests two motions *move-by(body-ground-site, forward, F1, world)* and *orient-by(torso-up-vector, forward, Ang2, pelvis-center)* for the forward component goal of the shoulder, and one motion *orient-by(torso-up-vector, forward, Ang1, pelvis-center)* for the downward component goal of the shoulder. If the two sets of motions do not interfere with each other with respect to the achievement of the two parallel goals, the motion postulation is successful. But this is not the case. When motion *orient-by(torso-up-vector, forward, Ang1, pelvis-center)* is simulated to achieve the downward motion component *DDist*, the shoulder goes below the horizontal plane passing through the pelvis-center (Figure 5.42). It therefore also contributes negatively to the forward mo-

tion component *FDist*, partly violating the goal *move-by(right.shoulder, forward, FDist)*. The **motion postulator** first attempts to resolve this goal interference by modifying distance parameters of motions in the current partial plan (goal tree). (If the rebinding of motion parameters fails, the **motion postulator** will try other combinations of contributing motions.) When the **motion postulator** modifies the subplans, subplans with more contributing motions are tried earlier than are those with fewer motions. In particular, subplans with single motions cannot be rebound without destroying the goals they achieved. Consider a subplan with more than one contributing motion. If the distance of one motion is modified to avoid the goal interference, this also causes the violation of the goal of the subplan. But the distances of the other motions can be modified to compensate for that violation. In the current example, the motion postulator keeps the subplan for the downward goal of the shoulder, because it has only one motion *orient-by(torso-up-vector, forward, Ang2, pelvis-center)*. This decision affects motion *orient-by(torso-up-vector, forward, Ang1, pelvis-center)* in the subplan for the forward goal of the shoulder, with *Ang1* := *Ang2*. (This decision in fact turns out to be the same as the initial arbitrary decision used to simulate the two subplans.) Simulate the two subplans thus obtained. Get the distance of the negative contribution from the resulting simulated situation. Let the distance be *NegDist*. The distance can be achieved by adding an additional motion *move-by(body-ground-site, forward, NegDist, world)*. This motion compensates for the distance *DegDist* without doing any harm to the downward goal of the shoulder. But the **motion postulator** is supposed to see first that modifying the distance parameters of the current plans will work, before trying to add other motions. That is possible in this case by modifying motion *move-by(body-ground-site, forward, FDist, world)* to *move-by(body-ground-site, forward, FDist + NegDist, world)*.

6. After the shoulder goals are achieved, the current motions in the goal tree to be considered are the downward and forward motions of the palm-center with respect to (the current position of) the shoulder. Simulate these motions. Both motion components are achieved with equal importance given to each of them. They will be achieved if there are no hindrances (constraints or obstacles) at all, because the position of the shoulder has been obtained based on that assumption. If there are hindrances, the base of the palm-center (the shoulder) needs to be relocated as the palm-center is moved to intermediate goals. The intermediate goals are found to avoid the hindrances while achieving the goal of the palm-center.

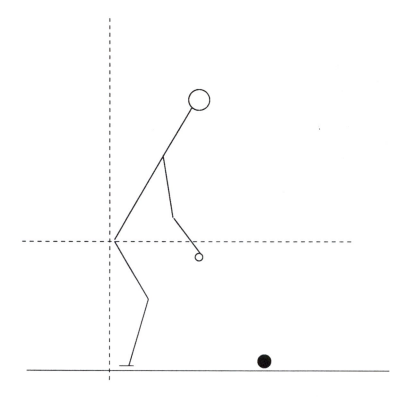

Figure 5.38: The Initial Situation for a Given Goal.

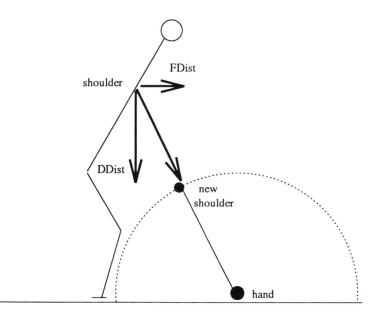

Figure 5.39: The Two Components of the Shoulder Difference Vector.

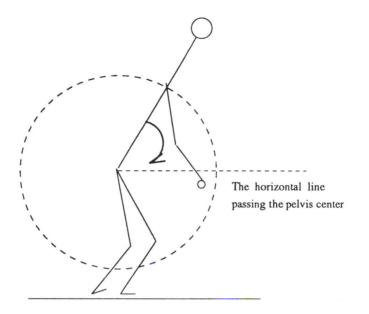

Figure 5.40: As Long as the Shoulder is Above the Horizontal Line, Bending the Torso-Up-Vector Moves the Shoulder Forward.

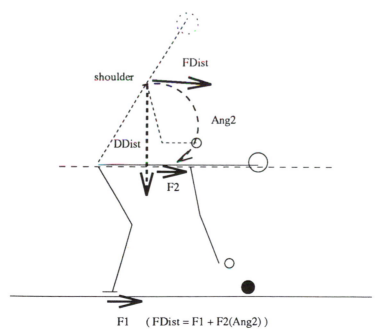

$$F1 \quad (\text{FDist} = F1 + F2(\text{Ang2}))$$

Figure 5.41: Achieving the Forward Component: By Moving the Body-Ground-Site and Bending the Torso.

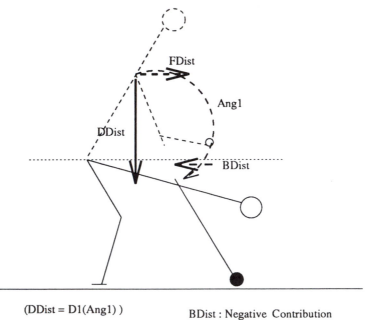

(DDist = D1(Ang1))   BDist : Negative Contribution
                                of Bending the Torso

Figure 5.42: Achieving the Downward Component: By Rotating the Torso-Up-Vector Forward, Which Violates the Forward Component by Distance *BDist*.

Chapter 6

Task-Level Specifications

So far we have been talking about real-time interactive display and manipulation of human figures, with the goal of enabling human factors engineers to augment their analyses of designed environments by having human figures carry out tasks intended for those environments. This chapter explores the use of task-level specifications as an alternative to direct manipulation for generating task simulations.

By now, the reader should be convinced of the value of being able to simulate, observe and evaluate agents carrying out tasks. The question is what is added by being able to produce such simulations from high-level task specifications. The answer is efficient use of the designer's expertise and time. A designer views tasks primarily in terms of what needs to be accomplished, not in terms of moving objects or the agent's articulators in ways that will eventually produce an instance of that behavior – e.g., in terms of slowing down and making a left turn rather than in terms of attaching the agent's right hand to the clutch, moving the clutch forward, reattaching the agent's right hand to the steering wheel, then rotating the wheel to the left and then back an equal distance to the right. As was the case in moving programming from machine-code to high-level programming languages, it can be more efficient to leave it to some computer system to convert a designer's high-level goal-oriented view of a task into the agent behavior needed to accomplish it. Moreover, if that same computer system is flexible enough to produce agent behavior that is appropriate to the agent's size and strength and to the particulars of any given environment that the designer wants to test out, then the designer is freed from all other concerns than those of imagining and specifying the environments and agent characteristics that should be tested.

This chapter then will describe a progression of recent collaborative efforts between the University of Pennsylvania's Computer Graphics Research Lab and the LINC Lab (Language, INformation and Computation) to move towards true high-level task specifications embodying the communicative richness and efficiency of Natural Language instructions.

The first section will describe our earliest work on using simple Natural

Language commands to drive task animation. This work also dealt with an aspect of performance simulation that is rarely communicated in task specifications: how long an action will take an agent to perform. Section 6.2 describes our next effort at using Natural Language commands to drive task animation, focusing on how kinematic and spatial aspects of desired behavior are conveyed in Natural Language commands.

One of the consequences of these first two studies is understanding the value of a stratified approach to mapping from language to behavior: it is not efficient for, say, the language understanding components to make decisions that commit the agent moving a hand or a knee in a particular way, unless those movements are stated explicitly (but rarely) in the text. Because of this recognized need for intermediate representations between Natural Language descriptions and animation directives, an experiment was performed, described in Section 6.3, in which an intermediate level compositional language was created for specifying task-actions and generating task-level animated simulations from scripts written in this language. This demonstration paves the way for the ultimate connection between the behavioral simulation structure of the preceding Chapter and the conceptual structures of this one.

Each of these early efforts focused on individual commands in Natural Language. Task specifications, on the order of Natural Language instructions, go beyond individual commands in specifying what an agent should (and shouldn't) do. Since our current work is aimed at generating task animations from specifications as rich as Natural Language instructions, we devote the discussion in Section 6.4 to describing some features of instructions and what an understanding system requires in order to derive from them what a person would in understanding and acting in response to instructions.

6.1 Performing Simple Commands

[1]Our first work on driving task animation through Natural Language commands was a prototype system developed by Jeffrey Esakov that explored simple relations between language and behavior [EBJ89]. In this case, the desired behaviors were simple arm reaches and head orientation (view) changes on the part of the animated figures. While seemingly very easy, these tasks already demonstrate much of the essential complexity underlying language-based animation control.

6.1.1 Task Environment

In Esakov's work, the tasks to be animated center around a control panel (i.e. a finite region of more or less rigidly fixed manually-controllable objects) – here, the remote manipulator system control panel in the space shuttle with its variety of controls and indicators. Because Esakov was producing task animations for task performance analysis, he needed to allow performance

---
[1] Jeffrey Esakov.

to depend upon the anthropometry of the agent executing the task. In the experiments, all the controls were in fact reachable without torso motion by the agents being animated: failure situations were not investigated and the fully articulated torso was not yet available. An animation of one of the experiments can be found in [EB91].

6.1.2 Linking Language and Motion Generation

The primary focus of this work was to combine Natural Language task specification and animation in an application-independent manner. This approach used the following Natural Language script:

```
John is a 50 percentile male.
Jane is a 50 percentile female.
John, look at switch twf-1.
John, turn twf-1 to state 4.
Jane, look at twf-3.
Jane, look at tglJ-1.
Jane, turn tglJ-1 on.
John, look at tglJ-2.
Jane, look at twf-2.
Jane, turn twf-2 to state 1.
John, look at twf-2.
John, look at Jane.
Jane, look at John.
```

(The abbreviations denote *thumbwheels* such as **twf-1** and *toggle switches* such as **tglJ-1**. Thumbwheels have states set by rotation; toggles typically have two states, **on** or **off**.)

This type of script, containing simple independent commands, is common to checklist procedures such as those done in airplanes or space shuttles [Cen81]. The verb "look at" requires a view change on the part of the figure, and the verb "turn" requires a simple reach. (Fine hand motions, such as finger and wrist rotations, were not animated as part of this work.) The two primary problems then are specifying reach and view goals, and connecting object references to their geometric instances.

6.1.3 Specifying Goals

For these reach tasks the goal is the 3D point which the fingertips of the hand should touch. A view goal is a point in space toward which one axis of an object must be aimed. Spatially, such goals are just Peabody sites and must be specified numerically with respect to a coordinate system. Within the natural language environment, goals are not seen as coordinates, but rather as the objects located there – for example,

```
John, look at switch twF-1.
Jane, turn switch tglJ-1 on.
```

Because the exact locations of the switches is unimportant at the language level, in creating an animation, the switch name `tglJ-1` must be mapped to the appropriate switch on the panel in the animation environment. The same process must be followed for the target object toward which an object axis must be aligned in a view change. This problem reduces to one of object referencing.

6.1.4 The Knowledge Base

In general, all objects have names. Since the names in the task specification environment may be different from those in the animation environment, there must be a mapping between the names. The knowledge base that Esakov used contained information about object names and hierarchies, but not actual geometry or location. He used a frame-like knowledge base called DC-RL to store symbolic information [Ceb87]. For example, the DC-RL code for an isolated toggle switch, `tglJ-1`, follows:

```
{ concept tglJ-1 from control
  having (
     [role name with [value = "TOGGLE J-1"]]
     [role locative with [value = panel1]]
     [role type-of with [value = switch]]
     [role sub-type with [value = tgl]]
     [role direction with [value = (down up)]]
     [role states with [value = (off on)]]
     [role movement with [value =
           (discrete mm linear ((off on) 20 5))]]
     [role current with [value = off]])
}
```

To reference this switch from within the animation environment, a mapping file was generated at the same time the graphical object was described.

```
{ concept ctrlpanel from panelfig
  having (
     [role twF-1 with
           [ value = ctrlpanel.panel.twf_1 ]]
     [role twF-2 with
           [ value = ctrlpanel.panel.twf_2 ]]
     [role twF-3 with
           [ value = ctrlpanel.panel.twf_3 ]]
     [role tglJ-1 with
           [ value = ctrlpanel.panel.tglj_1 ]]
     [role tglJ-2 with
           [ value = ctrlpanel.panel.tglj_2 ]]
  )
}
```

The names `twF-1`, `twF-2`, `tglJ-1` correspond to the names of switches in the existing knowledge base panel description called `panelfig`. These names are mapped to the corresponding names in the animation environment (e.g., `ctrlpanel.panel.twf_1`, etc.) and are guaranteed to match.

6.1.5 The Geometric Database

The underlying geometric database is just Peabody code. The salient toggle and thumbwheel locations were simply mapped to appropriate sites on a host segment representing the control panel object. The relevant part of the Peabody description of the panel figure is shown:

```
figure ctrlpanel {
  segment panel {
    psurf = "panel.pss";
    site base->location =
         trans(0.00cm,0.00cm,0.00cm);
    site twf_1->location =
         trans(13.25cm,163.02cm,80.86cm);
    site twf_2->location =
         trans(64.78cm,115.87cm,95.00cm);
    site twf_3->location =
         trans(52.84cm,129.09cm,91.43cm);
    site tglj_1->location =
         trans(72.36cm,158.77cm,81.46cm);
    site tglj_2->location =
         trans(9.15cm,115.93cm,94.98cm);
  }
}
```

This entire file is automatically generated by a modified paint program. Using the panel as a texture map, switch locations are interactively selected and the corresponding texture map coordinates are computed as the site transformation. The panel itself is rendered as a texture map over a simple polygon and the individual sites then refer to the appropriate visual features of the switches.

6.1.6 Creating an Animation

Linking the task level description to the animation requires linking both object references and actions. A table maps the names of objects from the task description environment into the psurf geometry of the animation environment. In this simple problem domain the language processor provides the other link by associating a single key pose with a single animation command. Each part of speech fills in slots in an animation command template. Simple *Jack* behaviors compute the final posture required by each command which are then strung together via simple joint angle interpolation.

6.1.7 Default Timing Constructs

Even though the basic key poses can be generated based upon a Natural Language task description, creating the overall animation can still be difficult. We have already discussed posture planning and collision avoidance issues, but there is yet another problem that bears comment. From the given command input, the *timing* of the key poses is either unknown, unspecified, or arbitrary.

Action timings could be explicitly specified in the input, but (language-based) task descriptions do not normally indicate time. Alternatively, defining the time at which actions occur can be arbitrarily decided and iterated until a reasonable task animation can be produced. In fact, much animator effort is normally required to temporally position key postures. There are, however, more computational ways of formulating a reasonable guess for possible task duration.

Several factors effect task performance times, for example: level of expertise, desire to perform the task, degree of fatigue (mental and physical), distance to be moved, and target size. Realistically speaking, all of these need to be considered in the model, yet some are difficult to quantify. Obviously, the farther the distance to be moved, the longer a task should take. Furthermore, it is intuitively accepted that performing a task which requires precision work should take longer than one not involving precision work: for example, threading a needle versus putting papers on a desk.

Fitts [Fit54] and Fitts and Peterson [FP64] investigated performance time with respect to two of the above factors, distance to be moved and target size. It was found that amplitude (A, distance to be moved) and target width (W) are related to time in a simple equation:

$$\text{Movement Time} = a + b \log \frac{2A}{W} \tag{6.1}$$

where a and b are task-dependent constants. In this formulation, an index of movement difficulty is manipulated by the ratio of target width to amplitude and is given by:

$$\text{ID} = \log \frac{2A}{W} \tag{6.2}$$

This index of difficulty shows the speed and accuracy tradeoff in movement. Since A is constant for any particular task, to decrease the performance time the only other variable in the equation W must be increased. That is, the faster a task is to be performed, the larger the target area and hence the movements are less accurate.

This equation (known as Fitts' Law) can be embedded in the animation system, since for any given reach task, both A and W are known. The constants a and b are linked to the other factors such training, desire, fatigue, and body segments to be moved; they must be determined empirically. For button tapping tasks, Fitts [FP64] determined the movement time (MT) to be

$$MT_{\text{arm}} = 74ID - 70 msec \tag{6.3}$$

Task Duration Times (msec)				
Actor	Action	ID	Fitts Duration	Scaled Duration
John	Look twf-1	2.96	321	963
John	Turn twf-1	5.47	335	1004
John	Look tglJ-2	4.19	566	1697
John	Look twf-2	4.01	530	1590
John	Look Jane	4.64	655	1966
Jane	Look twf-3	4.28	584	876
Jane	Look tglJ-1	3.64	456	685
Jane	Turn tglJ-1	5.39	329	493
Jane	Look twf-2	4.16	560	840
Jane	Turn twf-2	4.99	299	449
Jane	Look John	4.33	594	891

Table 6.1: Task Durations Using Fitts' Law.

In determining this equation, it was necessary to filter out the extraneous factors. This was done by having the subjects press the button as quickly as possible and allowing them to control the amount of time between trials. Jagacinski and Monk [JM85] performed a similar experiment to determine the movement time for the head and obtained the following equation

$$\text{MT}_{\text{head}} = 199ID' - 268msec \tag{6.4}$$

$$ID' = \log \frac{2A}{W - W_0} \tag{6.5}$$

This equation is the result of equating the task to inserting a peg of diameter W_0 into a hole of diameter W, and resulted in a better fit of the data.

For our purposes the above constants may not apply. Since it was our desire to have the man in our animation move sluggishly and the woman move quickly (but not too quickly), we scaled Equations 6.3 and 6.4 by differing constants.

$$
\begin{aligned}
MT_{\text{man(arm)}} &= 3 * MT_{\text{arm}} \\
MT_{\text{man(head)}} &= 3 * MT_{\text{head}} \\
MT_{\text{woman(arm)}} &= 1.5 * MT_{\text{arm}} \\
MT_{\text{woman(head)}} &= 1.5 * MT_{\text{head}}
\end{aligned}
$$

This width of the target, W in equation 6.2 was chosen to be 1cm. For head movements, we chose $W_0 = .33°$ after [JM85]. This results in the action durations shown in Table 6.1.

Although Fitts' Law has been found to be true for a variety of movements including arm movements ($A = 5 - 30cm$), wrist movements ($A = 1.3cm$)

[Dru75, JM85, LCF76], and head movements ($A = 2.45 - 7.50°$) [JM85] the application to 3D computer animation is only approximate. The constants differ for each limb and are only valid within a certain movement amplitude *in 2D space*, therefore the extrapolation of the data outside that range and into 3D space has no validated experimental basis. Nonetheless, Fitts' Law provides a reasonable and easily computed basis for approximating movement durations.

While it may seem odd at first to have attacked both Natural Language interpretation and timing constructs as part of the same research, Esakov's work foreshadows our more recent work on language and animation by focusing on the fact that the same instruction, given to agents with different abilities, will be carried out in different ways. Language tells an agent what he or she should attempt to do: how he or she does it depends on them.

6.2   Language Terms for Motion and Space

[2]The next piece of work that was done on driving task animation through Natural Language commands was Jugal Kalita's work on how Natural Language conveys desired motion and spatial aspects of an agent's behavior. In English, the primary burden falls on verbs and their modifiers. Kalita's work showed how verbs and their modifiers can be seen as conveying spatial and kinematic constraints on behavior, thereby enabling a computer to create an animated simulation of a task specified in a Natural Language utterance. This work is described at greater length in [Kal90, KB90, KB91].

6.2.1   Simple Commands

To understand Kalita's contribution, consider the following commands:

- *Put the block on the table.*

- *Turn the switch to position 6.*

- *Roll the ball across the table.*

Each of these commands specifies a task requested of an agent. Performing the task, requires *inter alia* that the agent understand and integrate the meanings of the verbs (*put, turn, open, roll*) and the prepositions (*on, to, across*). This requires understanding the significant geometric, kinematic or dynamic features of the actions they denote.

In Kalita' approach to physically based semantics, a motion verb denotes what may be called a *core* or *kernel* action(s). This kernel representation is then used with object knowledge and general knowledge about actions to obtain semantic representations and subsequent task performance plans which are specific to a context – for example,

---

[2]Jugal Kalita.

- The core meaning of the verb *put* (as in *Put the block on the table*) establishes a geometric constraint that the first object (here, the block) remains geometrically constrained to (or, brought in contact with and supported by) a desired position on the second object (here, the table).

- The core meaning of the verb *push* (as in *Push the block against the cone*) involves applying a force on the manipulated object (here, the block) through the instrument object (here, the hand). The prepositional phrase specifies the destination of the intended motion.

- The verb *roll* (as in *Roll the ball across the table*) involves two related motions occurring simultaneously—one rotational about some axis of the object, and the other translational, caused by the first motion. The rotational motion is repeated an arbitrary number of times.

6.2.2   Representational Formalism

Geometric relations and geometric constraints

The meanings of locative prepositions are represented using a template called a *geometric-relation*. A simple geometric relation is a frame-slot structure:

geometric-relation: spatial-type:
                      source-constraint-space:
                      destination-constraint-space:
                      selectional-restrictions:

Spatial-type refers to the type of the geometric relation specified. Its values may be *positional* or *orientational*. The two slots called *source-constraint-space* and *destination-constraint-space* refer to one or more objects, or parts or features thereof, which need to be related. For example, the command *Put the cup on the table* requires one to bring the bottom surface of the cup into contact with the top surface of the table. The command *Put the ball on the table* requires bringing an arbitrary point on the surface of the ball in contact with the surface of the table top. Since the items being related may be arbitrary geometric entities (i.e., points, surfaces, volumes, etc.), we call them *spaces*. The first space is called the *source-constraint space* and the second, the *destination-constraint space*. The slot *selectional-restrictions* refers to conditions (static, dynamic, global or object-specific) that need to be satisfied before the constraint can be executed.

More complex geometric relations require two or more geometric relations to be satisfied simultaneously:

geometric-relation:
 { **g-union**
            g-relation-1
            g-relation-2
            · · ·
            g-relation-n }

where *g-relation-i* is simple or complex.

Geometric relations are also used in the specification of *geometric con-straints*, which are geometric goals to be satisfied:

Geometric-constraint: execution-type:
                       geometric-relation:

Geometric constraints are distinguished by their *execution-type* slot, which can take one of four values: *achieve, break, maintain* or *modify*.

Kinematics

The frame used for specifying kinematic aspects of motion is the following:

Kinematics: motion-type:
             source:
             destination:
             path-geometry:
             velocity:
             axis:

Motions are mainly of two types: *translational* and *rotational*. In order to describe a translational motion, we need to specify the source of the motion, its destination, the trajectory of its path (path-geometry), and the velocity of the motion. In the case of rotational motion, path-geometry is circular, and velocity, if specified, is angular. Rotational motion requires an axis of rotation. If not specified, it is inferred by consulting geometric knowledge about the object concerned.

Kernel actions

The central part of an action consists of one or more components: *dynamics, kinematics* and *geometric-constraints*—along with control structures stating its other features. The control structures used in the examples that follow are: *repeat-arbitrary-times* and *concurrent*. The keyword *concurrent* is speci-fied when two or more components, be they kinematic, dynamic or geometric constraints, need to be satisfied or achieved at the same time. The keyword *repeat-arbitrary-times* provides a means for specifying the frequentation prop-erty of certain verbs where certain sub-action(s) are repeated several times. The verbs' semantic representation need not specify how many times the ac-tion or sub-action may need to be repeated. However, since every action is presumed to end, the number of repetitions of an action will have to be computed from simulation (based on tests for some suitable termination con-ditions), or by inference unless specified linguistically as in *Shake the block about fifty times.*

6.2.3 Sample Verb and Preposition Specifications

Many of the features of Kalita's representation formalism can be seen in his representation of the verbs "roll" and "open" and the prepositions "in" and "across". Others can be seen in the worked example in Section 6.2.4.

A kinematic verb: *roll*

The verb *roll* refers to two motions occurring concurrently: a rotational motion about the longitudinal axis of the object and a translational motion of the object along an arbitrary path. The rotational motion is repeated an arbitrary number of times. The verb *roll* is thus specified as:

roll (l-agent, l-object, path-relation)←
        agent: l-agent
        object: l-object
        kernel-action:
            concurrent {{ **{** kinematic:
                        motion-type: rotational
                        axis: longitudinal-axis-of (l-object)
                  } **repeat-arbitrary-times }**
                  { kinematic:
                        motion-type: translational
                        path: path-relation **} }**
           selectional restrictions: has-circular-contour (l-object,
                                            longitudinal-axis-of (l-object))

A verb that removes constraints: *open*

One sense of *open* is *to move (as a door) from closed position.* The meaning is defined with respect to a specific position of a specific object. The closed position of the object can be viewed as a *constraint* on its position or orientation. Thus, this sense of *open* involves an underlying action that undoes an existing *constraint*. The object under consideration is required to have at least two parts: a solid 2D part (the *cover*) and an unfilled 2D part defined by some kind of frame (the *hole*). The meaning must capture two things: (1) that at the start of the action, the object's cover must occupy the total space available in object's hole in the constrained position, and (2) that the result of the action is to remove the constraint that object's cover and its hole are in one coincident plane. This is fulfilled by requiring that the two sub-objects (the hole and the cover) are of the same shape and size.

    The definition for *open* is:

open (Ag, Obj) ←
    agent: Ag
    object: Obj
    kernel-action:
        geometric-constraint:

```
            execution-type:     break
            spatial-type:       positional
            geometric-relation: source-constraint-space:  Obj • hole
                                destination-constraint-space:  Obj • cover
  selectional-restrictions:  contains-part (Obj, hole)
                             contains-part (Obj, cover)
                             area-of (Obj • cover)  = area-of (Obj • hole)
                             shape-of (Obj • cover) = shape-of (Obj • hole)
```

A locative preposition: *in*

The sense of *in* captured here is *within the bounds of, contained in or included within*. According to Herskovits [Her86], this use type for *in* is *spatial entity in a container*. This meaning of *in* is specified as

```
in (X,Y) ⟵
    geometric-relation:
        spatial-type:              positional
        source-constraint-space:     volume-of (X)
        destination-constraint-space:interior-of (Y)
        selectional-restrictions:
            or (container-p (Y), container-p (any-of (sub-parts-of (Y))))
            size-of (X) ≤ size-of (Y)
            normally-oriented (Y)
```

A *container* is an object which can hold one or more objects such that the object is "surrounded by" the volume defined by the boundaries of the container. It is a concept which is difficult to define clearly, although heuristics can be devised to recognize whether an object is a container. For our purposes, if an object or any of its part(s) can work as container(s), it will be so labeled in the *function* slot of its representation. The second selectional restriction is due to Cooper [Coo68]. The third restriction is due to Herskovits, who explains its necessity by stating that the sentence *The bread is in the bowl* is pragmatically unacceptable if the bowl is upside down and covers the bread under it [Her86].

A path preposition: *across*

Path is a part of kinematic specification of a motion or an action. A complete definition of path requires specifying its source, destination and path geometry, which Kalita does, using a structure called a *path-specification*:

```
path-specification:
    source:
    destination:
    path-geometry:
```

Across is one of several path prepositions in English. Others include *from, to, around, round* and *along*. *Across* has two types of meanings—dynamic and static (locative) meaning. The dynamic meaning implies a journey across an object, whereas the static meaning implies a location between two lines (edges) perpendicular to them and touching, and (possibly) extending beyond them. The dynamic sense of *across* is seen in:

- Roll/Slide/Move the block/ball across the board.

This dynamic sense of *across* specifies all three components required for path specification.

across (X, Y) ⟵ path-specification:
   source: any-of (exterior-edges-of (Y, parallel-to (longitudinal-axis (Y))))
   destination:any-of (exterior-edges-of (Y, parallel-to (longitudinal-axis (Y))))
   path-geometry: straight-line
   selectional-restrictions:
      destination ≠ source
      has-axis (X, longitudinal)
      angle-between (path-geometry, longitudinal-axis (Y), 90°)
      length (Y) ≥ width (Y)
      length (Y) > dimension-of (X,along-direction (longitudinal-axis (Y)))

The *longitudinal axis* of an object is the axis along which the *length* of an object is measured. There are a number of selectional restrictions imposed on the objects X and Y also. For example, the reason for the fourth selectional restriction can be gauged from the two phrases: *across the road* and *along the road*.

6.2.4 Processing a sentence

The sentence *Put the block on the table* can be used to show how Kalita's system obtains a meaning for a whole sentence from the meanings of its parts, i.e., the lexical entries of its constituent words.

The lexical entry for *put* specifies the achievement of a geometric relationship between an object and a location specified by a prepositional phrase. The meaning of the verb is specified in terms of a yet-unspecified geometric relation between two objects. The preposition *on* along with the objects involved leads to the sense that deals with support.

A bottom-up parser [FW83] returns the logical meaning representation as (*put you block-1 (on block-1 table-1)*). In this representation, the verb *put* takes three arguments: a subject, an object and the representation for a locative expression. Entities *block-1* and *table-1* are objects in the world determined to be the referents of the noun phrases. The logical representation has *you* as the value of the subject since the sentence is imperative.

Now, to obtain the intermediate meaning representation, the arguments of *put* in the logical representation are matched with the arguments in the following lexical entry for *put*:

put (l-agent, l-object, l-locative) ⟵
    agent: l-agent
    object: l-object
    kernel-actions:
        geometric-constraint:
            execution-type: achieve
            geometric-relation: l-locative

This lexical entry has three arguments. After matching, *l-agent* has the value
you, *l-object* has the value *block-1*, and *l-locative* has the value (*on block-1
table-1*). The value of the *geometric-relation* slot (of the *kernel-actions* slot in
the representation) is filled in by the semantic representation for the *l-locative*
argument which is created from the meaning of "on the table", using the
following definition of "on":

on (X,Y) ⟵
    geometric-relation:
        spatial-type: positional
        source-constraint-space: any-of (self-supporting-spaces-of (X))
        destination-constraint-space: any-of (supporter-surfaces-of (Y))
    selectional-restrictions:
        horizontal-p (destination-constraint-space)
        equal (direction-of (normal-to
           destination-constraint-space), "global-up")
        free-p (destination-constraint-space)

As a result, the intermediate meaning representation of "put the block on
the table" is:

agent: you
object: block-1
kernel-actions:
    geometric-constraint:
        execution-type: achieve
        geometric-relation:
            spatial-type: positional
            source-constraint-space: any-of
                (self-supporting-spaces-of (block-1))
            destination-constraint-space: any-of
                (supporting-surfaces-of (table-1))
        selectional-restrictions:
            horizontal-p (destination-constraint-space)
            equal (direction-of (normal-to
               destination-constraint-space), "global-up")
            free-p (destination-constraint-space)

In order to execute the action dictated by this sentence, the program looks
at the knowledge stored about the block to find a part of the block on which

it can support itself. It observes that it can be supported on any one of its faces and no face is more salient than any other. A cube (the shape of the block) has six faces and one is chosen randomly as the support area. Next, the program consults the knowledge stored about the table and searches for a part or feature of the desk which can be used to support other objects. It gathers that its function is to support "small" objects on its top. This top surface is also horizontal. As a result, finally, the system concludes that one of the sides of the cube has to be brought in contact with the top of the table.

The final meaning for the sentence obtained is

agent: you
object: block-1
kernel-actions:
    geometric-constraint:
        execution-type: achieve
        geometric-relation:
            spatial-type: positional
            source-constraint-space: block-1•side-2
            destination-constraint-space: table-1•top-1

block-1•side-2 represents a specific face of a specific block. *table-1•top-1* represents the top surface of a specific table. This final representation is then sent to a planner [JKBC91] which produces a plan for performing the task by an animated agent in a given workspace. The plan is taken up by a simulator [BWKE91] which establishes connection with *Jack* and then produces an animation:

> The block is initially sitting on top of a closed box. The agent reaches for it with his right hand, grasps it, moves it to a point near the top of a table to his left, places it on the table, and moves his hand back.

As with Esakov's work, there were still unfortunate capability gaps in the simulator available to Kalita. In particular, the lack of a flexible torso, unchecked collisions with the environment, and no balance constraints led to some painful-looking postures and object trajectories which passed through obstacles.

6.2.5 Summary

This section has discussed the representation of meanings of some verbs and prepositions, emphasizing the importance of geometric information such as axes of objects, location of objects, distance or angle between objects, path of object motion, physical contact between objects, etc., in the meaning representation of prepositions. Elsewhere it is shown that such geometric considerations are important for not only representing verbs and prepositions, but also adverbs [KB90].

In the work described here, the operational meanings of action verbs and their modifiers have been represented in terms of components pertaining to constraints and kinematic/dynamic characterization. For additional examples of decomposition see [Kal90].

6.3   Task-Level Simulation

[3]The third experiment tested the feasibility of using what might be viewed as low-level task primitives to create task animations [Lev91]. If successful, this would have two advantages:

- Since we viewed some kind of low-level task primitives as being the output specification language of any language processing stages, it would allow us to design and test a set of primitives in parallel with the other system components.

- This kind of lower-level specification language might itself be usable by an engineer to generate animations in terms of task-level actions rather than having to specify particular body movements.

To illustrate the latter contrast, consider a scene with an animated agent, a table, and a cup on a shelf next to the table. The animator–engineer wants to create an animation of the agent moving the cup from the shelf to the table. A task-level specification could enable the animator–engineer to produce the desired behavior, using a set of **task-action** specifications. For example, the sequence

> **grasp-action** (*hand cup*)
> **position-action** (*cup table-top*)

could be used to generate an animation of the agent's hand grasping the cup, followed by a positioning of the cup on the top of the table.

As a test environment we used an expanded version of some written instructions to remove a Fuel Control Valve (FCV) from an imaginary aircraft fuselage (Figure 6.1).

Fuel Control Valve Removal Instructions:

1. With right hand, remove socket wrench from tool belt, move to front of body. With left hand, reach to tool belt pocket, remove 5/8 inch socket, move to wrench, engage. Adjust ratchet for removal.

2. Move wrench to left hand bottom hole, apply pressure to turn in a loosening motion, repeat approximately 7 times to loosen threaded bolt.

3. Move wrench away from bolt, with left hand reach to bolt and remove bolt and washer from assembly, move left hand to belt pouch, place bolt and washer in pouch.

---

[3]Libby Levison.

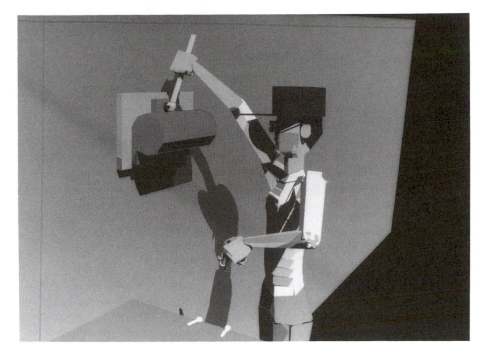

Figure 6.1: A Frame from the Fuel Control Valve Removal Task. The FCV is the Cylindrical Object Mounted to the Flat Plate.

4. Move wrench to bottom right hand bolt, apply pressure to turn in a loosening motion, repeat approximately 7 times to loosen threaded bolt.

5. Repeat operation 3.

6. Move wrench to top bolt, apply pressure to turn in a loosening motion, repeat approximately 6 times to loosen threaded bolt. Move left hand to grasp assembly, loosen the bolt the final turn. Move wrench to tool belt, release. With right hand reach to bolt, remove bolt and washer, place in pouch. Return right hand to assembly, with both hands move Fuel Control Valve to movable cart and release.

6.3.1 Programming Environment

The work area, tools and parts for the scene were modeled with *Jack*. Just as the engineer who currently writes the instruction manuals has knowledge of the task and knows, for example, that a Phillips head screwdriver is required, it is assumed that the engineer-animator will have the knowledge required to lay out the scene of the animation. It is also assumed that a skilled engineer is already trained in analyzing tasks and developing instruction sets for the domain. This project simply provides a different medium in which the engineer can explain the task.

The task simulation is based on **Yaps**, a symbolic process simulator [EB90, BWKE91]. **Yaps** provides *animation-directives* which access *Jack*'s behaviors. These animation-directives are not only ordered and sequenced via **Yaps'** temporal and conditional relationships [KKB88], but can also be composed to produce parameterized simulation procedures. These procedures, called **task-actions**, are defined for a number of parameters (agent, object, location, etc.). The same task-action can thus be used at various times with different parameters to create distinct animation segments. The possibility of defining and reusing these procedures simplifies the animation programming problem for the engineer. By extending these procedural compositions, high-level procedures could be generated so that the mapping from the instructions to these procedures would be straightforward.

KB [Esa90] is a frame-based, object-oriented knowledge system which establishes symbolic references to *Jack*'s geometric data. While *Jack* maintains and manipulates the geometric model of the world, **KB** maintains the symbolic information. **Yaps** uses **KB**'s symbolic representation to manipulate the geometric model. (These symbolic **KB** representations are passed to the **Yaps** task-actions as parameters.) This frees **Yaps** from "knowing" the specific world coordinates of an object or the object's exact geometric representation. For instance, if *Jack* contains a model of a cup, **KB** would have an entry which identified *cup* as that particular *Jack* entity. **Yaps** has no knowledge of the object's location; **KB**'s mapping from symbolic to geometric representation will resolve any ambiguity. Thus the animator need not talk about *the-cup-on-the-table-at-world-coordinates-(x,y,z)*, but can reference the symbolic entity, *cup*. Should the *cup* move during the course of the action, **KB** resolves the problem of the *cup*'s exact location.

6.3.2   Task-actions

At the time of this research, **Yaps** provided only three low-level animation-directives with which to access *Jack* behaviors. These are *generate-motion*, *create-constraint* and *delete-constraint*. *Generate-motion* causes an object (not necessarily animate) to move from its current location to another. (No path planning was performed in the *Jack* version of the time, and **Yaps** handled frame-to-frame timing directly as described in Section 6.1.) *Create-constraint* establishes a physical link between two (not necessarily adjacent) objects. If two objects are linked together and one of the objects is moved, the second object moves along with it. The physical constraint (relation) between the objects is maintained. *Create-constraint* can be further specified to use *positional* and/or *orientational* alignments. *Delete-constraint* removes the specified constraint between two objects.

Yaps provides a mechanism for building animation templates by combining or composing the above animation-directives. Using different combinations of *generate-motion*, *create-constraint*, and *delete-constraint*, and varying the agents and the objects of these *animation-directives* as well as their temporal and causal relations, it is possible to build a set of task-actions. Task-actions can themselves be composed into more complex task-actions. As the procedures acquire more specification, the task-actions approach task-level descriptions. It is important to note, however, that task-actions simply define templates; an animation is realized by instantiating the task-actions, supplying parameters as well as timing constraints and other conditions. The composability of the task-actions allows for the definition of some abstract and high-level concepts. It is these high-level animation descriptions which will allow the engineer to program an animation at the task-level.

6.3.3 Motivating Some Task-Actions

The first templates to be defined were simply encapsulations of the *Jack* animation-directives: **reach-action**(*agent object*), **hold-action**(*agent object*) and **free-object-action** (*object*) – were just *generate-motion*, *create-constraint* and *delete-constraint*, respectively. (Although the names chosen for the task-actions do make some attempt to elicit their definition, there was no attempt to come up with definitive definitions of these actions in this segment of the research project.) In the following, the use of *agent* and *object* is simply for readability; for example, a **hold-action** can be applied between two objects (*e.g.*, **hold-action** (*wrench-head 5-8th-socket*)).

Consider trying to describe the actions inherent in the example:

> *Move the cup to the table*

assuming that the agent is not currently holding the cup. The agent must first hold the cup before he can move it. How is this animation specified? Explicitly stating the sequence of actions:

> **reach-action** (*agent cup*)
> **hold-action** (*agent cup*)

to cause the agent to reach his hand to the location of the cup and to constrain his hand to the cup seems awkward. Composing two task-actions allows a new task-action **grasp-action** to be defined:

> (deftemplate **grasp-action** (*agent object*)
>   **reach-action** (*agent object*)
>   **hold-action** (*agent object*)).

(This is the actual **Yaps** definition. `Deftemplate` is the **Yaps** command to define a new task-action template.) **Grasp-action** is a sequence of instantiations of two primitive task-actions.

Now that the agent can grasp the cup, how can he move the cup? A second action, **position-action**, is defined to relocate the cup to a new location and constrain it there:

> (deftemplate **position-action** (*object1 location*)
>   **reach-action** (*object1 location*)
>   **hold-action** (*object1 location*)).

If a previous action had left an object (the cup) in the agent's hand, this task-action could be used to move the object to a new location (**position-action** *cup table*). (In this instruction set, the only use of the instruction "move something that is already being held" required that the object be constrained to the new location. This is the justification of the **hold-action** in this definition.) Note here that *location* could be the location of *object2*.

Thus, to animate the instruction:

> *Move the cup to the table*

the *animation-script* could be:

> **grasp-action** (*agent-right-hand cup*)
> **position-action** (*cup table-top*).

It is still necessary to specify a list of commands, since no high-level task-action has been defined for *move*, and therefore the action must be described in increments. However **move-action** could be defined as:

> (deftemplate **move-action** (*agent object1 location*)
>   **grasp-action** (*agent object1*)
>   **position-action** (*object1 location*)).

In other words, grasp (reach to and hold) *object1*, and position (move to and constrain) *object1* at *location* (where *location* might be the location of some *object2*). In the *Move the cup* example, the instantiation required to achieve the desired animation would be:

> **move-action** (*agent-right-hand cup table-top*).

This conciseness is one benefit of task-action composition.

Once the *cup* is actually on the *table*, it can be "un-grasped" by using:

> **free-object-action** (*cup*)

which breaks the constraint between the *hand* and the *cup*. If the *hand* is later moved, the *cup* will no longer move with it.

The final *animation script* for *Move the cup to the table* becomes:

> **move-action** (*agent-right-hand cup table-top*)
> **free-object-action** (*cup*).

6.3.4   Domain-specific task-actions

The *Move the cup to the table* example motivated a few fundamental task-action definitions. Some of these are actions common to many instructional tasks and milieus; this set of task-actions is also usable in the instruction set describing the FCV removal. However, it was also necessary to return to the instruction set and develop **Yaps** definitions for actions specific to the domain in question. These task-actions can be either primitive (see **turn-action** below) or compositional (see **ratchet-action**). The first new task-action, **attach-action**, is defined as:

> (deftemplate **attach-action** (*agent object1 object2*)
>   **move-action** (*agent object1 object2*)
>   **hold-action** (*object1 object2*)).

This allows the agent to grasp *object1*, move it to the location of *object2*, and establish a constraint between *object1* and *object2*. The expansion of this task-action is the command string:

> **reach-action, hold-action, reach-action, hold-action.**

Attach-action could have been equivalently defined as:

> (deftemplate **attach-action** (*agent object1 object2*)
>   **grasp-action** (*agent object1*)
>   **position-action** (*object1 object2*))

which would expand to exactly the same *Jack* animation-directive command string as above. The task-action definitions are associative; this provides flexibility and power to the system, and increases the feasibility of defining a minimal set of task-actions to be used throughout the domain.

The FCV removal instructions also require: **turn-action** (*object degrees*). **Turn-action** causes the *object* to rotate by the specified number of *degrees*. The geometric definition of the object includes information on its DOFs; for example, around which axis a bolt will be allowed to rotate. At the time that this research was done, the system did not have a feedback tool to monitor *Jack* entities; instead of testing for an ending condition on an action (a bolt being free of its hole), actions had to be specified iteratively (the number of times to turn a bolt). **Turn-action** is actually a support routine, used in the final task-action needed to animate the FCV instructions: **ratchet-action**. This is defined as:

> (deftemplate **ratchet-action** (*object degrees iterations*)
>   **turn-action** (*object degrees*)
>   **turn-action** (*object −degrees*)
>   **ratchet-action** (*object degrees iterations−1*)).

Ratchet-action is used to animate of a socket wrench ratcheting back and forth.[4]

---

[4] Having to explicitly state a number of degrees is not an elegant programming solution; it would have been preferable to take advantage of *Jack*'s collision detection algorithms to determine the range of the ratchet movement. Processing considerations at the time the work was done required this rather rough implementation.

The complete set of task-actions is listed below. With this set of only nine task-actions, it was possible to program the entire animation script from the natural language instructions (see Table 6.2 for an excerpt of the final animation script).

- **reach-action** (*agent object*)

- **hold-action** (*agent object*)

- **free-object-action** (*object*)

- **grasp-action** (*agent object*)

- **move-action** (*agent object location*)

- **attach-action** (*agent object1 object2*)

- **position-action** (*object1 object2*)

- **turn-action** (*object degrees*)

- **ratchet-action** (*object degrees iterations*)

6.3.5 Issues

Where Does Task-Action Decomposition Stop?

There is an interesting question as to whether, in defining task-actions, one needs to be concerned with variations that arise from differences in agents and their abilities.

Because our work is embedded in *Jack*, variations in agent ability at the animation specification level is not a concern. As long as the animation is within the agent's capabilities (and thus the animation is "solvable"), substituting different agents gives different valuations of the tasks. By testing different agents with varying abilities, one can analyze the task requirements and gather information on human factors issues. Similarly, it is possible to vary workplace geometry, tools, and agent placement.

Note the comparison here between innate and planned action. In reaching to grab a cup, we do not think about how to control the muscles in the forearm; we do, however, consider the goal of getting our hand to the same location as the cup. This distinction between cognizant motion and action is internal in this animation; *Jack* manages the motor skills. The same distinction is found in the level of detail of the instructions. One does not tell someone:

> *Extend your hand to the cup by rotating your shoulder joint 40° while straightening your elbow joint 82° degrees. Constrain your hand to the cup by contracting fingers ....*

Rather, we give them the goal to achieve and allow that goal to lend information as to how to accomplish the instruction. The hierarchy of the task-actions captures some of this knowledge.

The task-actions have been defined in such a way that they are not concerned with the abilities of a specific agent, but rather allow for interpretation

Table 6.2: Animation Script Excerpt.

```
;;;   No. 1
;;;    With right hand, remove socket wrench from tool belt,
;;;    move to front of body.  With left hand, reach to tool belt
;;;    pocket, remove 5/8" socket, move to wrench, engage.
;;;    Adjust ratchet for removal.
;
; with the right hand, grasp the wrench from the tool belt,
; and move it to site-front-body
;
(instantiate move-action
      (fred-rh wrench-handle fred-front-body-site planar)

   :instancename "r0-wrench-to-front"

   :time-constraints '((start now)
                       (duration
                           (eval(+(fitts fred-rh wrench-handle)
                                  (fitts wrench-handle
                                     fred-front-body-site)))))

; with the left hand, attach socket to wrench handle.
;  an attach entails, reaching for the socket, grasping
;  it and moving it to the wrench head.
;  if successful, free the left hand from the socket.
;
(instantiate attach-action
      (fred-lh 5-8th-socket wrench-head
                 attach-socket-time planar oriented)

   :instancename "r5-attach-socket"

   :time-constraints '((start (end "r0-wrench-to-front"))
                       (duration (eval
                            (+ (fitts fred-lh 5-8th-socket)
                               (fitts fred-left-pocket
                                    fred-front-body-site)
                             attach-socket-time))))

   :on-success '(progn
                   (free-object-action fred-lh)
                   (free-object-action 5-8th-socket)
                   (hold-action wrench-head 5-8th-socket
                        :orientation-type '("orientation")))
```

based on each agent's capabilities. Not only does this allow the same animation script to be used for different agents, generating different analyses, but it also means that the definitions of the task-actions decomposition stops at the level of innate action. There is no need to have multiple task-action definitions for various physical attributes; *Jack* handles this issue for us.

Instruction Translation

We noted earlier that one advantage of a **task-action** level of specification was that it might allow an engineer/animator to animate tasks directly. In terms of the above task-actions, moving the cup to the table (noted in the introduction) could be animated by issuing either of two command sequences:

>   **grasp-action** (*agent-right-hand cup*)
>   **position-action** (*cup table-top*)
>   **free-object-action** (*cup*)

or:

>   **move-action** (*agent-right-hand cup table-top*)
>   **free-object-action** (*cup*).

In both cases, the engineer has decided to release the constraint between the *agent* and the *cup* as soon as the *cup* is on the *table-top*. The engineer has also described the required animation at the task-level.

Sequencing Sub-tasks

Yaps is a simultaneous language; that is, all task-action instantiations are resolved concurrently. To sequence the actions and force them to occur in a specific order, the engineer/animator must use the *timing-constraints* option provided by **Yaps**. This construct allows the user to specify starting, ending and duration conditions for the instantiation of each action. It is possible to achieve the ordering needed to create a sequential animation by predicating the starting condition of instruction-2 on the ending condition of instruction-1; but a task-action template, which is defined as a series of other task-actions, has the sequencing automatically built in via the instantiation process. If this were not the case, defining **grasp-action**, for example, would be impossible because achieving and completing the **reach-action** before starting the **hold-action** could not be guaranteed.

The actions do not need to be performed discretely. Other **Yaps** timing constructs allow the actions to be overlapped and delayed by specifying *(start (after 5 min))* or *(start now)*, for example [KKB88]. Nor is defining a discrete linear order on the sub-tasks the only possibility. The simultaneous nature of **Yaps** is used to animate actions (such as moving an object with both hands) by simultaneously animating:

>   **move-action** (*agent-left-hand box*)
>   **move-action** (*agent-right-hand box*).

The **Yaps** timing constraints provide a powerful mechanism for specifying the relationships among the task-actions in the animation. Timing is one of the most critical issues involved in generating realistic animations; the power that **Yaps** provides in resolving timing issues greatly enhances the potential of the *Jack* animation system.

Task Duration

The **Yaps** timing constraints provide a powerful mechanism for specifying the inter-relationships among the task-actions in the animation script. Timing is one of the most critical issues involved in generating realistic animations. We have already noted that it is not sufficient to simply list all the actions; they must be times, sequenced and connected temporally. As in Esakov's work, adaptations of Fitts' Law were used to determine mimimum action times. Fitts' Law was used to calculate the duration of all **reach-action** instantiations. Thus, time requirements were cumulative (i.e., the sum of the sub-task-action times). **Create-constraint** uses a small default constant time to estimate sub-task duration. Although Fitts' Law only approximates the action times in this domain and must be further scaled by a motivation factor, it does give reasonable estimates. Relative to one another, the sub-task times make sense. Although the length of each **task-action** might not be correct, the animation does appear to be temporally coherent.

6.3.6   Summary

Recent work in defining *animation behaviors* reviewed earlier in this book greatly expands the set of animation directives available in *Jack*. In our current work, we will investigate using the new animation behaviors to script animations. Since animation directives form the semantical basis for our action definitions, a more powerful set of animation directives provides us with a richer language with which to work. As it becomes easier to define new task-actions, the animator will spend less time coordinating sub-actions.

Finally, this new vocabulary will allow us to express tasks (or define task-actions) which differ from the earlier work in their semantic content. Our first attempt at rescripting the instruction set resulted in a more realistic animation, in that the new behaviors allowed us to include such low-level actions as `take step to maintain balance` when the animated agent was reaching beyond his comfort range. We need to compare the expressive powers of the previous animation directives with the enhanced set of animation behaviors.

6.4   A Model for Instruction Understanding

[5]The three experiments described in the previous sections were all concerned with the operational semantics of *single-clause commands*. But the range of

---

[5]Barbara Di Eugenio, Michael White, Breck Baldwin, Chris Geib, Libby Levison, Michael Moore.

tasks that can be communicated to an agent with such commands is very limited – the less expertise and experience on an agent's part, the more he needs to be told. A telling example of this is given in [Pri81]. Here, Prince compares a recipe for stuffed roast pig given in a nineteenth century French cookbook with that given in Rombauer's contemporary *The Joy of Cooking*. The former says, essentially, "Roast pig. Stuff with farce anglaise." Rombauer's instructions go on for two pages: she assumes very little culinary experience with pigs on the part of today's men and women.

Multi-clause commands are very common in maintenance and assembly instructions, such as the following examples from Air Force maintenance manual T.O. 1F-16C-2-94JG-50-2:

> "With door opened, adjust switch until roller contacts cam and continuity is indicated at pins A and B. Verify positive switch contact by tightening bottom nut one additional turn." (p. 5-24)

> "Hold drum timing pin depressed and position entrance unit on drum. Install three washers and three bolts, release drum timing pin, and torque bolts to 60-80 inch-pounds." (p. 6-14)

Now just as multi-clause texts are commonly organized into paragraphs, multi-clause instructions are commonly organized into *steps*. In fact, the above multi-clause commands are actually single steps from longer, multi-step instructions. While there are no firm guidelines as to what a single instruction step should encompass, there is a strong tendency at least for steps to be organized around small coherent sub-tasks (such as adjusting a switch or installing a component, as in the above examples). A typical step may specify several actions that need to be performed together to accomplish a single subtask, or several aspects of a single complex action (e.g. its purpose, manner, things to watch out for, appropriate termination conditions, etc.). The agent must develop some degree of understanding of the whole step before starting to act.

In our current work on instruction understanding, we add to this sub-task sense of step, the sense that a step specifies behavior that the agent must attend to continuously: while carrying out a step, the agent's attention is fixed on the task at hand. Communication with the instructor is not allowed until completion (or failure) of the current step. Because of this, a step defines the extent of the instructions that must be processed *before* the agent begins to act on them. (With some reflection on one's own confrontations with new instructions, it is easy to recall situations where one has tried to understand too much or to act on too little understanding. It is not always obvious when one should begin to act.)

While our focus is on multi-clause instructions, it turns out that many of their important features can be demonstrated simply with two-clause instructions. (As in many things, the biggest leap is from one to two.) The two-clause example we will use here to describe our framework for instruction understanding and animation is:

"Go into the kitchen to get me the coffee urn."

This example will be used to illustrate, among other things:

- expectations raised by instructions;

- the need for *incremental* generation of sub-goals (plan expansion) in order to act in accordance with instructions;

- the need to accommodate the agent's behavior in carrying out actions, to the objects being acted upon; and

- the need to develop plans at more than one level.

Figure 6.2 shows a schematic diagram of the AnimNL (ANIMation from Natural Language) architecture. Before going through the example, we want to call attention to the system's overall structure – in particular, to the fact that it consists of two relatively independent sets of processes: one set of which produces commitments to *act* for a particular purpose, what we call *animated task actions* – e.g.

- goto(door1, open(door1)) – "go to door1 for the purpose of opening it"

- grasp(urn1, carry(urn1)) – "grasp urn1 for the purpose of carrying it"

and the other set of which figures out how the agent should *move* in order to act for that purpose. In this framework, instructions lead to initial commitments to act, and actions once embarked upon allow further commitments to be made and acted upon. (While our discussion here will be in terms of single-agent procedures, it can be extended to multi-agent procedures by adding communicative and coordinating actions. As shown in earlier chapters, both *Jack* and its behavioral simulator can support the activity of multiple agents. However, extending the upper set of processes to delineate the communication and coordination required of multiple agents cooperating on a task requires solution of many problems currently under investigation by members of the AI planning community.

We now begin by giving AnimNL the instruction step:

"Go into the kitchen to get me the coffee urn."

A picture of the agent in its starting situation, when it is given the instruction, is shown in Plate 6.

Steps are first processed by a parser that uses a combinatory categorial grammar (CCG) [Ste90] to produce an action representation based on Jackendoff's *Conceptual Structures* [Jac90]. We are using CCG because of its facility with conjoined constituents, which are common in instructions – for example

"Clear and rope off an area around the aircraft and post warning signs." [Air Force Maintenance manual T.O. 1F-16C-2-94JG-50-2]

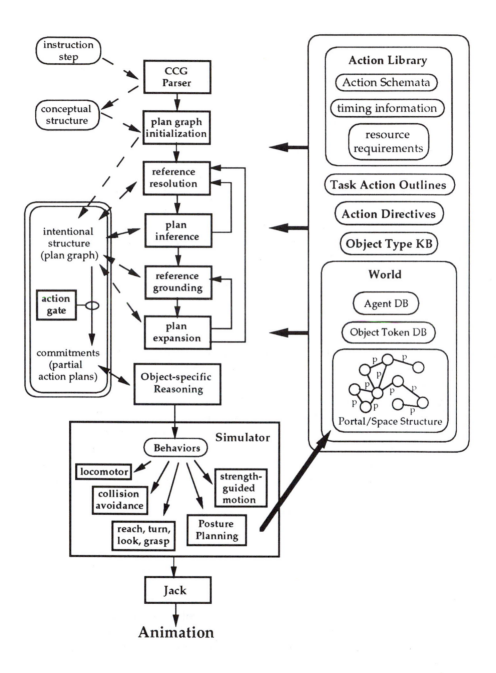

Figure 6.2: AnimNL System Architecture.

We are using Jackendoff's Conceptual Structures for two reasons: first, the primitives of his decompositional theory capture important generalizations about action descriptions and their relationships to one another, and second, they reveal where information may be missing from an utterance and have to be provided by inference. For the instruction step "Go into the kitchen to get me the coffee urn", the parser produces the following structure:

$$\left[\begin{array}{l} \text{GO}_{\text{Sp}}([\text{AGENT}]_i, [\text{TO}([\text{IN}([\text{KITCHEN}])])]) \\ \text{FOR}(\beta) \end{array} \right]_\alpha$$

$$[\text{CAUSE}(i, [\text{GO}_{\text{Sp}}([\text{COFFEE-URN}]_j, k)])]_\beta$$

$$\left[\begin{array}{l} \text{FROM}([\text{AT}(j)]) \\ \text{TO}(l) \end{array} \right]_k$$

This representation makes explicit the fact that getting the coffee urn involves its moving from its current location to a new one (which should be the location of the instructor). The FOR-function (derived from the *to*-phrase) encodes the purpose relation holding between the *go*-action α and the *get*-action β. Indices indicate different instances of a single conceptual type [ZV92].

From these indexed conceptual structures, an initial *plan graph* is constructed to represent the agent's intentions, beliefs and expectations about the task it is to perform. To do this, the system consults the agent's knowledge of actions and plans (the *Action KB* and *Plan Library* in Figure 6.2), to develop hypotheses about the instructor-intended relationships between the specified actions (e.g., temporal relations, enablement relations, generation relations, etc.). The initial plan graph for our running example is shown in Figure 6.3.

This initial plan graph is further elaborated through processes of *reference resolution*, *plan inference*, *reference grounding*, *plan expansion* and *performance* (through *simulation*). To show the interaction between these processes and how they are used to elaborate the plan graph, we will contrast our example

"Go into the kitchen to get me the coffee urn."

with a somewhat different but related example

"Go into the kitchen and wash out the coffee urn."

In the first case, recall from the conceptual structure produced by the parser, that "get me" is interpreted as an instance of a "cause something to go somewhere" action. One recipe that the system has in its *Plan Library* for accomplishing this is shown in Figure 6.4. With respect to this recipe, "go" can be seen as a substep of "get" – which is one way it can serve the purpose of "get". (This action representation and the plan graph are described in greater detail in [EW92].)

Getting an object from one place to another requires first going to its location. This leads to the assumption, noted in Figure 6.3, that the coffee

A1: BE(urn, IN([other-room]))

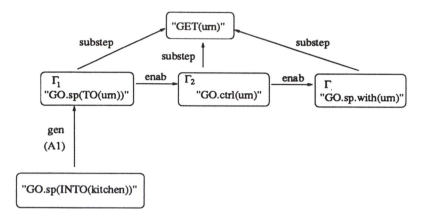

Figure 6.3: Initial Plan Graph: "Go into the kitchen and get me the coffee urn."

urn is in the kitchen. (The role of plan inference in instruction understanding is discussed in more detail in [Di 92, DW92].) Reference resolution cannot contribute any further constraints to the description "the coffee urn", since (1) there is no urn in the discourse context (nor anything that has a unique coffee urn associated with it), and (2) the assumption that the urn is in the kitchen is incompatible with its being unique in the current spatio-temporal context (which is the room next to the kitchen). Reference grounding does not attempt to associate this description with an object in the current spatio-temporal context, for the same reason. In fact, the agent will not attempt to ground this referring expression until it has entered the kitchen. (Whether the agent then succeeds immediately in grounding the expression will depend on whether the urn is perceivable – i.e., out in full view. We will discuss this shortly. In any case, the agent *expects* to be able to get access to the urn when it gets to the kitchen. This is what will drive it to *seek* the urn, if it is not in view when it gets to the kitchen.)

In the contrasting example "Go into the kitchen and wash out the coffee urn", the system again hypothesizes that the purpose relation between *go* and *wash-out* is a substep relation – but in this case, it is because washing out an object requires being at a washing site (e.g., a sink or tub). That kitchens usually have sinks gives further weight to this hypothesis.

Reference resolution may now contribute something to the agent's understanding of the definite expression "the coffee urn". While the discourse context does not provide evidence of a unique coffee urn, either directly or by association, there is also no evidence *against* the hypothesis that the urn is in the current spatio-temporal context. An initial hypothesis added by reference resolution that the urn is in the current space, if confirmed by reference

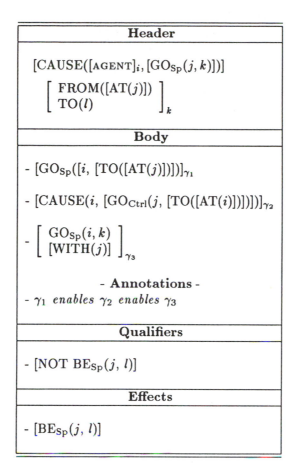

Figure 6.4: A *Move Something Somewhere* Action.

grounding, would lead plan expansion (through sub-goal generation) to get the agent over to its location. Failure of that hypothesis would lead to the alternative hypothesis that the coffee urn is in the kitchen. This is the same hypothesis as in the original example – it has just arisen in a different way.

The next thing to discuss is how the plan graph is expanded, and why it is expanded incrementally, as actions are performed in accordance with earlier elements of the plan graph. *How* it is expanded is through subgoal generation down to what we have called *annotated task actions*. This process makes use of a new kind of planner that (1) eschews pre-conditions in favor of decisions based on the agent's positive and negative intentions, and (2) takes upcoming intentions into account when deciding how to expand current goals, so as to put the agent in the best position with respect to satisfying those intentions. This planner, called *ItPlanS*, is described in more detail in [Gei92]. It is also

Figure 6.5: The Urn is Not Visible, so Cabinets will be Opened.

the source of the annotations of purpose in annotated task actions.

The main reason *why* the plan graph is expanded incrementally is that the agent does not have sufficient knowledge, before beginning to act, of what it will need to do later. In particular, AnimNL assumes that an agent cannot have up-to-date *knowledge* of any part of its environment that is outside its direct perception. (An AnimNL agent may know what non-visible parts of its environment *were* like, when it saw them earlier, and have expectations about what they *will be* like, when it sees them next, but its *knowledge* is limited to general truths about the world and to its direct perceptions.) As for the extent of the agent's perception, it is assumed that an agent cannot see into any space that has no *portal* open into the space the agent occupies. Thus AnimNL agents have to open doors, closets, boxes, etc., if they want to know what is inside, or go into other rooms to find out what is there.

What this means in our example is that only the plan graph node corresponding to "go into the kitchen" can be expanded – in this case, to "go over to the door", "open door", and "enter kitchen" – before the agent begins to act. The node corresponding to "go to the location of the coffee urn" cannot be expanded until the door has been opened and the agent can see whether or not the urn is visible. If it is visible, the agent can go to its location (Plate 6). If it is not visible, this same node must be expanded with actions corresponding to finding the urn – going through the kitchen cabinets one at a time looking for the urn, until it is found or all cabinets have been searched (Figure 6.5).

When an annotated task action becomes sufficiently specified for the agent

to be ready to commit to it and temporal dependencies permit such commitment, it is gated, triggering other, low-level planning processes (see Figure 6.2
below the "action gate"). An annotated task action is sufficiently specified if

- the action is "executable" (i.e., a *task action*, as described in Section 6.3).

- all actions temporally prior to it have been committed to. (Note that
  previous actions need not be completed before a new action is committed
  to: an agent can be (and usually is) doing more than one thing at a
  time.)

- its purpose has been determined.

It is worthwhile saying a bit more here about these purpose annotations,
since we have come to believe they play a large part in low-level decisions
about how to act. The kind of observations that motivates them are the
following:

- when told to pick up a book and hand it to someone, an agent will grasp
  it one way;

- when told to pick up the same book and turn it over, an agent will
  commonly grasp it in quite a different way;

- when told to pick up the book and open to page 70, the agent will grasp
  it yet a third way.

- when just told to pick up the book, and nothing further, agents commonly grasp it, lift it up and wait expectantly for the next command.

These variations in grasp extend to such low-level features as grasp site and
wrist position.

What we have tentatively concluded from such observations is that when
agents don't know the purpose of some action they are told to perform, they
put themselves into a position that easily supports subsequent action. Of
course, always going into a position in which an agent is poised for subsequent action is very inefficient, especially when the agent knows what that
subsequent action will be. In that case, he or she acts in such a way to
smoothly and efficiently transition from one to the other. In AnimNL, purpose annotations (including "PFA" or *poised for action*) are there to allow the
simulator, upon action commitment, to come up with the most effective ways
of moving the agent's body for the given purpose. It is also why the system is
designed to delay commitment until it knows the purpose of any task action
or knows that the only thing it *can* know is PFA.

When an action is committed to, there is still further work to be done
in order to determine the agent's behavior. In particular, one result of the
experiment described in the previous section (Section 6.3) was our recognition
of the need for tailoring an agent's behavior in carrying out an action to the

type of object given as an argument to that action. This follows from the fact that the same Natural Language verb is commonly used with different objects to denote very different behavior on an agent's part, and for a task animation to be correct, these differences must be depicted.

Consider, for example, the following definition (from [JCMM73]) of the word "remove" and sentences illustrating its use:

Remove: to perform operations necessary to take an equipment unit out of the next larger assembly or system; to take off or eliminate; to take or move away.

     1a. Remove bleed air shutoff valves.

     1b. Remove bolts from nuts.

     2. Remove paint.

     3. Remove covers.

For each different object, the behavior needed to effect a "remove" is quite different. The question is whether to define a single *remove-action*, to use in animating both *Remove the paint* and *Remove the bolt*? The alternative – defining a multitude of animation procedures (e.g. *remove-paint, remove-bolt, remove-nut, remove-nail, remove-boxtop*, etc.) – appears expensive in terms of time and effort, and prone to error.

The solution we are adopting is to build a hybrid system. Instead of specifying complete definitions for each verb, we can identify the *core* or *kernel* action for a verb like *remove* in a fashion similar to that described in Section 6.2. We will use this core meaning, central to many different instantiations of the verb, in building the task-action. The missing information can be supplied by the verb's object: The knowledge base is object-oriented and so can store relevant information about individual objects. For example, one slot of information might be the DOFs an object has – a bolt "knows" (i.e., its geometric constraints specify) around which axis it turns. Joint and rotation information is already available in *Jack*.

The hybrid system would process an instruction by combining the information in the two representations – the underspecified definitions of the task-actions, in conjunction with the object-oriented knowledge base. By identifying which information is lacking in the task-actions, the system can try to supply that information from the knowledge base.

The advantages of a hybrid system is economy of both action definitions and of the object feature information to be stored. We no longer need to worry about developing separate definitions for each animation movement based on distinct verb/object pairs. Instead we take advantage of the compositional nature of the task-actions, and the object-oriented, hierarchical knowledge-base. Using these utilities, we can define a single animation definition for *remove* which will allow us to animate both *Remove the bolt* and *Remove nuts from bolts* while still distinguishing the instruction *Remove covers*.

Our work on using complex Natural Language instructions to motivate the behavior of animated agents is still in its infancy. There is much more to be done before it is a useful tool in the hands of task designers and human factors engineers. On the other hand, we have begun to demonstrate its potential flexibility in accommodating the task behavior of an agent to the environment in which the task is being carried out and the agent's own capabilities.

Chapter 7

Epilogue

[1]To define a future for the work described in this book, it is essential to keep in mind the broad goals which motivated the efforts in the first place. Useful and usable software is desired, to be sure, but the vision of manipulating and especially *instructing* a realistically behaved animated agent is the greater ambition. Some of our visions for the near future are presented, not just for the sake of prognostication, but for its exciting prospects and possibilities.

Any discussion of the future of software must take into account the extraordinary pace of developments in the hardware arena. Even conservative predictions of hardware capabilities such as speed and capacity over the five year term lead one perilously close to science fiction. Accordingly, predictions of "better, faster, cheaper, more reliable, more fault tolerant, more highly parallel computers" are easy to make but do little to inform us of the applications these fantastic machines will facilitate. Rather, as general purpose computers improve in all these ways, specialized hardware solutions will decrease in importance and robust, usable software and symbiotic human-computer interfaces will remain the crucial link between a task and a solution.

Transforming research into practice is a lengthy process, consisting of a flow of concepts from ideas through algorithms to implementations, from testing and analysis through iterated design, and finally transfer of demonstrably workable concepts to external users and actual applications. This entire process may span years, from the initial description of the concept to a fielded system. The publication of initial results often breeds over-optimism and has been known to lead researchers to allow false expectations to arise in the minds of potential users, with unfortunate results. (Automatic machine translation of text, speech understanding, and early promises of Artificial Intelligence problem solving are good examples of premature speculations.) At the other end of the spectrum, however, are concepts which take a long time to work their way into mainstream technological consciousness. (3D computer graphics is a good example where concepts and even working systems pre-dated

---

[1]With the help of Mark Steedman.

widespread commercial availability by more than a decade.) So we will attempt to strike a balance in making speculations: while looking toward a long term research plan we will generally consider technology transfer to occur when serious but sympathetic users can experiment and accomplish real work with it. Our experience with software in the past is both our model and our promise for expecting new concepts to eventually reach potential users for evaluation and feedback.

7.1 A Roadmap Toward the Future

We seek to study the conceptual structure and limits of "virtual agents" in "simulated tasks" (VAST): the software and interface systems necessary to permit a user to describe, control, animate, analyze, interact with, and cooperate with multiple virtual computer-synthesized human models. We will remain cognizant of anticipated developments in underlying computer capabilities, but our principal intention will be to probe the intelligent software and user-interface issues. VAST focuses on the simulated human figure not just as a graphical entity but as an active, behaviorally complex *agent* who can follow instructions and autonomously negotiate its own way in the world.

Recall that our introduction emphasized certain simulation goals:

- Create an interactive computer graphics human model;

- Endow it with reasonable biomechanical properties;

- Provide it with "human-like" behaviors;

- Use this simulated human as an agent to effect changes in its world;

- Describe and guide its tasks through natural language instructions;

VAST augments this list to further improve the symbiosis between user and virtual agents:

- Control the agent through natural manual interfaces;

- Automatically generate explications or commentary on its behavior as sub-titles (text), voice-over or its own speech;

- Coordinate the activity of multiple agents engaged in a task.

We have probed the state-of-the-art in the first set of goals, but many problems and prospects remain for study. Indeed, there are other efforts that are advancing human modeling and animation. But our emphasis on interactivity and usability, especially by non-animators, outweighs mere visual beauty.

7.1.1 Interactive Human Models

While we are currently partway toward this goal with *Jack*, there are enhancements that are necessary before a virtual human looks and behaves realistically. Increases in hardware capability will certainly aid in the presentation of highly detailed models with smooth real-time response. The realistic and beautiful human models created by the Thalmanns [MTT90, MTT91a] are illustrative of the surface veracity possible under non-real-time conditions.

7.1.2 Reasonable Biomechanical Properties

Joint limits prevent unnatural adjacent body segment postures, but do nothing to prevent non-adjacent collisions. Collision-avoidance should be an implicit part of interactive manipulation for body integrity and natural appearance. In addition, clothing or equipment worn by the virtual human should demonstrate similar collision-free behavior.

Realistic strength models for the whole body and especially the torso should be incorporated into the model not only as a source of data but as an active resource for body motions. Preliminary work on strength-guided motion has shown feasibility, but more study of joint torque distribution strategies under comfort and loading constraints is needed. Ongoing "performance" models of the virtual human should be maintained throughout an interactive session or animation so that realistic assessments of workload and fatigue may be monitored.

7.1.3 Human-like Behaviors

We must continue to build a "primitive" behavior library so that the "innate" motion vocabulary of the virtual figure is as broad as possible. Ideally the behaviors can be "taught" to the figure rather than procedurally coded. Each behavior should enumerate the consequences of its execution so that higher level planning activities may take its potential effects into account.

Posture planning should take into account the spatial organization of the world and the virtual agent's desire to maximize effective behavior while minimizing useless movements (work). This can be done, in part, by having effective collision-avoidance schemes for articulated figures and, in part, by using symbolical spatial information to prune the high-dimensional numerical search space and move the figure into predictably useful postures. We already realize that classical AI planning paradigms are too weak for posture planning, and more reactive, incremental planners with "mental motion simulation" are needed.

Moving a virtual figure around an environment requires more than simple locomotion behavior: the behavioral repertoire and planner should understand crawling, climbing, jumping, sliding, etc. With this large repertoire of possible behaviors, a planner will be busy coordinating them all and sorting out priorities, even for simple activities.

7.1.4   Simulated Humans as Virtual Agents

The notion of skill level should be quantified with notions of context-sensitive execution time and [optimal] motion smoothness. Synthesized animations should be customized to the user's own body size and capabilities (or limitations) for training situations.

The environment in which the virtual humans work must be imported from any number of external CAD systems, preferably through standardized interfaces. During importation, perceptually and behaviorally significant features such as articulations, handles, removable parts, and open spaces (holes) should be recognized from the geometric model. We can expect some CAD systems to offer some of this data, but in general we should expect to build enhanced semantics into the models interactively or semi-automatically ourselves. For example, handles are needed to determine likely grasp points, and articulations, parts, and holes are needed for automatic generation of disassembly behaviors given only the object descriptions.

7.1.5   Task Guidance through Instructions

For a designer to use Natural Language instructions to describe and guide a virtual agent through a task, the overall system must know how to *understand* instructions and to *use* them appropriately in a given environment. Instructions must be understood in terms of intention – what is meant to be *achieved* in the world – and in terms of positive and negative constraints on the behavior used to achieve it. Instructions must be used to interpret features of the environment and to coordinate the agent's task-level knowledge and skills in acting to achieve its given goals. Advances in AI planning and execution are coming at a rapid rate, independent of our own work, and we will be incorporating those advances into VAST, to make the bridge to actual behavior.

7.1.6   Natural Manual Interfaces and Virtual Reality

The virtual figure should exist in a virtual 3D world that is accessible to a user with a minimum of training and little, if any, computer expertise. While mouse and keyboard input to *Jack* addresses some of these goals, it is still too "low level." By taking advantage of novel 3D, 6D, multiple 6D, and hand posture sensor input devices, the user's movements can be translated directly into virtual figure behaviors. The trick is *not* to make the mapping one-to-one, so the user exhausts herself flailing arms and twisting her body as the current Virtual Reality paradigms would have one do. Rather the mapping should have considerable intelligent "multipliers" so that the suggestion of action is enough to precipitate complete behaviors in the virtual human. We can already control the center of mass of the figure to effect a significant multiplier of input effort, this needs to be extended to arm gestures, view focus, and locomotion generation. We envision a strong corroborating role from our animation from instructions work, such as speech-based commands. Minimal device encumbrances on the user are deemed essential.

7.1.7 Generating Text, Voice-over, and Spoken Explication for Animation

Animation for purposes of instruction in the performance of a task frequently requires spoken or written text, as well as graphic presentation, if it is to be understood. Negative instructions such as "warnings" or "cautions" provide an obvious example. While written captions can be adequate for some purposes, presenting few problems for animation, spoken language is more efficient and more engaging of the viewers' attention. For certain purposes even, a human face speaking in accompaniment to action is the most efficient and attention-holding device of all. Among the problems involved in including linguistic information in an on-going animation are: appropriately allocating information to the different modalities; integration of the two modalities over time; limitations of existing speech synthesizers with respect to intonation; integration of a facial animation with speech. All of these are tasks which the animator can in principle take over, but all of them, especially the last, are laborious. It would be highly desirable to automate all of them, especially if they are to be used in highly interactive animations, in which model-based synthesis-by-rule is required, rather than image based techniques.

One of the extensions to *Jack* is an animated facial model with a programming language for integrating its movements with a segmental representation of speech [PBS91, Pel91]. This effort is now focused on the following extensions:

- Provide an improved programming language for facial animation of speech.

- Provide a discourse semantics for spoken intonation in terms of appropriate knowledge representations.

- Perform automatic generation from such semantic representations of phonological representations of spoken explications, including appropriate intonational markers of contrast and background, for input to a speech synthesizer, with or without the facial animation program.

7.1.8 Coordinating Multiple Agents

Our principle goal has been getting a single agent to *behave plausibly* in response to multi-clause instruction steps. One goal for the longer term involves producing *sensible behavior* on the part of a single virtual agent and plausible behavior from a group of virtual agents engaged in a multi-agent task.

Coordinated multi-person simulations will be the next [large] step after an individual agent's actions can be effectively determined. Such simulations require physical, task and cognitive coordination among the agents. For physical coordination, our particular efforts will focus on determining timing coordination, strength and workload distribution, and mutual achievement of spatial goals. In these multi-agent tasks, the interactive user may or may not be one of the participating agents.

Task coordination requires augmenting our task knowledge base with information on multi-agent tasks. This is essential both for understanding the text of multi-agent task instructions and for interpolating between explicit instructions, since instructions cannot (by virtue of not knowing the precise circumstances under which they will be carried out) specify everything.

For cognitive coordination among the agents, communication may be necessary to determine or alter the leadership role, initiate activity, keep it moving along, interrupt or abort it, or rest on imminent fatigue. Research on communication for coordinating multi-agent tasks is being carried on at other institutions [GS89, CL91, Loc91]. In the longer term, we look to importing the results of this research and incorporating it into the VAST framework. Until then, we will focus on single virtual agents or centrally-controlled multiple agents engaged in tasks in which communication is not required for coordination.

7.2   Conclusion

There are a multitude of other directions for virtual agent work. Some of these are automatic view control, a perceptual "sense," spatial reasoning for improved posture planning, recognizing and accommodating task failures, skill acquisition, flexible object interactions, animation presentation techniques, behaving with common sense, enriched instruction understanding, and speech-based agent animation. But all that's for a sequel.

Bibliography

[AAW74]   M. A. Ayoub, M. M. Ayoub, and A. Walvekar. A biomechanical model for the upper extremity using optimization techniques. *Human Factors*, 16(6):585–594, 1974.

[Abb53]   Edwin A. Abbott. *Flatland; a romance of many dimensions*. Dover, New York, NY, 1953.

[ABS90]   T. Alameldin, N. Badler, and T. Sobh. An adaptive and efficient system for computing the 3-D reachable workspace. In *Proceedings of IEEE International Conference on Systems Engineering*, pages 503–506, 1990.

[AC87]   Phillip Agre and David Chapman. Pengi: An implementation of a theory of activity. *Proceedings of the AAAI-87 Conference*, pages 268–272, June 1987.

[AD90]   T.L. Anderson and M. Donath. Animal behavior as a paradigm for developing robot autonomy. In Pattie Maes, editor, *Designing Autonomous Agents*, pages 145–168. MIT Press, 1990.

[AG85]   W. W. Armstrong and Mark Green. The dynamics of articulated rigid bodies for purposes of animation. *The Visual Computer*, 1(4):231–240, 1985.

[AGL87]   William Armstrong, Mark Green, and R. Lake. Near-real-time control of human figure models. *IEEE Computer Graphics and Applications*, 7(6):52–61, June 1987.

[AGR+81]   M. M. Ayoub, C. F. Gidcumb, M. J. Reeder, M. Y. Beshir, H. A. Hafez, F. Aghazadeh, and N. J. Bethea. Development of an atlas of strengths and establishment of an appropriate model structure. Technical Report (Final Report), Institute for Ergonomics Research, Texas Tech Univ., Lubbock, TX, Nov. 1981.

[AGR+82]   M. M. Ayoub, C. F. Gidcumb, M. J. Reeder, H. A. Hafez, M. Y. Beshir, F. Aghazadeh, and N. J. Bethea. Development of a female atlas of strengths. Technical Report (Final Report), Institute for Ergonomics Research, Texas Tech Univ., Lubbock, TX, Feb. 1982.

[AHN62]   E. Asmussen and K. Heeboll-Nielsen. Isometric muscle strength in relation to age in men and women. *Ergonomics*, 5(1):167–169, 1962.

[Ala91]   Tarek Alameldin. *Three Dimensional Workspace Visualization for Redundant Articulated Chains*. PhD thesis, Computer and Information Science, Univ. of Pennsylvania, Philadelphia, PA, 1991.

[Alb81]   James S. Albus. *Brains, Behavior, and Robotics*. BYTE Books, McGraw-Hill, 1981.

[Ali90]   Alias Research, Inc. *ALIAS V3.0 Reference Manual*, 1990.

[AM71]   B. Anson and C. McVay. *Surgical Anatomy*. Saunders, Philadelphia,

PA, 1971.

[And60]　E. Anderson. A semigraphical method for the analysis of complex problems. *Technometrics*, 2:381–391, 1960.

[And72]　D. F. Andrews. Plots of high-dimensional data. *Biometrics*, 28(125), 1972.

[Ayo91]　M. Ayoub. From biomechanical modeling to biomechanical simulation. In Edward Boyle, John Ianni, Jill Easterly, Susan Harper, and Medhat Korna, editors, *Human-Centered Technology for Maintainability: Workshop Proceedings*. Wright-Patterson Air Force Base, Armstrong Laboratory, June 1991.

[Bad75]　Norman I. Badler. *Temporal scene analysis: Conceptual descriptions of object movements*. PhD thesis, Computer Science, Univ. of Toronto, Toronto, Canada, 1975. (Univ. of Pennsylvania, Computer and Information Science, Tech. Report MS-CIS-76-4).

[Bad76]　Norman I. Badler. Conceptual descriptions of physical activities. *American Journal of Computational Linguistics*, Microfiche 35:70–83, 1976.

[Bad89]　Norman I. Badler. A representation for natural human movement. In J. Gray, editor, *Dance Technology I*, pages 23–44. AAHPERD Publications, Reston, VA, 1989.

[Bar89]　David Baraff. Analytical methods for dynamic simulation of non-penetrating rigid bodies. *Computer Graphics*, 23(3):223–232, 1989.

[BB78]　Norman I. Badler and Ruzena Bajcsy. Three-dimensional representations for computer graphics and computer vision. *Computer Graphics*, 12(3):153–160, Aug. 1978.

[BB88]　Ronen Barzel and Alan H. Barr. A modeling system based on dynamic constraints. *Computer Graphics*, 22(4):179–188, 1988.

[BBA88]　P. G. Bullough and O. Boachie-Adjei. *Atlas of Spinal Diseases*. Lippincott, Philadelphia, PA, 1988.

[BBB87]　Richard H. Bartels, John C. Beatty, and Brian A. Barsky. *An Introduction to Splines for Use in Computer Graphics and Geometric Modeling*. Morgan Kaufmann, Los Altos, CA, 1987.

[BBH+90]　C. Blanchard, S. Burgess, Y. Harvill, J. Lanier, A. Lasko, M. Oberman, and M. Teitel. Reality built for two: A virtual reality tool. *Computer Graphics*, 24(2):35–36, 1990.

[BC68]　R. Beckett and K. Chang. An evaluation of the kinematics of gait by minimum energy. *Journal of Biomechanics*, 1:147–159, 1968.

[BC89]　Armin Bruderlin and Tom W. Calvert. Goal-directed, dynamic animation of human walking. *Computer Graphics*, 23(3):233–242, 1989.

[BCS90]　R. D. Beer, H. J. Chiel, and L. S. Sterling. A biological perspective on autonomous agent design. In Pattie Maes, editor, *Designing Autonomous Agents*, pages 169–186. MIT Press, 1990.

[Bec92]　Welton M. Becket. Simulating adaptive autonomous behavior with recurrent neural networks. Technical report, Computer and Information Science, Univ. of Pennsylvania, Philadelphia, PA, 1992. To appear.

[BEK+81]　P. Bapu, S. Evans, P. Kitka, M. Korna, and J. McDaniel. User's guide for COMBIMAN programs. Technical Report AFAMRL-TR-80-91, Univ. of Dayton Research Institute, Jan 1981. U.S.A.F. Report.

[Ber83]　J. Bertin. *Semiology of Graphics, translated by W. J. Berg*. The Univ. of Wisconsin Press, 1983.

[BG86]　Norman I. Badler and Jeffrey S. Gangel. Natural language input for human task description. In *Proc. ROBEXS '86: The Second International Workshop on Robotics and Expert Systems*, pages 137–148. Instrument Society of America, June 1986.

[BHJ+83] Michael Brady, John M. Hollerbach, Timothy L. Johnson, Tomas Lozano-Pérez, and Matthew T. Mason, editors. *Robot Motion: Planning and Control*. MIT Press, Cambridge, MA, 1983.

[Bie86] Eric Allan Bier. Snap-dragging. *Computer Graphics*, 20(3):233–240, 1986.

[Bie87] Eric Allan Bier. Skitters and jacks: Interactive positioning tools. In *Proceedings of 1986 ACM Workshop on Interactive 3D Graphics*, Chapel Hill, NC, Oct. 1987.

[Bie90] Eric Allan Bier. Snap-dragging in three dimensions. *Computer Graphics*, 24(2):193–204, March 1990.

[BKK+85] Norman I. Badler, Jonathan Korein, James U. Korein, Gerald Radack, and Lynne Brotman. Positioning and animating human figures in a task-oriented environment. *The Visual Computer*, 1(4):212–220, 1985.

[BKT86] K. Boff, L Kaufmann, and J Thomas, editors. *The Handbook of Perception and Human Performance*. John Wiley and Sons, New York, NY, 1986.

[BL88] Kenneth R. Boff and Janet E. Lincoln, editors. *Engineering Data Compendium*. Harry G. Armstrong Aerospace Medical Research Laboratory, Wright-Patterson Air Force Base, OH, 1988.

[BL89] J. Barraquand and J. Latombe. Robot motion planning: A distributed representation approach. Technical Report STAN-CS-89-1257, Computer Science, Stanford Univ., Stanford, CA, May 1989.

[Bli82] James F. Blinn. A generalization of algebraic surface drawing. *ACM Transactions on Graphics*, 1(3):235–256, July 1982.

[BLL89a] J. Barraquand, B. Langlois, and J. Latombe. Numerical potential field techniques for robot path planning. Technical Report STAN-CS-89-1285, Computer Science, Stanford Univ., Stanford, CA, 1989.

[BLL89b] J. Barraquand, B. Langlois, and J. Latombe. Robot motion planning with many degrees of freedom and dynamic constraints. In *Fifth Intl. Sym. on Robotics Research (ISRR), Tokyo*, pages 1–10, 1989.

[BLP78] Edward G. Britton, James S. Lipscomb, and Michael E. Pique. Making nested rotations convenient for the user. *Computer Graphics*, 12(3):222–227, August 1978.

[BLP83] Rodney A. Brooks and Tomas Lozano-Pérez. A subdivision algorithm in configuration space for findpath with rotation. In *Proc. 8th Int. Joint Conf. Artificial Intelligence*, pages 799–806, 1983.

[BMB86] Norman I. Badler, Kamran H. Manoochehri, and David Baraff. Multidimensional input techniques and articulated figure positioning by multiple constraints. In *Proc. Workshop on Interactive 3D Graphics*, New York, NY, Oct. 1986. ACM.

[BMTT90] R. Boulic, Nadia Magnenat-Thalmann, and Daniel Thalmann. A global human walking model with real-time kinematic personification. *The Visual Computer*, 6:344–358, 1990.

[BMW87] Norman I. Badler, Kamran Manoochehri, and G. Walters. Articulated figure positioning by multiple constraints. *IEEE Computer Graphics and Applications*, 7(6):28–38, 1987.

[BN88] L. S. Brotman and A. N. Netravali. Motion interpolation by optimal control. *Computer Graphics*, 22(4):309–315, 1988.

[Bob88]   J. E. Bobrow. Optimal robot path planning using the minimum-time criteria. *IEEE Journal of Robotics and Automation*, 4(4):443–450, August 1988.

[Bod77]   Margaret Boden. *Artificial Intelligence and Natural Man*. Basic Books, New York, NY, 1977.

[BOK80]   Norman I. Badler, Joseph O'Rourke, and Bruce Kaufman. Special problems in human movement simulation. *Computer Graphics*, 14(3):189–197, July 1980.

[BOT79]   Norman I. Badler, Joseph O'Rourke, and Hasida Toltzis. A spherical representation of a human body for visualizing movement. *IEEE Proceedings*, 67(10):1397–1403, Oct. 1979.

[BP88]   Alain Berthoz and Thierry Pozzo. Intermittent head stabilization during postural and locomotory tasks in humans. In B. Amblard, A. Berthoz, and F. Clarac, editors, *Posture and Gait: Development, Adaptation, and Modulation*. Excerpta Medica, 1988.

[Bra84]   Valentino Braitenberg. *Vehicles: Experiments in Synthetic Psychology*. The MIT Press, 1984.

[Bre89]   David E. Breen. Choreographing goal-oriented motion using cost functions. In N. Magnenat-Thalmann and D. Thalmann, editors, *State-of-the-Art in Computer Animation*, pages 141–151. Springer-Verlag, New York, NY, 1989.

[Bro83a]   Rodney A. Brooks. Planning collision-free motions for pick-and-place operations. *Int. Journal of Robotics Research*, 2(4):19–44, Winter 1983.

[Bro83b]   Rodney A. Brooks. Solving the find-path problem by good representation of free space. *IEEE Transactions on Systems, Man and Cybernetics*, SMC-13(3):190–197, Mar 1983.

[Bro86]   Rodney A. Brooks. A robust layered control system for a mobile robot. *IEEE Journal of Robotics and Automation*, pages 14–23, April 1986.

[Bro90]   Rodney A. Brooks. Elephants don't play chess. In Pattie Maes, editor, *Designing Autonomous Agents*, pages 3–18. MIT Press, 1990.

[Bru88]   Armin Bruderlin. Goal-directed, dynamic animation of bipedal locomotion. Master's thesis, Simon Fraser Univ., Vancouver, Canada, 1988.

[BS76]   Maxine Brown and Stephen W. Smoliar. A graphics editor for Labanotation. *Computer Graphics*, 10(2):60–65, 1976.

[BS79]   Norman I. Badler and Stephen W. Smoliar. Digital representations of human movement. *ACM Computing Surveys*, 11(1):19–38, March 1979.

[BS91]   Jules Bloomenthal and Ken Shoemake. Convolution surfaces. *Computer Graphics*, 25(4):251–256, 1991.

[BSOW78]   Norman I. Badler, Stephen W. Smoliar, Joseph O'Rourke, and Lynne Webber. The simulation of human movement. Technical Report MS-CIS-78-36, Computer and Information Science, Univ. of Pennsylvania, Philadelphia, PA, 1978.

[BW76]   N. Burtnyk and M. Wein. Interactive skeleton techniques for enhancing motion dynamics in key frame animation. *Communications of the ACM*, 19(10):564–569, Oct. 1976.

[BW90]   Aijaz A. Baloch and Allen M. Waxman. A neural system for behavioral conditioning of mobile robots. *IEEE International Joint Conference on Neural Networks*, 2:723–728, 1990.

[BwDL80]   Irmgard Bartenieff and (with Dori Lewis). *Body Movement: Coping with the Environment*. Gordon and Breach, New York, NY, 1980.

[BWKE91] Norman I. Badler, Bonnie L. Webber, Jugal K. Kalita, and Jeffrey Esakov. Animation from instructions. In Norman I. Badler, Brian A. Barsky, and David Zeltzer, editors, *Making Them Move: Mechanics, Control, and Animation of Articulated Figures*, pages 51–93. Morgan-Kaufmann, San Mateo, CA, 1991.

[CA84] D. B. Chaffin and G. B. J. Andersson. *Occupational Biomechanics*. John Wiley & Sons, 1984.

[Cal91] Tom Calvert. Composition of realistic animation sequences for multiple human figures. In Norman I. Badler, Brian A. Barsky, and David Zeltzer, editors, *Making Them Move: Mechanics, Control, and Animation of Articulated Figures*, pages 35–50. Morgan-Kaufmann, San Mateo, CA, 1991.

[Car72] Sven Carlsoo. *How Man Moves*. William Heinemann Ltd, 1972.

[Cat72] Edwin Catmull. A system for computer generated movies. In *Proceedings of ACM Annual Conference*, pages 422–431, August 1972.

[Cat78] E Catmull. The problems of computer-assisted animation. *Computer Graphics*, 12(3):348–353, August 1978.

[CB92] Wallace Ching and Norman I Badler. Fast motion planning for anthropometric figures with many degrees of freedom. In *IEEE Intl. Conf. on Robotics and Automation*, May 1992.

[CBR] K. Corker, A. Bejczy, and B. Rappaport. *Force/Torque Display For Space Teleoperation Control Experiments and Evaluation*. Cambridge, MA.

[CCP80] Tom Calvert, J. Chapman, and A. Patla. The integration of subjective and objective data in the animation of human movement. *Computer Graphics*, 14(3):198–203, July 1980.

[CCP82] Tom Calvert, J. Chapman, and A. Patla. Aspects of the kinematic simulation of human movement. *IEEE Computer Graphics and Applications*, 2(9):41–50, Nov. 1982.

[Ceb87] David Cebula. The semantic data model and large information requirements. Technical Report MS-CIS-87-72, Computer and Information Science, Univ. of Pennsylvania, Philadelphia, PA, 1987.

[Cen81] NASA Johnson Space Center. Space Shuttle Flight Data File Preparation Standards. Flight Operations Directorate, Operations Division, 1981.

[Che73] H. Chernoff. The use of faces to represent points in k-dimensional space graphically. *J. of the American Statistical Assoc.*, 68(342), 1973.

[CJ71] E. Y. Chao and D. H. Jacobson. Studies of human locomotion via optimal programming. *Mathematical Biosciences*, 6:239–306, 1971.

[CL91] P. Cohen and H. Levesque. Teamwork. *Nôus*, 25, 1991.

[CMS88] Michael Chen, S. Joy Mountford, and Abigail Sellen. A study in interactive 3-D rotation using 2-D control devices. *Computer Graphics*, 22(4):121–129, August 1988.

[Coo68] G.S. Cooper. A semantic analysis of English locative prepositions. Technical Report Report No. 1587, BBN: Clearinghouse for Federal Scientific and Technical Information, Springfield, VA, 1968.

[Del70] Cecily Dell. *A Primer for Movement Description*. Dance Notation Bureau, Inc., New York, NY, 1970.

[DH55] Jacques Denavit and Richard Hartenberg. A kinematic notation for lower pair mechanisms based on matrices. *Journal of Applied Mechanics*, 23, 1955.

[Di 92]   Barbara Di Eugenio. Goals and actions in Natural Language instructions. Technical Report MS-CIS-92-07, Computer and Information Science, Univ. of Pennsylvania, Philadelphia, PA, 1992.

[DLRG91]   Bruce R. Donald, Jed Lengyel, Mark Reichert, and Donald Greenberg. Real-time robot motion planning using rasterizing computer graphics hardware. *Computer Graphics*, 25(4):327–336, July 1991.

[Don84]   Bruce Donald. Motion planning with six degrees of freedom. Technical Report 791, MIT AI Lab, 1984.

[Don87]   B. Donald. A search algorithm for motion planning with six degrees of freedom. *Artificial Intelligence*, 31:295–353, 1987.

[Doo82]   Marianne Dooley. Anthropometric modeling programs – A survey. *IEEE Computer Graphics and Applications*, 2(9):17–25, Nov. 1982.

[Dru75]   C. Drury. Application of Fitts' Law to foot-pedal design. *Human Factors*, 17, 1975.

[DW92]   B. Di Eugenio and B. Webber. Plan recognition in understanding instructions. In *Proc. First Int'l Conference on Artificial Intelligence Planning Systems, College Park MD*, pages 52–61, June 1992.

[DX89]   Bruce Donald and Patrick Xavier. A provably good approximation algorithm for optimal-time trajectory planning. In *IEEE Intl. Conf. on Robotics and Automation*, pages 958–963, 1989.

[EB90]   Jeffrey Esakov and Norman I. Badler. An architecture for high-level human task animation control. In P. A. Fishwick and R. S. Modjeski, editors, *Knowledge-Based Simulation: Methodology and Application*, pages 162–199. Springer-Verlag, New York, NY, 1990.

[EB91]   Jeffrey Esakov and Norman I. Badler. Animation from instructions – video tape. In Norman I. Badler, Brian A. Barsky, and David Zeltzer, editors, *Making Them Move: Mechanics, Control, and Animation of Articulated Figures*. Morgan-Kaufmann, San Mateo, CA, 1991. Videotape.

[EBJ89]   Jeffery Esakov, Norman I. Badler, and M. Jung. An investigation of language input and performance timing for task animation. In *Graphics Interface '89*, pages 86–93, San Mateo, CA, June 1989. Morgan-Kaufmann.

[EC86]   S. M. Evans and D. B. Chaffin. Using interactive visual displays to present ergonomic information in workspace design. In W. Karwowski, editor, *Trends in Ergonomics/Human Factors III*. Elsevier Science Publishers B.V. (North-Holland), 1986.

[EI91]   Jill Easterly and John D. Ianni. Crew Chief: Present and future. In Edward Boyle, John Ianni, Jill Easterly, Susan Harper, and Medhat Korna, editors, *Human-Centered Technology for Maintainability: Workshop Proceedings*. Wright-Patterson Air Force Base, Armstrong Laboratory, June 1991.

[Emm85]   Arielle Emmett. Digital portfolio: Tony de Peltrie. *Computer Graphics World*, 8(10):72–77, Oct. 1985.

[EP87]   Ali Erkan Engin and Richard D. Peindl. On the biomechanics of human shoulder complex – I: Kinematics for determination of the shoulder complex sinus. *Journal of Biomechanics*, 20(2):103–117, 1987.

[EPE88]   S. M. Evans, S. L. Palmiter, and J. Elkerton. The edge system: Ergonomic design using graphic evaluation. The Annual Meeting of the Human Factors Society, Los Angeles, CA, Oct. 1988.

[Esa90]   Jeffrey Esakov. KB. Technical Report MS-CIS-90-03, Univ. of Pennsylvania, Philadelphia, PA, 1990.

[ET89]   Ali Erkan Engin and S. T. Tumer. Three-dimensional kinematic modelling of the human shoulder complex – I: Physical model and determination of joint sinus cones. *Journal of Biomechanical Engineering*, 111:107–112, May 1989.

[ETW81]   Kenneth B. Evans, Peter Tanner, and Marceli Wein. Tablet based valuators that provide one, two or three degrees of freedom. *Computer Graphics*, 15(3):91–97, 1981.

[Eva85]   Susan M. R. Evans. *Ergonomics in manual workspace design: Current practices and an alternative computer-assisted approach*. PhD thesis, Center for Ergonomics, Univ. of Michigan, Ann Arbor, MI, 1985.

[Eva88]   S. M. Evans. Use of biomechanical static strength models in workspace design. In *Proceedings for NATO Workshop on Human Performance Models in System Design*, Orlando, FL, May 1988.

[EW92]   Barbara Di Eugenio and Michael White. On the interpretation of Natural Language instructions. In *Proceedings of 1992 International Conference on Computational Linguistics (COLING-92)*, Nantes, France, 1992.

[Far88]   Gerald Farin. *Curves and Surfaces for Computer Aided Geometric Design*. Academic Press, San Diego, CA, 1988.

[Fav84]   Bernard Faverjon. Obstacle avoidance using an octree in the configuration space of a manipulator. In *IEEE Intl. Conf. on Robotics and Automation*, pages 504–512, 1984.

[FB85]   K. Fishkin and B. Barsky. An analysis and algorithm for filling propagation. In *Proceedings Graphics Interface*, pages 203–212, 1985.

[Fet82]   William Fetter. A progression of human figures simulated by computer graphics. *IEEE Computer Graphics and Applications*, 2(9):9–13, Nov. 1982.

[Fey86]   Carl R. Feynman. Modeling the appearance of cloth. Master's thesis, Massachusetts Institute of Technology, 1986.

[Fis86]   Paul A. Fishwick. *Hierarchical Reasoning: Simulating Complex Processes over Multiple Levels of Abstraction*. PhD thesis, Computer and Information Science, Univ. of Pennsylvania, Philadelphia, PA, 1986.

[Fis88]   Paul A. Fishwick. The role of process abstraction in simulation. *IEEE Transactions on Systems, Man and Cybernetics*, 18(1):18–39, Jan/Feb. 1988.

[Fis90]   K. Fishkin. Filling a region in a frame buffer. In A. Glassner, editor, *Graphics Gems*, pages 278–284. Academic Press, Cambridge, MA, 1990.

[Fit54]   P. Fitts. The information capacity of the human motor system in controlling the amplitude of movement. *Journal of Experimental Psychology*, 47:381–391, 1954.

[FKU77]   H. Fuchs, Z. Kedem, and S. Uselton. Optimal surface reconstruction from planar contours. *Communications of the ACM*, 20(10):693–702, Oct. 1977.

[Fle70]   R. Fletcher. A new approach to variable metric algorithms. *Computer Journal*, 13:317–322, 1970.

[FLP89]   H. Fuchs, M. Levoy, and M. Pizer. Interactive visualization of 3D medical data. *IEEE Transactions on Computers*, pages 46–57, August 1989.

[FMHR87] S.S. Fisher, M. McGreevy, J. Humphries, and W. Robinett. Virtual environment display system. In *Proceedings of 1986 ACM Workshop on Interactive 3D Graphics*, Chapel Hill, NC, Oct. 1987.

[FP64]   P. Fitts and J. Peterson. Information capacity of discrete motor responses. *Journal of Experimental Psychology*, 67(2), 1964.

[FS91]   James A. Freeman and David M. Skapura. *Neural Networks: Algorithms, Applications, and Programming Techniques*. Addison Wesley, 1991.

[FvDFH90] James D. Foley, Andries van Dam, Steven K. Feiner, and John F. Hughes. *Computer Graphics: Principles and Practice*. Addison-Wesley, Reading, MA, 1990. Second Edition.

[FW83]   T. W. Finin and B. L. Webber. BUP – A Bottom Up Parser. Technical Report MS-CIS-83-16, Computer and Information Science, Univ. of Pennsylvania, Philadelphia, PA, 1983.

[FW88]   David R. Forsey and Jane Wilhelms. Techniques for interactive manipulation of articulated bodies using dynamic analysis. In *Proceedings of Graphics Interface '88*, 1988.

[Gal80]   C. R. Gallistel. *The Orginization of Action: A New Synthesis*. Lawrence Elerbaum Associates, Publishers, Hillsdale, NJ, 1980. Distributed by the Halsted Press division of John Wiley & Sons.

[Gan85]   Jeffrey S. Gangel. A motion verb interface to a task animation system. Master's thesis, Computer and Information Science, Univ. of Pennsylvania, Philadelphia, PA, August 1985.

[Gei92]   Christopher Geib. Intentions in means-end planning. Technical Report MS-CIS-92-73, Dept. of Computer and Information Science, Univ. of Pennsylvania, Philadelphia, PA, 1992.

[GFS71]   R. M. Goldwyn, H. P. Friedman, and T. H. Siegel. Iteration and interaction in computer data bank analysis. *Computer in Biomedical Research*, 4:607–622, 1971.

[Gir87]   Michael Girard. Interactive design of 3D computer-animated legged animal motion. *IEEE Computer Graphics and Applications*, 7(6):39–51, 1987.

[Gir91]   Michael Girard. Constrained optimization of articulated animal movement in computer animation. In Norman I. Badler, Brian A. Barsky, and David Zeltzer, editors, *Making Them Move: Mechanics, Control, and Animation of Articulated Figures*, pages 209–232. Morgan-Kaufmann, San Mateo, CA, 1991.

[GL90]   Michael P. Georgeff and Amy L. Lansky. Reactive reasoning and planning. In James Allen, James Hendler, and Austin Tate, editors, *Readings in Planning*, pages 729–734. Morgon Kaufmann Publishers, Inc., 1990.

[GM85]   Michael Girard and A. A. Maciejewski. Computational modeling for the computer animation of legged figures. *Computer Graphics*, 19(3):263–270, 1985.

[GM86]   Carol M. Ginsberg and Delle Maxwell. Graphical marionette. In N. I. Badler and J. K. Tsotsos, editors, *Motion: Representation and Perception*, pages 303–310. Elsevier, North Holland, New York, NY, 1986.

[GMTT89] Jean-Paul Gourret, Nadia Magnenat-Thalmann, and Daniel Thalmann. Simulation of object and human skin deformations in a grasping task.

Computer Graphics, 23(3):21–30, 1989.

[Gol69]   D. Goldfarb. Extension of Davidon's variable metric method to maximization under linear inequality and equality constraints. *SIAM Journal of Appl. Math.*, 17:739–764, 1969.

[Gol70]   D. Goldfarb. A family of variable metric methods derived by variational means. *Math. Computation*, 24:23–26, 1970.

[Gom84]   Julian E. Gomez. Twixt: A 3D animation system. In *Proc. Eurographics '84*, pages 121–133, New York, NY, July 1984. Elsevier Science Publishers B.V.

[Gou84]   Laurent Gouzenes. Strategies for solving collision-free trajectories problems for mobile and manipulator robots. *Int. Journal of Robotics Research*, 3(4):51–65, Winter 1984.

[GP88]   Ralph Guggenheim and PIXAR. Tin Toy (excerpt). *SIGGRAPH Video Review*, 38, 1988.

[GQB89]   Marc Grosso, Richard Quach, and Norman I. Badler. Anthropometry for computer animated human figures. In N. Magnenat-Thalmann and D. Thalmann, editors, *State-of-the Art in Computer Animation*, pages 83–96. Springer-Verlag, New York, NY, 1989.

[GQO⁺89]   Marc Grosso, Richard Quach, Ernest Otani, Jianmin Zhao, Susanna Wei, Pei-Hwa Ho, Jiahe Lu, and Norman I. Badler. Anthropometry for computer graphics human figures. Technical Report MS-CIS-89-71, Computer and Information Science, Univ. of Pennsylvania, Philadelphia, PA, 1989.

[GR82]   K. Gupta and B. Roth. Design considerations for manipulator workspace. *ASME Journal of Mechanical Design*, 104:704–711, Oct. 1982.

[GRB⁺85]   S. M. Goldwasser, R. A. Reynolds, T. Bapty, D. Baraff, J. Summers, D. A. Talton, and E. Walsh. Physician's workstation with real-time performance. *IEEE Computer Graphics and Applications*, 5(12):44–57, Dec. 1985.

[GS89]   Barbara Grosz and Candice Sidner. Plans for discourse. In J. Morgan, P. Cohen, and M. Pollack, editors, *Intentions in Communication*. MIT Press, 1989.

[Gup86]   K. Gupta. On the nature of robot workspace. *Int. Journal of Robotics Research*, 5:112–122, 1986.

[Gup90]   Kamal Kant Gupta. Fast collision avoidance for manipulator arms: A sequential search strategy. *IEEE Transactions on Robotics and Automation*, 6(5):522–532, Oct 1990.

[Hac77]   R. J. Hackathorn. ANIMA II: A 3-D color animation system. *Computer Graphics*, 11(2):54–64, July 1977.

[Hah88]   James K. Hahn. Realistic animation of rigid bodies. *Computer Graphics*, 22(4):299–308, August 1988.

[Har75]   J. A. Hartigan. Printer graphics for clustering. *Journal of Statistical Computation and Simulation*, 4:187–213, 1975.

[Hau89]   Edward J. Haug, editor. *Concurrent Engineering of Mechanical Systems: Volume I*. The Univ. of Iowa, Iowa City, IA, 1989.

[HBD80]   R. Harris, J. Bennet, and L. Dow. CAR-II – A revised model for crew assesment of reach. Technical Report 1400.06B, Analytics, Willow Grove, PA, 1980.

[HC90]   Adele E. Howe and Paul R. Cohen. Responding to environmental change. *Proceedings of the ARPA Workshop on Planning, Scheduling, and Control*, pages 85–92, Nov. 1990.

[HE78]   Don Herbison-Evans. NUDES2: A numeric utility displaying ellipsoid solids. *Computer Graphics*, 12(3):354–356, Aug. 1978.

[HE82]   Don Herbison-Evans. Real-time animation of human figure drawings with hidden lines omitted. *IEEE Computer Graphics and Applications*, 2(9):27–34, 1982.

[Her86]   Annette Herskovits. Language and spatial cognition. In Aravind Joshi, editor, *Studies in Natural Language Processing*. Cambridge Univ. Press, Cambridge, England, 1986.

[HH87]   C. Hoffmann and R. Hopcroft. Simulation of physical systems from geometric models. *IEEE Journal of Robotics and Automation*, RA-3(3):194–206, 1987.

[Hir77]   Vicki Hirsch. Floorplans in Labanotation. Master's thesis, Computer and Information Science, Univ. of Pennsylvania, Philadelphia, PA, 1977.

[HJER86]   V. H. Heyward, S. M. Johannes-Ellis, and J. F. Romer. Gender differences in strength. *Research Quarterly for Exercise and Sport*, 57(2):154–159, 1986.

[HKP91]   John Hertz, Anders Krogh, and Richard G. Palmer. *Introduction to the theory of neural computation*. Addison Wesley, 1991.

[Hol81]   W. H. Hollinshead. *Functional Anatomy of the Limbs and Back*. Saunders, Philadelphia, PA, 1981.

[Hol82]   W. H. Hollinshead. *Anatomy for Surgeons*. Harper & Row, Philadelphia, PA, 1982.

[HP88]   David R. Haumann and Richard E. Parent. The behavioral testbed: Obtaining complex behavior from simple rules. *The Visual Computer*, 4(6), 1988.

[HS85a]   Pat Hanrahan and David Sturman. Interactive animation of parametric models. *The Visual Computer*, 1(4):260–266, 1985.

[HS85b]   J. M. Hollerbach and K. C. Suh. Redundancy resolution of manipulators through torque optimization. In *IEEE Intl. Conf. on Robotics and Automation*, pages 1016–1021, St. Louis, MO, 1985.

[Hut70]   Ann Hutchinson. *Labanotation*. Theatre Arts Books, New York, NY, 1970.

[Hut84]   Ann Hutchinson. *Dance Notation*. Dance Horizons, New York, NY, 1984.

[Ibe87]   T. Iberall. The nature of human prehension: Three dextrous hands in one. In *IEEE Intl. Conf. on Robotics and Automation*, pages 396–401, 1987.

[IC87]   Paul M. Isaacs and Michael F. Cohen. Controlling dynamic simulation with kinematic constraints. *Computer Graphics*, 21(4):215–224, 1987.

[Imr83]   S. N. Imrhan. *Modelling Isokinetic Strength of the Upper Extremity*. PhD thesis, Texas Tech Univ., 1983.

[IRT81]   Verne T. Inman, Henry J. Ralston, and Frank Todd. *Human Walking*. Williams and Wilkins, Baltimore, MD, 1981.

[Jac90]   Ray Jackendoff. *Semantic Structures*. MIT Press, Cambridge, MA, 1990.

[JCMM73]   Reid Joyce, Andrew Chenzoff, Joseph Mulligan, and William Mallory. Fully proceduralized job performance aids. Technical Report AFHRL-

           Tr-73-43(I), Air Force Human Resources Laboratory, Wright-Patterson AFB, 1973.

[JKBC91]   Moon Jung, Jugal Kalita, Norman I. Badler, and Wallace Ching. Simulating human tasks using simple natural language instructions. In *Proc. Winter Simulation Conf.*, Phoenix, AZ, 1991.

[JM85]   R. J. Jagacinski and D. L. Monk. Fitts' Law in two dimensions with hand and head movements. *Journal of Motor Behavior*, 17, 1985.

[Joh76]   G. Johansson. Spatial-temporal differentiation and integration in visual motion perception. *Psychology Research*, 38:379–383, 1976.

[Jun92]   Moon Jung. *Human-Like Agents with Posture Planning Ability*. PhD thesis, Computer and Information Science, Univ. of Pennsylvania, Philadelphia, PA, 1992.

[Kae90]   Leslie P. Kaelbling. An architecture for intelligent reactive systems. In James Allen, James Hendler, and Austin Tate, editors, *Readings in Planning*, pages 713–728. Morgon Kaufmann Publishers, Inc., 1990.

[Kal90]   Jugal Kumar Kalita. *Natural Language Control of Animation of Task Performance in a Physical Domain*. PhD thesis, Computer and Information Science, Univ. of Pennsylvania, Philadelphia, PA, 1990.

[Kar87]   Robin Karlin. SEAFACT: A semantic analysis system for task animation of cooking operations. Master's thesis, Computer and Information Science, Univ. of Pennsylvania, Philadelphia, PA, Dec. 1987.

[Kar88]   Robin Karlin. Defining the semantics of verbal modifiers in the domain of cooking tasks. In *Proc. of the 26st Annual Meeting of ACL*, pages 61–67, 1988.

[KB82]   James U. Korein and Norman I. Badler. Techniques for goal directed motion. *IEEE Computer Graphics and Applications*, 2(9):71–81, Nov. 1982.

[KB90]   Jugal Kalita and Norman I. Badler. Semantic analysis of a class of action verbs based on physical primitives. In *Proc. 12th Annual Conference of the Cognitive Science Society*, pages 412–419, Boston, MA, July 1990.

[KB91]   Jugal Kalita and Norman I. Badler. Interpreting prepositions physically. In *Proc. AAAI-91*, pages 105–110, Anaheim, CA, 1991.

[Kee82]   Steve W. Keele. Learning and control of coordinated motor patterns: The programming perspective. In J.A. Scott Kelso, editor, *Human Motor Behavior*. Lawrence Erlbaum Associates, 1982.

[KH81]   B. Kleiner and J. A. Hartigan. Representating points in many dimensions by trees and castles. *Journal of American Statistical Association*, 76(374):260–269, 1981.

[KH83]   C.A. Klein and C.H. Huang. Review of pseudoinverse control for use with kinematically redundant manipulators. *IEEE Transactions on Systems, Man and Cybernetics*, 13(2), 1983.

[Kha86]   O. Khatib. Real-time obstacle avoidance for manipulators and mobile robots. *Int. Journal of Robotics Research*, 5(1):90–98, 1986.

[Kha87]   O. Khatib. A unified approach for motion and force control of robot manipulators: The operational space formulation. *IEEE Journal of Robotics and Automation*, RA-3(1):43–53, 1987.

[KKB88]   Scott Kushnier, Jugal Kalita, and Norman I. Badler. Constraint-based temporal planning. Technical report, Computer and Information Science, Univ. of Pennsylvania, Philadelphia, PA, 1988.

[KN87]   K. Kazerounian and A. Nedungadi. An alternative method for mini-
           mization of driving forces in redundant manipulators. In *IEEE Intl.
           Conf. on Robotics and Automation*, pages 1701–1706, Raleigh, NC,
           1987.

[Kor85]   James U. Korein. *A Geometric Investigation of Reach*. MIT Press,
           Cambridge, MA, 1985.

[KR79]   M. E. Kahn and B. Roth. The near-minimum time control of open loop
           articulated kinematic chains. *Transactions of the ASME: Journal of
           Dynamic Systems, Measurement, and Control*, 93(3):164–172, 1979.

[KSC81]   E. Kingsley, N. Schofield, and K. Case. SAMMIE – A computer aid
           for man-machine modeling. *Computer Graphics*, 15(3):163–169, Aug.
           1981.

[KTV⁺90]   James P. Karlen, Jack M Thompson, Havard I. Vold, James D. Far-
           rell, and Paul H. Eismann. A dual-arm dexterous manipulator system
           with anthropomorphic kinematics. In *IEEE Intl. Conf. on Robotics and
           Automation*, 1990.

[Kum80]   A. Kumar. *Characterization of Manipulator Geometry*. PhD thesis,
           Univ. of Houston, 1980.

[KW81]   A. Kumar and K. Waldron. The workspace of a mechanical manipula-
           tor. *ASME Journal of Mechanical Design*, 103:665–672, July 1981.

[KZ86]   Kamal Kant and Steven W. Zucker. Toward efficient trajectory plan-
           ning: The path-velocity decomposition. *Int. Journal of Robotics Re-
           search*, 5(3):72–89, Fall 1986.

[Lau76]   L. L. Laubach. Comparative muscular strength of men and women: A
           review of the literature. *Aviation, Space, and Environmental Medicine*,
           47(5):534–542, 1976.

[LCF76]   G. D. Langolf, D. B. Chaffin, and J. A. Foulke. An investigation of
           Fitts' Law using a wide range of movement amplitudes. *Journal of
           Motor Behavior*, 8, 1976.

[Lee92]   Philip L. Y. Lee. *Modeling Articulated Figure Motion with Physically-
           and Physiologically-Based Constraints*. PhD thesis, Mechanical Engi-
           neering and Applied Mechanics, Univ. of Pennsylvania, Philadelphia,
           PA, 1992.

[Lev77]   Marc Levoy. A color animation system based on the multi-plane tech-
           nique. *Computer Graphics*, 11(2):64–71, July 1977.

[Lev91]   Libby Levison. Action composition for the animation of Natural Lan-
           guage instructions. Technical Report MS-CIS-91-28, Computer and
           Information Science, Univ. of Pennsylvania, Philadelphia, PA, 1991.

[Lif91]   Kinetic Effects, Inc., Seattle, WA. *Life Forms User Manual*, 1991.

[Loc91]   K. Lochbaum. An algorithm for plan recognition in collaborative dis-
           course. In *Proc. 29ᵗʰ Annual Meeting of the Assoc. for Computational
           Linguistics*, pages 33–38, Berkeley, CA, June 1991.

[Lou83]   R. Louis. *Surgery of the Spine*. Springer-Verlag, New York, NY, 1983.

[LP81]   Tomas Lozano-Pérez. Automatic planning of manipulator transfer
           movements. *IEEE Transactions on Systems, Man and Cybernetics*,
           SMC-11(10):681–698, Oct 1981.

[LP83]   Tomas Lozano-Pérez. Spatial planning: A configuration space ap-
           proach. *IEEE Transactions on Computers*, c-32(2):26–37, Feb 1983.

[LP87]   Tomas Lozano-Pérez. A simple motion planning algorithm for general
           robot manipulators. *IEEE Journal of Robotics and Automation*, RA-

3(3):224–238, June 1987.

[LPW79] T. Lozano-Pérez and M. A. Wesley. An algorithm for planning collision-free paths among polyhedral obstacles. *Communications of the ACM*, 22(10):560–570, Oct. 1979.

[LRM88] Timothy Lohman, Alex Roche, and Reynaldo Martorell. *Anthropometric Standardization Reference Manual*. Human Kinetic Books, Champaign, IL, 1988.

[LWZB90] Philip Lee, Susanna Wei, Jianmin Zhao, and Norman I. Badler. Strength guided motion. *Computer Graphics*, 24(4):253–262, 1990.

[LY83] T. Lee and D. Yang. On the evaluation of manipulator workspace. *Journal of Mechanisms, Transmissions, and Automation in Design*, 105:70–77, March 1983.

[Mae90] Pattie Maes. Situated agents can have goals. In Pattie Maes, editor, *Designing Autonomous Agents*, pages 49–70. MIT Press, 1990.

[Mau91] Ruth A. Maulucci. Personal communication, 1991.

[MB77] M. A. MacConaill and J. V. Basmajian. *Muscles and Movements, a Basic for Human Kinesiology*. R. E. Krieger, Huntington, NY, 1977.

[MB91] G. Monheit and N. Badler. A kinematic model of the human spine and torso. *IEEE Computer Graphics and Applications*, 11(2):29–38, 1991.

[McD89] J. W. McDaniel. Modeling strength data for CREW CHIEF. In *Proceedings of the SOAR 89 (Space Operations, Automation, and Robotics)*, Johnson Space Center, Houston, TX, July 1989.

[Mil88] Gavin S. P. Miller. The motion dynamics of snakes and worms. *Computer Graphics*, 22(4):169–178, 1988.

[Mil91] Gavin Miller. Goal-directed animation of tubular articulated figures or how snakes play golf. In Norman I. Badler, Brian A. Barsky, and David Zeltzer, editors, *Making Them Move: Mechanics, Control, and Animation of Articulated Figures*, pages 209–233. Morgan-Kaufmann, San Mateo, CA, 1991.

[Min86] Marvin Minsky. *The Society of Mind*. Simon and Schuster, 1986.

[MK85] A. A. Maciejewski and C. A. Klein. Obstacle avoidance for kinematically redundant manipulators in dynamically varying environments. *Int. Journal of Robotics Research*, 4(3):109–117, 1985.

[MKK+88] J. McDaniel, M. Korna, P. Krauskopf, D. Haddox, S. Hardyal, M. Jones, and J. Polzinetti. User's Guide for CREW CHIEF: A computer graphics simulation of an aircraft maintenance technician. Technical report, Armstrong Aerospace Medical Research Laboratory, Human Systems Division, Air Force System Command, Wright-Patterson Air Force Base, OH, May 1988.

[MPZ90] Michael McKenna, Steve Pieper, and David Zeltzer. Control of a virtual actor: The roach. *Computer Graphics*, 24(2):165–174, 1990.

[MS86] A. Mital and N. Sanghavi. Comparison of maximum volitional torque exertion capabilities of males and females using common hand tools. *Human Factors*, 28(3):283–294, 1986.

[MTT85] Nadia Magnenat-Thalmann and Daniel Thalmann. *Computer Animation: Theory and Practice*. Springer-Verlag, New York, NY, 1985.

[MTT90] Nadia Magnenat-Thalmann and Daniel Thalmann. *Synthetic Actors in 3-D Computer-Generated Films*. Springer-Verlag, New York, NY, 1990.

[MTT91a] Nadia Magnenat-Thalmann and Daniel Thalmann. Complex models for animating synthetic actors. *IEEE Computer Graphics and Applications*,

11(5):32–44, Sept. 1991.

[MTT91b] Nadia Magnenat-Thalmann and Daniel Thalmann. Human body deformations using joint-dependent local operators and finite-element theory. In Norman I. Badler, Brian A. Barsky, and David Zeltzer, editors, *Making Them Move: Mechanics, Control, and Animation of Articulated Figures*, pages 243–262. Morgan-Kaufmann, San Mateo, CA, 1991.

[Muj87] C. Mujabbir. Workspaces of serial manipulators. Master's thesis, Mechanical Engineering and Applied Mechanics, Univ. of Pennsylvania, 1987.

[NAS78] NASA. *The Anthropometry Source Book*. NASA Reference Publication 1024, Johnson Space Center, Houston, TX, 1978. (Two volumes).

[NAS87] NASA. Man-System Integration Standards. NASA-STD-3000, March 1987.

[Nel85] Greg Nelson. Juno, a constraint-based graphics system. *Computer Graphics*, 19(3):235–243, 1985.

[NHK⁺85] H. Nishimura, M. Hirai, T. Kawai, T. Kawata, I. Shirakawa, and K. Omura. Object modeling by distribution function and a method of image generation. In *Proc. Electronics Communication Conf.*, volume J68-D(4), 1985. (in Japanese).

[NHK86] NHK. Caron's world. *SIGGRAPH Video Review*, 24, 1986.

[NO87] Gregory Nielson and Dan Olsen Jr. Direct manipulation techniques for 3D objects using 2D locator devices. In *Proceedings of 1986 ACM Workshop on Interactive 3D Graphics*, Chapel Hill, NC, Oct. 1987.

[OB80] Joseph O'Rourke and Norman I. Badler. Model-based image analysis of human motion using constraint propagation. *IEEE Trans. on Pattern Analysis and Machine Intelligence*, 2(6):522–536, Nov. 1980.

[OO81] T. J. O'Donnell and Arthur J. Olson. GRAMPS – A graphics language interpreter for real-time, interactive, three-dimensional picture editing and animation. *Computer Graphics*, 15(3):133–142, 1981.

[Ota89] Ernest Otani. Software tools for dynamic and kinematic modeling of human motion. Technical Report MS-CIS-89-43, Computer and Information Science, Univ. of Pennsylvania, Philadelphia, PA, 1989. (MSE Thesis, Mechanical Engineering and Applied Mechanics, Univ. of Pennsylvania).

[Pau81] Richard Paul. *Robot Manipulators: Mathematics, Programming, and Control*. MIT Press, Cambridge, MA, 1981.

[PB88] Cary Phillips and Norman I. Badler. Jack: A toolkit for manipulating articulated figures. In *Proceedings of ACM SIGGRAPH Symposium on User Interface Software*, pages 221–229, Banff, Canada, Oct. 1988.

[PB91] Cary B. Phillips and Norman I. Badler. Interactive behaviors for bipedal articulated figures. *Computer Graphics*, 25(4):359–362, 1991.

[PBS91] Catherine Pelachaud, Norman I. Badler, and Mark Steedman. Issues in facial animation. In *Computer Animation '91*, Geneva, Switzerland, 1991.

[Pel91] Catherine Pelachaud. *Communication and coarticulation in facial animation*. PhD thesis, Computer and Information Science, Univ. of Pennsylvania, Philadelphia, PA, 1991. Tech. Report MS-CIS-91-82.

[Pen86] Alex Pentland. Perceptual organization and the representation of natural form. *AI Journal*, 28(2):1–38, 1986.

[PMA⁺91] A. Pandya, J. Maida, A. Aldridge, S. Hasson, and B. Woolford. Development of an empirically based dynamic biomechanical strength model. In *Space Operations Applications and Research Conf. Proc.*, pages 438–444, 1991. Vol. 2.

[Pot91] Caren Potter. The human factor. *Computer Graphics World*, pages 61–68, March 1991.

[Pow70] M. J. D. Powell. A hybrid method for nonlinear equations. In P. Rabinowitz, editor, *Numerical Methods for Nonlinear Algebraic Equations*. Gordon and Breach Science, 1970.

[PR90] Martha E. Pollack and Marc Ringuette. Introducing Tileworld: Experimentally evaluating an agent architecture. *Proceedings of the 8th National Conference on Artificial Intelligence*, pages 183–189, 1990.

[Pra84] P. Prasad. An overview of major occupant simulation models. In *Proceedings of Society of Automotive Engineers*, 1984. Paper No. 840855.

[Pri81] Ellen Prince. Toward a taxonomy of given/new information. In P. Cole, editor, *Radical Pragmatics*, pages 223–255. Academic Press, New York, NY, 1981.

[PW89] A. Pentland and J. Williams. Good vibrations: Modal dynamics for graphics and animation. *Computer Graphics*, 23(3):215–222, 1989.

[PZB90] Cary Phillips, Jianmin Zhao, and Norman I. Badler. Interactive real-time articulated figure manipulation using multiple kinematic constraints. *Computer Graphics*, 24(2):245–250, 1990.

[RA90] David F. Rogers and J. Alan Adams. *Mathematical Elements for Computer Graphics*. McGraw-Hill, New York, NY, 1990. Second Ed.

[Ree83] William T. Reeves. Particle systems – A technique for modelling a class of fuzzy objects. *Computer Graphics*, 17(3):359–376, July 1983.

[Rey82] Craig W. Reynolds. Computer animation with scripts and actors. *Computer Graphics*, 16(3):289–296, July 1982.

[Rey87] Craig W. Reynolds. Flocks, herds, and schools: A distributed behavioral model. *Computer Graphics*, 21(4):25–34, 1987.

[Rey88] Craig W. Reynolds. Not bumping into things. SIGGRAPH course 27 notes: Developements in Physically-Based Modeling, 1988. G1–G13.

[RG91] Hans Rijpkema and Michael Girard. Computer animation of hands and grasping. *Computer Graphics*, 25(4):339–348, July 1991.

[RMTT90] Olivier Renault, Nadia Magnenat-Thalmann, and Daniel Thalmann. A vision-based approach to behavioral animation. *The Journal of Visualization and Computer Animation*, 1(1):18–21, 1990.

[Ros60] J. B. Rosen. The gradient projection method for nonlinear programming – I: Linear constraints. *SIAM Journal of Appl. Math.*, 8:181–217, 1960.

[Ros91] David A. Rosenbaum. *Human Motor Control*. Academic Press, 1991.

[Rot75] B. Roth. Performance evaluation of manipulators from a kinematics viewpoint. *NBS Special Publication*, pages 39–61, 1975.

[SB85] Scott Steketee and Norman I. Badler. Parametric keyframe interpolation incorporating kinetic adjustment and phrasing control. *Computer Graphics*, 19(3):255–262, 1985.

[Sch72] F. T. Schanne. *Three Dimensional Hand Force Capability Model for a Seated Person*. PhD thesis, Univ. of Michigan, Ann Arbor, MI, 1972.

[Sch82a] Richard Schmidt. More on motor programs. In J.A. Scott Kelso, editor, *Human Motor Behavior*. Lawrence Erlbaum Associates, 1982.

[Sch82b] Richard Schmidt. The schema concept. In J.A. Scott Kelso, editor, *Human Motor Behavior*. Lawrence Erlbaum Associates, 1982.

[Sch83]   Christopher Schmandt.   Spatial input/display correspondence in a
            stereoscopic computer graphics workstation.   *Computer Graphics*,
            17(3):253–261, July 1983.
[Sch90]   J. H. Schmidhuber.   Making the world differentiable: On using su-
            pervised learning fully recurrent networks for dynamic reinforcement
            learning and planning in non-stationary environments. Technical Re-
            port FKI-126-90, Technische Universität München, Febuary 1990.
[SEL84]   SELF. The first 3-D computer exercises, Sept. 1984.
[SH86]   G. Sahar and J. M. Hollerbach. Planning of minimum-time trajectories
            for robot arms. *Int. Journal of Robotics Research*, 5(3):90–100, 1986.
[Sha70]   D. F. Shanno. Conditioning of quasi-Newton methods for function min-
            imization. *Math. Computation*, 24:647–664, 1970.
[Sha80]   U. Shani. Filling regions in binary raster images: A graph-theoretic
            approach. *Computer Graphics*, 14(3):321–327, 1980.
[Sha88]   Lokendra Shastri. A connectionist approach to knowledge representa-
            tion and limited inference. *Cognitive Science*, 12(3):331–392, 1988.
[Sho92]   Ken Shoemake.   ARCBALL: A user interface for specifying three-
            dimensional orientation using a mouse. In *Proceedings of SIGCHI '92*,
            1992.
[Sim81]   Herbert A. Simon. *The Sciences of the Artificial*. MIT Press, 2 edition,
            1981.
[SL87]   S. Singh and M. C. Leu.   Optimal trajectory generation for robotic
            manipulators using dynamic programming. *Transactions of the ASME:
            Journal of Dynamic Systems, Measurement, and Control*, 109:88–96,
            1987.
[SP86]   Thomas W. Sederberg and Scott R. Parry. Free-form deformation of
            solid geometric models. *Computer Graphics*, 20(4):151–160, August
            1986.
[SS83a]   J. T. Schwartz and M. Sharir. On the piano movers' problem – I: The
            case of a two dimensional rigid polygonal body moving amidst polygonal
            barriers. *Communications on Pure and Applied Mathematics*, 36:345–
            398, 1983.
[SS83b]   J. T. Schwartz and M. Sharir. On the piano movers' problem – II: Gen-
            eral techniques for computing topological properties of real algebraic
            manifolds. *Advances in Applied Mathematics*, 4:298–351, 1983.
[SSSN85]   D. Schmitt, A. H. Soni, V. Srinivasan, and G. Naganthan. Optimal mo-
            tion programming of robot manipulators. *Transactions of the ASME:
            Journal of Mechanisms, Transmissions, and Automation in Design*,
            107:239–244, 1985.
[Ste83]   G. Stern. BBOP – A program for 3-Dimensional animation. In *Nico-
            graph '83*, Tokyo, Japan, 1983.
[Ste90]   Mark Steedman. Gapping as constituent coordination. *Linguistics and
            Philosophy*, 13:207–263, 1990.
[Stu84]   David Sturman. Interactive key frame animation of 3-D articulated
            models. In *Proc. Graphics Interface '84*, pages 35–40, Ottawa, Canada,
            1984.
[Sug81]   D. Sugimoto. Determination of extreme distances of a robot hand.
            ASME Journal of Mechanical Design, 103:631–636, July 1981.
[Sun91]   Ron Sun. Neural network models for rule-based reasoning. In *IEEE In-
            ternational Joint Conference on Neural Networks*, pages 503–508, Sin-

gapore, 1991.

[TA75]   G. J. Torotra and N. P. Anagnostakos. *Principles of Anatomy and Physiology*. Canfield Press, New York, NY, 1975.

[TJ81]   Frank Thomas and Ollie Johnson. *Disney Animation: The Illusion of Life*. Abbeville Press, New York, NY, 1981.

[TPBF87]   Demetri Terzopoulos, John Platt, Alan Barr, and Kurt Fleischer. Elastically deformable models. *Computer Graphics*, 21:205–214, 1987.

[TS81]   Y. Tsai and A. Soni. Accessible region and synthesis of robot arms. *ASME Journal of Mechanical Design*, 103:803–811, Oct. 1981.

[TS83]   Y. Tsai and A. Soni. An algorithm for the workspace of a general n-R robot. *ASME Journal of Mechanical Design*, 105:52–57, July 1983.

[Tsa86]   M. Tsai. *Workspace Geometric Characterization and Manipulability of Industrial Robots*. PhD thesis, Ohio State Univ., 1986.

[TST87]   Yosuke Takashima, Hideo Shimazu, and Masahiro Tomono. Story driven animation. In *CHI + GI '87 Proceedings*, pages 149–153. ACM SIGCHI, 1987.

[Tur63]   A. M. Turing. Computing machinery and intelligence. In E. A. Feigenbaum and J. Feldman, editors, *Computers and Thought*, pages 11–35. McGraw-Hill, New York, NY, 1963.

[VB90]   S. A. Vere and T. W. Bickmore. A basic agent. *Computational Intelligence*, 6:41–60, 1990.

[Vij85]   R. Vijaykumar. Robot manipulators – Workspaces and geometrical dexterity. Master's thesis, Mechanical Engineering, Ohio State Univ., Columbus, OH, 1985.

[Wav89]   Wavefront Technologies. *MODEL User's Manual Version 6.0*, 1989.

[WB85]   Jane Wilhelms and Brian A. Barsky. Using dynamics for the animation of articulated bodies such as humans and robots. In *Proc. Graphics Interface '85*, pages 97–104, Montreal, Canada, 1985.

[WB92]   Susanna Wei and Norman I. Badler. Graphical displays of human strength data. *Visualization and Computer Animation*, 3(1):13–22, 1992.

[Wei86]   Jerry Weil. The synthesis of cloth objects. *Computer Graphics*, 20(4):49–54, 1986.

[Wei90]   Susanna Wei. *Human Strength Database and Multidimensional Data Display*. PhD thesis, Computer and Information Science, Univ. of Pennsylvania, Philadelphia, PA, 1990.

[Wel71]   K. Wells. *Kinesiology, the Scientific Basis of Human Action*. Saunders, Philadelphia, PA, 1971.

[Wes73]   Barry D. Wessler. *Computer-assisted visual communication*. PhD thesis, Univ. of Utah, Salt Lake City, UT, 1973.

[WFB87]   Andrew Witkin, Kurt Fleisher, and Alan Barr. Energy constraints on parameterized models. *Computer Graphics*, 21(3):225–232, 1987.

[Whi72]   D. E. Whitney. The mathematics of coordinated control of prostheses and manipulators. *J. Dynamic Systems, Measurement, and Control, Transaction ASME*, 94:303–309, 1972. Series G.

[Wil75]   F. Wilson, editor. *The Musculoskeletal System*. Lippincott, Philadelphia, PA, 1975.

[Wil82]   K. D. Willmert. Visualizing human body motion simulations. *IEEE Computer Graphics and Applications*, 2(9):35–38, Nov. 1982.

[Wil86]   Jane Wilhelms. Virya – A motion editor for kinematic and dynamic animation. In *Proc. Graphics Interface '86*, pages 141–146, Vancouver, Canada, 1986.

[Wil87]　Jane Wilhelms. Using dynamic analysis for realistic animation of articulated bodies. *IEEE Computer Graphics and Applications*, 7(6):12–27, 1987.

[Wil91]　Jane Wilhelms. Dynamic experiences. In Norman I. Badler, Brian A. Barsky, and David Zeltzer, editors, *Making Them Move: Mechanics, Control, and Animation of Articulated Figures*, pages 265–279. Morgan-Kaufmann, San Mateo, CA, 1991.

[Win90]　David A. Winter. *Biomechanics and Motor Control of Human Movement*. Wiley Interscience, New York, NY, 1990. Second Edition.

[WK88]　A. Witkin and M. Kass. Spacetime constraints. *Computer Graphics*, 22(4):159–168, 1988.

[WMW86]　G. Wyvill, C. McPheeters, and B. Wyvill. Data structure for soft objects. *The Visual Computer*, 2:227–234, 1986.

[WS90]　Jane Wilhelms and Robert Skinner. A 'notion' for interactive behavioral animation control. *IEEE Computer Graphics and Applications*, 10(3):14–22, May 1990.

[WSB78]　Lynne Weber, Stephen W. Smoliar, and Norman I. Badler. An architecture for the simulation of human movement. In *Proc. ACM Annual Conf.*, pages 737–745, Washington, DC, 1978.

[WW90]　Andrew Witkin and William Welch. Fast animation and control of nonrigid structures. *Computer Graphics*, 24(4):243–252, 1990.

[Yeo76]　B. P. Yeo. Investigations concerning the principle of minimal total muscular force. *Journal of Biomechanics*, 9:413–416, 1976.

[YL83]　D. Yang and T. Lee. On the workspace of mechanical manipulators. *Journal of Mechanisms, Transmissions, and Automation in Design*, 105:62–69, March 1983.

[YN87]　V. Yen and M. L. Nagurka. Suboptimal trajectory planning of a five-link human locomotion model. In *Biomechanics Proceedings*, 1987.

[ZB89]　Jianmin Zhao and Norman I. Badler. Real time inverse kinematics with joint limits and spatial constraints. Technical Report MS-CIS-89-09, Computer and Information Science, Univ. of Pennsylvania, Philadelphia, PA, 1989.

[Zel82]　David Zeltzer. Motor control techniques for figure animation. *IEEE Computer Graphics and Applications*, 2(9):53–59, Nov. 1982.

[Zel84]　David Zeltzer. *Representation and Control of Three Dimensional Computer Animated Figures*. PhD thesis, The Ohio State Univ., 1984.

[Zel91]　David Zeltzer. Task-level graphical simulation: Abstraction, representation, and control. In Norman I. Badler, Brian A. Barsky, and David Zeltzer, editors, *Making Them Move: Mechanics, Control, and Animation of Articulated Figures*, pages 3–33. Morgan-Kaufmann, San Mateo, CA, 1991.

[ZV92]　J. Zwarts and H. Verkuyl. An algebra of conceptual structure: An investigation into Jackendoff's conceptual semantics. *Linguistics and Philosophy*, 1992. To appear.

Index